Baskets in Europe

Maurice Bichard

Émilien Métézeau.
Photo: RJ Whittick

i

ISBN 978-0-9560249-0-9

Published by Fyfield Wick Editions, The Farmhouse, Fyfield Wick, Abingdon, Oxon, OX13 5NB, UK. www.basketsineurope.co.uk

Printed by Information Press, Eynsham, Oxon, UK

European map courtesy of the University of Texas Libraries

Country maps from www.world66.com/myworld66/visitedEurope

Cover photo: van Pluis, Musselkanaal

Inside back cover photo: Anthony Blake

For Diana

Europe

Contents

Foreword and Acknowledgements

This survey of basketry traditions throughout Europe results from studies and collecting over almost 50 years, and travels through 25 of the 40 or more countries. For the first time it provides an overall European survey of basketry in a single language which is increasingly understood throughout the world. The story is far from complete, and I hope others will be encouraged to fill in the gaps.

My interests and activities have been in farming and food production at many levels. They embrace science-based intensive agriculture and horticulture, agricultural history, peasant life, woodland and hedge management, kitchen-gardening, bee-keeping, and baking. I have belonged to the Basketmakers' Association for over 20 years, have held office, and have benefited from friendships with many members, but have never tried to achieve proficiency as a maker. I have been a Visiting Research Fellow in the Rural History Centre at the University of Reading, but do not claim to be an historian.

This background has coloured the way I have approached the study. The book begins with a generalised historical survey of the way the craft has developed, expanded, and contracted since man first inhabited this continent. The materials used, their preparation, and the techniques employed to weave them into useful articles are then described. I will have missed many details, and make no attempt to teach the reader how to practise the craft.

The main contents are presented in 13 regional chapters which each follow the same pattern. Since similar baskets are often found in more than one region, there is a need to avoid excessive repetition. Probably the only consistent and logical classification of the many types of work would be based strictly on the technique employed and the specific material. I have preferred to adopt a more pragmatic, mixed description based mainly on these criteria, but sometimes on function. This identifies around 20 different types. I have then chosen to feature the three or four which seem to me to be particularly characteristic of each region. This of course omits others since they are covered in different chapters.

In addition, I have mentioned a few specific articles from each region, often because these represent other techniques or materials. Such a selection is bound to be personal, and obviously reflects my own interests and discoveries. My views and interpretation derive from the fact that I have lived most of my life in England.

The text is mine but the design and layout of the book have been the work of my wife Hannah. We have appreciated the freedom from external constraints which this solution has provided, but trust that this has not led to annoying excesses or omissions.

Professional work required me to travel extensively before retirement, and I have since supplemented these visits with more targeted trips. I am grateful to all those academic and other colleagues who have shared with me their knowledge of their countries' history and culture, or more specifically the basket traditions. I have amassed a collection of several hundred baskets and have been able to use photographs of these to illustrate many points. In this way I hope to share them with readers who have not had the chance to see and handle them in our gallery.

All photographs have been taken by us except where indicated. Numerous museums have opened up their stores or allowed their own images to be reproduced here. We have tried our best to contact them, and I apologise if I have failed to acknowledge any sources.

My primary debt has to be to the many previous authors of books and articles, many of which appeared in the quarterly newsletter of the Basketmakers' Association over the past 33 years. These are acknowledged at the ends of each chapter. In this sense the book is as much a review paper as a record of original research.

Many people have provided specific inputs in the form of advice and encouragement, research results, answers to technical queries, baskets, images, translation, discussion of their collections, transport, and hospitality, especially: Elizabeth Allnutt, Maria Rosa Bagnari, Guy Barbier, Ian Beaty, Bernard Bertrand, Katharine, Rosie, and Tom Bichard, Roy Brigden, Ann Brooks, Mary Butcher, Mimmo Cecere, Anna Champeney, Daniel Ciobanu, Elena Couto, Maria Dikiç, Füsun Ertug, Alison Fitzgerald, Ginet Godeau, Sally Goymer, Lluis Grau, José Ramiro Guitiérrez, Natalie Gutgessel, Beth Hardcastle, Jonas Hasselrot, Iris Hawkes, Joe Hogan, Arie van t'Hoog, Erik van t'Hull, Geraldine Jones, Owen Jones, Ebeltje Hartkamp-Jonxis, Ioan Ladosi, Andris Lapins, Steen Madsen, Colin Manthorpe, Émilien Métézeau, Michael and Ellen Musgrove, Bob de Nigtere, Dario Novellino, Anna Patrucco, Michèle Pichonnet, Maria Raimonda Pinna, Mia Pot-van Regteren Altena, Shuna Rendel, Angela Roumelioti, José Schilder, Alfred Schneider, Kit Seth, Inja Smerdel, Nikolai Todorov, Carel Toms, Antonio Campelo Trigo, Dick Whittick, Bernd Witzgall, Bernd Wollner, Felicity Wood, Sheila Wynter, Anna-Maria Väätäinen. But the one person who has enabled my story to move from a long-term aim into this tangible form by dint of long months of work at the computer screen is Hannah, to whom we must all be grateful.

Maurice Bichard
July 2008

The Evolution of Basketry

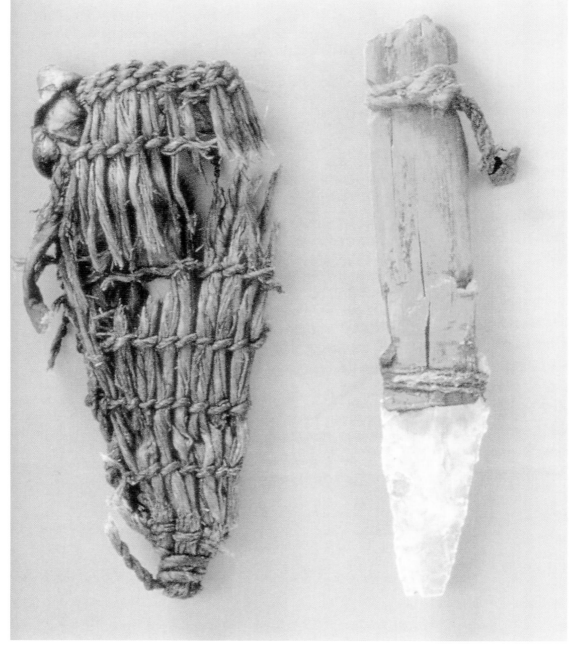

Small dagger with scabbard from Neolithic hunter preserved in ice in Ötztaler Alps for c5300 years. Scabbard woven from strips of bast sewn up at the side with a grass cord. Dagger with flint blade and oak handle bound together with sinew and grass cord around pommel.
Photo: Christin Beeck

Introduction

The production of basketry is known to date back at least 10-12,000 years, and this makes its antiquity second only to cordage and netting among the crafts that utilise perishable fibres. Unfortunately, only a very few fragments of early baskets have survived. Most were considered of little value and when broken were cast out. Furthermore, the materials used were fragile and disintegrated, decayed, or were consumed by fire. This decay was only avoided within very stable environments that were extremely dry, cold or wet where oxygen, insects, moulds, bacteria, and other destructive agents were absent. Occasionally charred remains have been preserved because, once burned, they resisted normal decay, and there are also examples recovered from under volcanic eruptions.

Imprints of coiled basketry have survived on Neolithic pottery fragments for over 9000 years, and there have been recent discoveries of conical fishing baskets in Scandinavia and Ireland dating from c5000 BC. Woven walls or roofs were also early constructions, and examples exist from Swiss lake dwellings built around 5000 years ago. There are many Greek and Roman illustrations, and even some actual Roman examples from the first and second century AD preserved in dry Mediterranean climates and in water-logged conditions elsewhere.

The range of articles, and the weaving and construction techniques used to make them, would have increased gradually as human society evolved into more complex and specialised activities. Thus, the requirements of a hunter-gatherer might be satisfied by a simple shelter, some fish or animal traps and containers for transporting food, and others for storage. Family members would have made these themselves. But by the 19th century, a European nation contained a vast number of specialist occupations and activities, urban, rural and seafaring, domestic and industrial, and huge quantities of goods needed to be moved around from producer to processor to market, and hence to consumer. Baskets of every description were employed and large numbers of specialised people were needed to grow or prepare the fibrous materials, to weave the articles, to market them and even to repair them.

This transition from self-sufficiency to dependence upon specialist craftsmen is, of course, just one example of the evolution that occurred in every facet of human society. It is difficult to put precise dates on each phase: not least because these were different between countries, between regions within countries, and between urban and rural communities. But it is worth tracing these changes and noting the dates at which they were occurring where recorded.

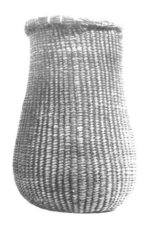

Containers woven from esparto grass made some 5,400 years ago and recovered from a cave near Albuñol, Spain

The change from hunter-gatherers to settled agriculture

In one sense there were men and women present in Europe at least 700,000 years ago. These first European hominoids and their successor species, including latterly Neanderthals, periodically advanced northwards before being beaten back by violent climatic changes. Yet these were not the direct ancestors of today's human population.

It is now believed that our own species, originating in Africa, took advantage of a lowering in the Red Sea level so that there was almost a land bridge exposed across the gulf between modern Eritrea and the Yemen[1]. A group made its way across around 80,000 BP (before present), and the descendants eventually replaced all previous genetic lines. They first moved along the coast to the Arabian Gulf. Some then travelled around the shore lines of Asia to reach as far as Australia by 70,000 BP. Europe was not colonised by them for a further 20,000 years, when a warm moist phase greened the Arabian desert sufficiently to allow them to migrate from the Gulf region to the eastern Mediterranean.

Europe was then populated by our species in two or three different ways. One route after 46,000 BP was through Turkey into Bulgaria, up the Danube, through the Alps, and then the Pyrenees to Portugal by around 38,000 BP. Other groups may have gone across the Caucasus up into Russia, or east from the Gulf into Kashmir, passed into Russia east of the Caspian Sea, and thence across the north European plain by perhaps 30,000 BP[2]. By this time our ancestors had developed skills in mining metal ores, in cave art, elaborate burials, specialised mammoth hunting and the use of bones both for house construction and to make tool sets. Their northern limits continued to be dictated by sudden and dramatic changes in climate where mean annual temperature could drop by 15°C in 10 years[3]. Only in the last 11,500 years has there been continuous occupation of most parts of the European land mass. But these same climatic changes had a much more far-reaching effect on Europe through the developments they produced a long way away to the south east.

With the onset of warmer, wetter weather about 13,000 years ago, growing conditions improved in the Fertile Crescent from the Jordan Valley up to south east Turkey and down towards the Persian Gulf. These improvements favoured the wild grasses whose seeds were important food sources for the hunter-gatherer people who lived in this region[4]. Open forests and grasslands expanded in area and so encouraged increases in the populations of the most important animal species hunted for food.

Three articles from the Old Kingdom period of Egypt (4700-4200 BP) in the Museum of Egyptian Antiquities, Cairo

Large oval lidded container in palm coiled work   Stool with woven seat probably in rush

Coiled jar with domed lid. Palm leaf core bound with split palm rib and stem

By 10,000 years ago, the Fertile Crescent was inhabited by a diverse array of societies; some in permanent year-round settlements, others spending different seasons in lowland (winter) campsites and highland settlements; but all relying on some combination of the wild plants and animals. The next 2000 years saw profound changes. Indeed it has been claimed that there occurred the one event in history which really did change the world - the invention of farming. These societies learned to domesticate three cereal species (emmer wheat, einkorn wheat, and barley), and also goats, sheep, pigs and cattle, and changed their ways of life to become village-based farmers. Then, as a result of interactions with their northern neighbours, between 8000 and 7000 years ago this new agricultural way of life was carried westward into the Balkans and around the shores of the Mediterranean basin, probably by trade rather than migration.

In some places, for example, southern Greece, north-west Sicily, and also along the southern French coast, the existing hunter-gatherer communities seem to have begun herding sheep and goats and planting wheat and barley, but otherwise lived much as before. In contrast, in other areas fully formed agricultural societies may have appeared abruptly between 7500 and 7000 BP, perhaps colonised by farmers from other parts. Examples have been found in south eastern Italy, and in Macedonia and Thessaly in Greece. This rapid development was probably aided by the ease with which Near-Eastern agriculture could be transferred around the Mediterranean. Many other parts even of southern Europe were not so accommodating, and there, hunting and gathering ways of life persisted for many centuries. This applied even more to the northerly latitudes. It was only around 6700 years ago, when people learned to sow their cereals in the spring and harvest them in the autumn (instead of the reverse), and to rely more on cattle than on sheep and goats, that farming could spread rapidly across central and western Europe. Thousands of farming villages appeared as far east as Russia and as far west as France by 6500 to 6000 BP. These were at first concentrated on the widely scattered bands of wind-deposited loess soils that were fertile, well-drained and easily cultivated.

Farming took hold even more slowly in northern and western Europe, Britain, and Ireland, where soil and climate were less favourable. Cereals, legumes, sheep and goats were adopted as minor additions to the former way of life until new systems were gradually evolved to suit the challenges and opportunities of local environments, and this may have been delayed until some 6000 years ago. Even so, there is new evidence of fishing activities well before this[5].

The destruction of the wildwood for cultivation began around that time, and continued throughout the Neolithic and Bronze ages, but probably reached its peak during the

Coiled dish with compartments in palm from Tutankhamun's tomb 3,350BP. Museum of Egyptian Antiquities, Cairo

early Iron Age (from 2750 BP). Surviving timberwork from this time shows that carpenters' joints, wheel-wrighting and each separate woodcraft had already "attained and sometimes surpassed the sophistication which it has today"[6]. Maybe this also applied to basketry?

Unfortunately, there is little clear evidence of the basketry articles made by these early European farmers. Some of the older Near-Eastern civilizations from whom they had acquired their new technology did leave behind both artistic representations and actual pieces preserved in extremely dry conditions. Reed huts and woven willow coffins have left their impressions in the clay from 4000 years ago in several settlements in Mesopotamia, the centre of the Fertile Crescent. Stone sculptures depict various baskets, often carried on the head with offerings for the gods or building materials.

In Egypt, to which settled agriculture had spread much earlier than Europe, coiled linings from pits or granaries sunk in the sand have been excavated and dated to 12,000–10,000 BP. The well-known tomb of Tutankhamun (c3350 BP) contained chairs with woven seats and coiled baskets in remarkable condition[7].

In Europe, comparably dry conditions were rare but existed in southern Spain. Small cylindrical baskets and crude sandals from a cave at Albuñol near Grenada have been dated to 5450 BP. They were woven from esparto grass[8]. Many more remains have survived in the opposite conditions, continuous waterlogging as in the base of wells or in moors and bogs, but these are frequently only fragments. The man preserved in ice for over 5000 years in the Alps before his discovery in 1991 was wearing a grass cloak held together by rows of fine twisted and woven cord, and beside him were lengths of grass rope, again twisted and woven[9]. He probably carried a back pannier with a wooden frame, an elaborate scabbard for his flint dagger woven from lime bast and grass cord, and two birch bark containers.

The productivity of these new farming systems would have gradually improved over the next millennia. Europeans selected for improvements in both plant and animal species. New technology was introduced from regions to the east and south where agriculture had developed sooner and had permitted the first civilisations to evolve. Wheeled vehicles, ploughs, and the use of the horse for riding and draught power were adopted. Metalworking spread: first copper then bronze, and finally iron adapted from the eastern Mediterranean and the Near East, reaching northern Europe around 2800 BP.

As productivity increased, so it became possible for a greater proportion of the population to cease full-time food production and specialise in other occupations, for at least part of the year. When each farming family can produce 125% of its needs, then

Above left: Three female basket bearers painted on a Greek black-figure vase.
© Trustees of the British Museum

Right: Part of a third century mosaic of a basketmaker working outside a Roman villa, and a second figure bringing a bolt of new rods, Saint-Romain-en-Gal. Photo: R.M.N. (Jean Schormans)

some 20% of the population is released and can adopt an urban existence as artisans, traders, soldiers, priests, or the professions. The earliest European cities were in Crete from 4000 BP: the classical Greek period was around 2900 to 2500 BP and the Roman empire from 2200 BP.

Evidence of the European basketmaking scene is greatly increased from these dates. The combination of large collections of sculptures, drawing, paintings, mosaics, and even writings begins to reveal the full richness of ancient craftsmanship even though rather few actual artefacts have survived.

Basketry in Greek and Roman culture

Quite clearly the craft was already highly developed in these sophisticated cultures with their urban communities, very far removed from subsistence agriculture. Several different forms were used in Greek religious ceremonies including the *liknon* and *vannus* both of which appear to have been originally made as winnowing fans for scooping up the corn and even for cradling a child[10]. Others were used for gathering grapes, straining cheeses and carrying possessions or provisions when travelling. This variety of forms demonstrates that there must have been specialist basketmakers in Greece at least 2500 years ago, since some of them could not have been efficiently made by an amateur.

Knowledge of basketmaking within Roman Gaul is even more extensive. Roman writers (including Pliny and Columella) advocated the use of willow and advised on the cultivation of the most suitable varieties in addition to the exploitation of wild material[11]. But other species were used: trees (hazel, birch, lime); shrubs (dogwood,

Third century Roman bas-relief of man using the winnowing fan to separate grain from chaff while another carries a round basket on his shoulders, Romisch-Germanisches Zentralmuseum de Mayence, Photo: Musée Archéologique de Dijon

broom); creepers (clematis, honeysuckle, bramble); rushes, reeds and esparto grass[12]. Baskets were made both by professionals and by peasant farmers in their slack times.

There was an active 'college' of weavers in Rome before 80 BC and members (often slaves) were sited near to a shrine in order to sell baskets to contain offerings to the gods. There are records of a fire in 36 AD in a district where the professionals worked. These men concentrated upon articles which were elegant, those difficult to make, and those approved as standard measures and no doubt worked mainly in willow. A very well preserved mosaic from the third century shows a seated basketmaker receiving a fresh bolt of willow.

The professionals' tools remained essentially similar from their first fashioning by Celtic peoples in central Europe at the dawn of the Iron Age until recent times[13]. These became almost identical all over Europe, north Africa and the Middle East. Differences between regions and countries were insignificant because of the trade routes which became the arteries of culture. The Greeks, Romans, Arabs and Crusaders communicated inventions made in one region to those living in others. The same tools were then used to produce the particular articles demanded in each region. By contrast, peasant workers, using simpler tools, were completely adapted to their local conditions and raw materials.

Knowledge of working techniques and of the forms of the articles made during Roman times is in part based upon monuments. Since these were usually religious or funerary, this means that they depict mainly items used in ceremonies, in various trades and in harvesting. In addition, the images may not convey exact details. Coiled work is evident (from Neolithic times) as is stake and strand. Many methods of carrying are shown: by hand (one or two people), on the shoulders or high on the back, around the neck (using a rope), on a pole between two persons' shoulders, on the backs of animals, or on wheels (carts and chariots). There are references to beehives, panniers, chairs, hoof protectors, ox muzzles, fishing signals, and others[14]. Guy Barbier, a basketmaker based in central France, has collaborated with local museums as well as some in Germany and Belgium, to recreate examples of many of these articles based upon representations on stones and on the few preserved specimens.

Roman products would undoubtedly have been carried throughout their empire so that the local people must have become aware of them and their construction. Naturally our knowledge of current basketry increased with these Roman invasions since they left behind written records.

Tools still used by basketmakers - beating iron, bodkin, shop and picking knives

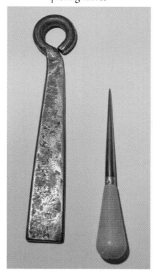

Two farm carts made by Guy Barbier in white willow and chestnut for the Musée d'Argentomagus, Saint-Marcel, based upon stone carvings from Roman Gaul. Photo: Gérard Przysiezna

Lidded willow basket with six glass bottles originally part of a toilet set from Roman or Coptic period, Museum of Egyptian Antiquities, Cairo

It has often been assumed that the forces which returned Europe to much less sophisticated civilisations in the fourth to fifth centuries would have reversed the emergence of specialised artisans and returned many crafts back to the peasant householder and his family. The barbarians who sacked Rome in 410 AD and again in 453 AD were unfamiliar with urban life, had little need for artisan or professional groups, and ended coinage. Their primary activity, apart from farming, was warfare, and coercion was their method of acquiring goods or services. There was rapid and fundamental depopulation of cities in the west, principally in Italy and southern France. But the Romans who returned to the Mediterranean were members of an upper governing class, while the people who could pass on technical skills were the ordinary folk and lower nobility, and these remained. In fact, there is evidence that technology continued to advance: for example, in the way plough and scythe designs changed after the disappearance of the large estates[15]. One can imagine that there would have been a reduction in the demand for baskets used in urban life and transport, but that some skilled professionals would have continued to work and ordinary people's needs were unchanged. In time, a new system of agriculture emerged. The estates, formerly managed using slave labour, were divided into a part run by the landowner and the remainder split into a number of dependent holdings.

Development of a market economy

After the decline of the Greek and Roman empires, written documents which might throw light on European life are rare. It is only from around 1150 AD that surviving records became steadily more abundant. Nevertheless, we do know that even in the ninth and tenth centuries, rural life was still universal in almost all of Europe. Entire countries like England and all the German lands were without towns. Even in other regions, such towns as existed had at most a few hundred permanent inhabitants and all these remained essentially countrymen. Villages and hamlets housed peasant communities under the control of the manors that were owned by wealthy families or religious orders.

The peasants would have been largely self-sufficient, building their own huts (often walled in wattle and daub), fashioning their own tools, making their clothing and household goods, cultivating food crops, and exploiting the unenclosed forests, wastes, rivers and lakes. Many of them owed dues to their manor, primarily labour, but this might take the form of objects upon which labour had been expended – firewood, stakes, simple tools, woollen cloth and, no doubt, baskets. Thus the rural household was for many years a workshop upon whose services the lord could call, and in return

Wall showing plaster (daub)
falling away and exposing the
inner wattle construction, Spain

Model of house construction in the 9th
century town of Hedeby (later replaced by
Schleswig). Wattle siding being installed.
Wikinger Museum Haithabu, Germany

the peasants received protection from the lord's castle and soldiers. This was not yet a wage-labour economy.

But the time came when the manor relinquished its claims on these handmade articles. This was before 1100 AD in Italy, 1100-1150 AD in France, and even later in England. The change was facilitated by the establishment of networks of markets in towns and villages, even before towns were fully developed. The manors could therefore break their dependence on their own peasants' output since small workshops had sprung up near these markets where such articles could be obtained more cheaply and of better quality. As standards of living were rising, customers were becoming more numerous and harder to please. They began to demand the products of specialists. The towns and their markets began to provide both the protection and trade opportunities previously given by the lords.

This change may have come about in several stages. A degree of specialisation grew up on the estates and their villages. Bakers, carpenters, cobblers, smiths and brewers emerged within most villages. At first these had been absolutely dependent upon their lords, but they gradually received permission to work for others as well. The workshops and equipment may have been rented from the lord, but it was their special skills that provided their livelihood. It became easier for families of cultivators to supplement their incomes by working part-time in the slack seasons of the agricultural calendar and by making at home a few articles for sale. As an example, woollen and linen cloth were carried to market, or offered to town dealers as soon as the lord ceased to call for it. Thus some trades and professions existed before the dawn of the urban revival around 1000 AD.

In western Europe there was also a movement of people away from the manors to the newly-emerging towns and cities. It occurred legally through payment of a small annual fee, or alternatively by runaways. This was an escape from serfdom to wage labour so

Women offering their produce for sale at market in
Betanzos, Galicia, Spain 1993

The daily produce market in
Zagreb, Croatia 1981

that for a time the gulf between the urban and rural economies was great. In England manor records from the 1270s show that this type of emigration was well established. On arrival in the towns, those with specialist skills often congregated in the same neighbourhood. Some would have prospered and even become employers. Rulers allowed these movements since trade and markets brought them revenue. But they also allowed some households to become free farmers because such liberated people would support the crown in its struggles with the local seigneurs.

During the 13th century in England, already established towns grew rapidly, and many new ones were added. The main occupations of town dwellers, in addition to administrative, military and ecclesiastical functions were manufacturing and trade.

The residents not only consumed agricultural surpluses and purchased raw materials from the hinterland, but also became producers of simple manufactured goods for distribution both within the towns and cities, and to rural populations. It was these exchanges, and the short distance transport thus created, which were the forces generating the multiplication of towns and markets. Some 2500 English market charters were granted in the century[16]. The increased demand for basket containers to service this trade must have been considerable.

In addition to the expected blacksmiths, shoemakers, bakers and butchers, the first recorded artisans in these small country towns at the end of the 12th and 13th centuries were more specialised workers such as wheelwrights, leatherworkers, tailors, locksmiths, farriers, dyers and millers. Basketmakers were seldom mentioned, either because their craft was held in such low esteem or perhaps because baskets were still largely made in villages and peasant households. We may appreciate the degree of organisation already present around 1300 in one town in eastern England.

"At Ipswich … There was an elaborate arrangement of separate markets. Imported cloth as well as cloth made in the town itself … together with linen, canvas and made-up garments, were sold in the cloth market. There was also a fish market, a wool market (where hides were also sold), a cheese market (where potters also disposed of their wares), a wood market for timber, domestic utensils made of wood, baskets, spades and cartwheels, a bread market, a flesh market for the retail sale of meat, and a market for livestock.

These urban markets … were links in a complex chain of exchanges. They enabled, in the first place, the townsfolk to procure essential foodstuffs. … On the other hand (they) accommodated rural as well as urban customers for goods made in the town … and also for imported goods including foreign cloth, fish, wine, oil, canvas, millstones,

Spanish and Normandy iron, perhaps even sea coal. Some of the goods … were sent elsewhere by sea: wool, hides and skins, herrings both to London and to France, cloth, butter and cheese. Some buyers in the markets, however, might be town craftsmen who needed (raw materials) to carry on their crafts."[17]

Eastern Europe

In contrast, Eastern Europe and Russia experienced quite different histories of mediaeval urbanisation. Waves of new town settlements were produced in Eastern Europe by colonising movements of the Germans in the 12th and 13th centuries. These peasants were initially more free than those who had remained in the west. The Slav populations often also enjoyed these good conditions since their secular and ecclesiastical lords had only small farms and did not need much servile labour.

In Russia, there had been a rapid growth of new towns in the period 1000-1240, but these developments ceased and the peasants were then largely pushed deeper into the forest heartlands by the nomadic Mongols[18]. It was only after the 1550s that Russian military might was able to secure the fertile steppe lands for agricultural settlement. But the period of the late Middle Ages was the turning point. The eastern seigneurs were then allowed to implement measures which would turn their peasants into bondsmen. They demanded ever higher payments and enlarged their own estates at their workers' expense while tying them permanently to the land. This effectively froze the further development of these vast lands and kept them in simple village societies. Serfdom only ceased in 1861 and peasants still constituted over 80 per cent of the population in 1897. With such continuing subsistence agriculture, it would be expected that most Russian basketmaking would have remained household-based, supplying a limited range of simple needs.

Craft organisations

Twelfth century sources provide the first documentary evidence of artisan employers and their wage-earning or apprenticed assistants. Nevertheless, most of these sources refer to earlier organisations, so their origins are unrecorded. A weavers' charter of 1149 suggests that in Cologne, one group of specialists was already splitting off from the existing guild[19]. The two most urbanised areas of Europe were the Low Countries and north Italy. The burghers of St Omer in Flanders obtained a charter in 1127 which confirmed old customs and freed their businesses from some traditional feudal controls. In London too, King Henry II (1154-89) formally gave the weavers the same rights as they had enjoyed during his grandfather's reign (1100-1135) including the exclusive

right to practice in the city. He also confirmed rights for other trades in Lincoln, Winchester and Oxford. These groups of craftsmen in the central Middle Ages reinvented guilds (first seen in Roman times) because they found unfettered competition for workers, markets and raw materials less desirable than cooperation.

Another way of understanding these new urban organisations is as continuations of the principles, attitudes, and values developed over the centuries on the rural manors from which the new townsfolk had just arrived. Just as in a bounded field where everyone grew the same crop in their individual strips, the peasants had to have an order which tried to prevent competition, since one man's gain was another's loss, so they now invented guilds for tradesmen and craftsmen. They brought a set of moral principles from village to town, a sense of resources being limited, and a priority of moral over commercial criteria[20].

The motivation of the masters was to limit the number of persons involved in any one place, in part to maintain quality standards, and in part to ensure the available work was not shared among too many workers. Both would help to maintain prosperity among the group of specialists in one locality, and limit competition from those outside the group whether locals, or those from another place. Workers in a given neighbourhood, often a whole city or town, formed themselves into a guild, fraternity, or company, and only members were allowed to practise their trade and sell their output except at the annual free markets and fairs.

Their workers were qualified wage earners (journeymen) and apprentices rather than slaves (except in some Mediterranean cities). Two prerequisites were necessary – the start of a cash economy and a respect for contracts. There are many examples of workers' contracts with their masters from a variety of trades preserved in notaries' records from Italian and French cities from early in the 13th century, and these are simultaneous with the statutes of the first guilds.

The laws and customs of the Parisian guilds from the 1260s contain the inner workings of some 101 trades. Similarly many guild records survive from London dated 1309-1312. Naturally, such rules and contracts were revised many times in subsequent years. The plague of 1348 caused a dramatic loss of people across Europe, particularly in the densely populated cities. The ranks of masters were thinned and wage rates increased in spite of efforts to keep them stable. The lengths of apprenticeships were reduced which suggests these were more about labour markets than the time needed to learn a craft.

Basketry as a specialist activity

It is not clear how far basketmaking falls into the category of crafts that began to be commercialised in the 11th and 12th centuries. For many basketry items, the essential materials could be gathered free by anyone, and the necessary tools consisted of little more than a sharp knife. This probably meant that country people at least continued to satisfy many of their own basketry needs long after they had begun to rely on other purchased goods which required more specialised equipment and training for their manufacture. On the other hand, it seems clear that the growing number of town dwellers would have increasingly turned to artisans for their basketry needs, using cash or barter, and no doubt the peasants would also obtain specialist articles when they attended the markets to sell their own produce.

It is therefore likely that specialist basketmakers became increasingly important both as trade increased and as more people left the land. Their output would include more complex articles as well as those requiring fine-quality workmanship. Some would be part-time, combining this activity with farming, fishing, or another trade; others would become full-time makers. While baskets continued to be made from a wide variety of naturally occurring materials dependent upon local climates and soils, the professionals in many countries would mainly use willow. This in turn led to concentrations of activity in regions particularly favourable for willow cultivation, especially river valleys. The plant was easily propagated, and could be confined to areas relatively near to the makers' workshops. Hence the most suitable varieties could be grown and protected from damage by grazing livestock and from other gatherers. The best material would come from carefully managed beds since single straight rods require annual cutting from good stools kept free of weeds, pests, and diseases. In regions where the lack of wild willow had given rise to the exploitation of other local plant species such as oak and chestnut, then even professionals might work with these materials.

French records from 1292 also list groups which specialised in different branches: beaten work (e.g. winnowing fans), general basketry, open work (e.g. fish traps) and bottle covering. A French royal statute of 1467 established the basketmakers' fraternity and laid down the system of apprentice (four years) and improver or journeyman (two years), and hence a minimum of six years supervised work before attaining the status of a master basketmaker. The earliest recorded basketmaker in England was one Johanne Hoo listed as subject to the Suffolk poll tax in Stowmarket in 1381 and perhaps an immigrant from The Netherlands[21]. In London, the humble position of the craft may account for the scanty records of any fraternity in mediaeval times. A clear hierarchy among guilds emerged in which some trades became noble and others vulgar. Contributing factors included the value of the raw materials, wage levels of employees, the quality and wealth of customers, and size of the guild and its chronology. No doubt basketmaking scored low on most of these criteria. In London, basketmakers were mentioned in a list compiled by the Brewers Company in 1422, but did not become established as a craft guild in their own right until 1569, by order of the City of London[22]. The guild was certainly involved in maintaining standards in the City. For example, in 1677 it collected a fine for defective workmanship and ordered the sub-standard baskets to be burned at Smithfield.

In Germany, most of the principal towns had their own guilds. Their formal charters seem only to have been conferred centuries after the initial groupings had evolved. Thus Cologne (1589) and Braunschwieg (1593) were some of the first to receive charters followed by many others in the next hundred years although a few were only established in the first half of the 19th century[23]. These guilds set the rules governing training and examinations, and also kept the peace among members when these were in competition with each other. They insisted that improvers must travel during their journeymen

years, and limited the number who could work for any master (one to three in different towns) and also the numbers of apprentices, presumably to prevent any one workshop becoming too large and taking work from other members. In the earliest guild times, formal measurements of skill at the end of the long training period were not common, but gradually it seems that the production of a 'masterpiece' was essential for those few journeymen lucky enough to advance to set up their own workshops.

The examination to become a master in Munich involved the submission of nine different articles specified to demonstrate competence across the whole range of normal work. In Kranichfeld, the rule specified several test-pieces for a candidate from outside the town, but only a single basket for local men. Each fraternity defended the interests of its own members and there were frequent disagreements between guilds.

In the Netherlands as elsewhere, the guilds had a strong religious element, adopted a patron saint, and were attached to particular churches for annual ceremonies[24]. Their ordinances came from the town authority, but the members might have to promise obedience to the Church, the Guild Master, and the Lord of the Manor. Dordrecht had such a guild from 1367. In the earliest times, each member (Master Basketmaker) had to possess a sword and protective clothing for defence of the town, and a bucket and ladder to help in fire fighting for the community. They each contributed money to guild funds upon admittance, thereafter annually, when taking an apprentice, and through fines for non-attendance or non-compliance with the rules. One surviving cash box from the guild in Alkmaar dates from 1643 and is decorated on three of its sides with a layette basket, a winnowing fan, and a text. The guild's reserves were available to help a master, his wife or children in case of illness or death – an early form of mutual insurance.

For several hundred years the guilds controlled the trade within the town or city, maintaining quality standards, and preventing excessive competition among masters while guarding their local market from incursions by others from outside the area. But by the second half of the 18th century, the guild records show very few new members as

Far left: Romanian peasant farmer weaving the base for a basket in semi-green willow for his own use. Transylvania 1986

Left: Antonio Campelo Trigo from Mondariz, Galicia, Spain, now retired. He worked in chestnut splint travelling around the region to make and repair the large grape harvesting baskets, 1995

the basketmakers wanted to free themselves from the restrictions imposed upon them. Eventually the masters lost their control over who could engage in the craft. The French profession was declared 'free' in 1776 and The Netherlands followed in 1798. The German guilds survived until the 19th century when the law gave men the right to follow any profession.

Basketry as a continuing rural craft

Nevertheless, a concentration upon the organisation and work of the city and town guilds surely gives a distorted picture of European basket making from the 13th to the 19th centuries. During all this time, many households must have continued to make their own for both domestic use and their own professional needs, as and when they were required, and sometimes to exchange a few with neighbours. Thus fishermen would be skilled in making their own traps for eels and crustaceans, and some types of fish (e.g. salmon). Retired or disabled workers would have had an even greater output, and some of these would have achieved high levels of skill. Often they utilised different materials from the professionals, either because good willow was not available, or because alternative fibres were abundant or actually preferred. Thus in Britain and other northern countries, oak, hazel, ash, and chestnut stems were harvested and normally split before use. Straw, usually rye or wheat, was used in coils bound with split bramble stems or other material. Freshwater rush was plaited or woven. In the Nordic countries tree roots were gathered, and in southern Europe many other tree stems including olive, cherry, and dogwood were used besides leaves of palm trees and esparto grass.

Another type of basketmaking has been described by Anna Champeney from her studies of peasant crafts in Galicia in north west Spain[25]. In some parts of Mondariz district, almost every man was a basketmaker, practising his craft on a semi-itinerant, seasonal basis. Leaving his wife and children to take care of the farm during the summer months, he would travel around the larger farms making and repairing baskets, in particular the *culeiros* or grape harvesting baskets. This system may once have been common in other regions. In the Lleyn peninsula of west Wales, older men travelled, stayed at the farm where the owner provided hazel and willow, and made frame baskets used in cattle feeding in return for a small wage and their keep[26].

A gypsy family offering their white willow and wood splint baskets for sale in Sofia market, Bulgaria 1972

The gypsies, or Roma, Europe's true itinerants, have also had a long tradition of making and selling baskets. When travelling they would cut willow rods from the wild and use them half-dried or semi-green. Where they settled, they often adopted the materials of the professional (boiled and stripped buff willow for example), and indeed in some countries like Bulgaria they dominate the profession today.

It is not surprising that different weaving techniques were used with different materials. Thus, willow was frequently employed in constructions where a skeleton of thicker rods is first woven around to form a separate base and this weaving is then continued up the side stakes finishing in a border. Many split woods were used in a frame technique. In this, the worker starts at the rigid frame or rim and gradually inserts carved ribs as the side weaving progresses from the top down to the base from each side (see techniques chapter). A feature of such basketry is the large amount of time taken to gather and prepare the material, but this was less important to people with slack periods, particularly in winter, and who were not trying to earn their major income from cash payments per finished article.

Basketry servicing the industrial revolutions

A clear picture of the organisation of basketmaking in Europe before 1900 is not yet available except from a few specific areas. Records survive for several regions of Germany[27]. In some other countries investigations from the early part of the 20th century are able to throw some light on previous times by looking backwards from the patterns which still existed. Thus the surveys carried out in England and Wales between 1919-1923 by staff from the Agricultural Economics Research Institute at Oxford, through their interviews with many people in the industry, reveal something of conditions and practices in the second half of the 19th century[28]. Several French studies, though concluded more recently, have also dealt with situations going back more than 100 years and are summarised in the chapter on France.

It is difficult today to realise just how slowly European life had evolved for the mass of its people since the loosening of the manorial system in the west during the 12th and 13th centuries. In 1700, only an estimated 16 per cent of the population in Britain lived in towns of more than 5000 people, and this figure was even lower in most other countries. The vast majority of the people were still rural with a high degree of self-sufficiency. Only the capital cities had developed the societies that needed many specialist services (London had over half a million residents). But population growth from 1750, combined with the expansion of industry, transformed some countries to predominantly urban societies. By 1900, 77 per cent of Britons lived in towns.

Not only did this cut off most people in these western cities from the materials and the skills necessary for basketmaking, it also increased enormously the movement of goods – food, raw materials, and finished products – and thus the need for containers which were still largely woven. This increasing demand would first have encouraged some rural people to develop their skills into a secondary occupation. Eventually, many of them would evolve into full-time makers in their own houses, and would cultivate their own willow beds. Frequently sons would work with their father, or brothers would work together throughout their lives. While the men mainly did the weaving, women and children helped with other jobs including stripping the bark from the willow rods, making bases, and perhaps splitting the rods and using the resultant willow 'skein' for fine work. The more successful businesses might employ extra hands in the form of hired men, and a few would eventually grow into substantial concerns with scores, or even hundreds, of workers. Some of these would be in central workshops, others were out-workers using their own houses, but weaving willow supplied by their employer. Payment would frequently be by piecework – an agreed sum for each completed article.

Merchants evolved to move the basketry to more distant markets, including exports. The makers delivered their output once or twice weekly to the market towns, collected their money and perhaps materials for the next batch. New materials might be imported from overseas. The successful merchants developed markets and encouraged increased output. In some of the less favoured areas of Germany where farms could not support much agricultural production, whole communities turned over to basketry. Different villages specialised in single products: pine chip baskets, cane carpet beaters, fine skeined willow work, or items made from palm leaf or raffia. While the merchants may have prospered, individual basketmakers were frequently exploited and had to work long hours under poor conditions to make a meagre living.

The same situation occurred elsewhere and, as in other industries, led to two developments. Those who continued as paid workers formed trade unions to improve their negotiating ability with their employers. A union for London journeymen was founded in 1816. It published lists of agreed prices paid for all types and sizes of baskets and continued on a national scale, publishing its last list in 1956. In other cases, some

Showroom of Cooperative at Bussières-les-Belmont, France

Ecole Nationale d'Osiericulture et de Vannerie, Fayl-Billot. The French National School

of the independent makers formed cooperatives with the idea of selling their collective output at better prices while retaining their independence as makers and perhaps willow growers also. In France, the cooperative at Villaines-les-Rochers, near Tours, was founded in 1849. Another is at Bussières-les-Belmont, in Haute-Marne, and both are still continuing today.

In spite of the huge impact of urbanisation and industrialisation, it would be wrong to conclude that all basketmaking moved into Europe's cities or into specialist villages and became part of that same industrial revolution. Large numbers of rural basketmakers were neither employers nor employees, but people working by themselves. While some would work on orders from merchants, others would service their local community making a wide range of articles and mending others. Naturally, these are the ones about whom least is known, or has been recorded.

Throughout history, perhaps because they were so ephemeral, destroyed either by rough use or by decay, baskets were seen as of low value. In addition the status of the craft and the people working at these occupations seems unfortunately to have reflected the status of the articles produced. Even though there is a high degree of skill required for the production of good work, the practitioners have not been highly regarded among other craft workers. A man with a lifetime of fine work behind him, from a family which specialised in the craft for a least five previous generations and with a father recognised as 'one of the best craftsmen in France', could still sum up his condition to me in 1990 using the words "I am only a basketmaker"[29].

Basketry training

One consequence of the decline of the old apprenticeship system, where new entrants had to undertake a long training period and perhaps pass final examinations, was a shortage of skilled workers in the 19th century. As a result, several countries established training schools where young people were formally taught both manual and design skills. A French school opened in Fayl-Billot in 1905 and evolved into the national school in 1912. The Austro-Hungarian Empire established many trade schools based on the first in Vienna in the late 19th century. The German national school in Lichtenfels began in 1904 but another seven regional schools had been founded between 1876 and 1882, at least one in The Netherlands (Noordwolde) and in Switzerland (St Gall). The decline in demand has meant that all of these are now closed or under threat.

Cutting one-year-old willow rods by machine, Sofia, Bulgaria 2003

A partially-automated stripping machine producing white willow rods in Villaines-les-Rochers, France 1991

The decline of the basketry industries

The high noon of the European basketmaking industries has passed. In the more prosperous western countries, this was around 1900, or even earlier for some products. The fundamental cause was the gradual substitution of other packaging materials and transport methods for the traditional basket. Many articles are today carried in disposable cardboard cartons, in plastic shopping bags, or in bulk containers. The disappearance of traditional western-made baskets has been hastened by cheaper imports from further east. Since willow growing and weaving are both highly labour intensive, the price needed for a basket is primarily dependent upon wage rates and output per worker. While mechanisation has recently helped the grower and processor, the actual weaving remains entirely manual. Wages have remained much lower in central and eastern European countries, and this effect was magnified after World War II as long as their centrally planned economies favoured exports in order to earn foreign currency. As a result, large-scale basketmaking industries survived much later in these eastern countries – indeed after 1990 in some. Today, even the basketry industries in Poland, Romania, the former East Germany and Hungary are suffering competition from those in the Far East where wage rates continue to be low and working hours and conditions may be very different from those that Europeans have come to expect.

This is not a new phenomenon. English makers were complaining of cheap imports before 1870 except during wars when supplies sometimes stopped! Dutch and Belgian fruit baskets then competed strongly so that by the 1920s some 90 per cent of all baskets in the Evesham fruit growing area in England were from The Netherlands. Changes in fashion, new inventions, and new materials have killed off other basketry products like fine willow skein handbags, carpet beaters, and perambulators with woven bodies. More details of the history of basketmaking in Europe's many countries and regions are given in subsequent chapters, particularly where these seem to deviate from this generalised account. In the concluding chapter an attempt is made to review the current position of the craft and the ways in which it is continuing to change.

Basket-making factory, Marginex, Gherla, Romania 1995 producing mainly domestic baskets in buff skeined willow

Notes and references

1. Oppenheimer, S. (2003) 'Out of Eden - the peopling of the world'. Constable.
2. Sykes, B. (2006) 'Blood of the Isles - exploring the genetic roots of our tribal history'. Bantam Press.
3. Stringer, C. (2006) 'Homo Britannicus - the incredible story of human life in Britain'. Allen Lane.
4. Smith, B.D. (1998) 'The Emergence of Agriculture'. Scientific American Library.
5. FitzGerald, M. (2007) 'Revolutionising our understanding of Prehistoric Basketry'. Seanda 2: 49-51 (National Roads Authority Magazine, Ireland. www.nra.ie/archaeology/); also Madsen, S. (2008) personal communication. This Danish basketmaker examined an eel trap, also dating back over 7000 years, which had been buried in the mud on the Swedish coastline opposite Copenhagen until its discovery in 2007. It was made from around 100 willow rods joined in a pairing weave of juniper roots.
6. Rackham, O. (2001) 'Trees and Woodland in the British Landscape'. Phoenix Press.
7. Bobart, H.H. (1997) 'Basketwork through the Ages'. The Basketmakers' Association.
8. Gaitzsch, W. (1986) 'Antike Korb und Seilerwaren'. Limesmuseum Aalen.
9. Spindler, K. (1995) 'The Man in the Ice'. Phoenix.
10. See 7, p36.
11. Okey, T. (1930) 'A Basketful of Memories - an autobiographical sketch'. J.M. Dent & Sons.
12. Blanc, N. and Gury, F. (1999) 'La Vannerie en Gaule Romaine' in La Vannerie à l'Époque Gallo-Romaine by Barbier, G., Blanc, N., Coulon, G., Gury, F., and Pichonnet, M. Musée d'Argentomagus; and Frayne, J.M. (1979) 'Subsistence Farming in Roman Italy'. Centaur Press.
13. Lerche, G. (1993) 'Documentation of Traditional Crafts' in Tools and Traditions, Ed. Cheape, H. National Museums of Scotland.
14. See 12 (Frayne), p134.
15. Brunner, K, (1995) 'Continuity and Discontinuity of Roman Agricultural Knowledge in the Early Middle Ages' in Agriculture in the Middle Ages, Ed. Sweeney, D. University of Pennsylvania Press.
16. Fox, H.S.A (1973) 'Going to Town in 13th Century England' in Man Made the Land, Eds. Baker, A.R.H. and Harley, J.B. David & Charles.
17. Miller, E. and Hatcher, J. (1978) 'Medieval England: Rural society and economic change 1086-1348'. Longman.
18. Moon, D. (1999) 'The Russian Peasantry 1600-1930'. Longman.
19. Epstein, S.A. (1991) 'Wage Labor and Guilds in Medieval Europe'. University of North Carolina Press.
20. Miller, E. and Hatcher, J. (1995) 'Medieval England: towns, commerce and crafts'. Longman.
21. See 7, p106.
22. The Basketmakers' Company is 52nd in order of preference among the Livery companies in the City of London, of which there are now over 100.
23. Dippold, G. (1994) 'Deutsches Korbmuseum Michelau (Begleitbuch zur Dauerausstelung)' Schriften des Deutschen Korbmuseums Nr 2.
24. My information on Dutch basketry guilds is based on extensive research by Mrs G.M. Pot-van Regteren Altena, and in particular a manuscript 'A Basketmakers' Guild in a Dutch Town' which she translated for me from her Dutch paper 'Een Nederig Ambacht'.
25. Champeney, A. (1996) 'On the Basketry Trail in Galicia'. BA NL **76** 2-4.
26. Jones, A.M. (1926) 'The Rural Industries of England and Wales IV: Rural industries in Wales'. OUP. Republished 1977 by EP Publishing Ltd.
27. See 23.
28. Fitzrandolph, H.E. and Doriel Hay, M. (1926) 'The Rural Industries of England and Wales II: Osier growing and basketry and some rural factories'. OUP. Republished 1977 by EP Publishing Ltd.
29. Emilien Métézeau belongs to a family of professional basketmakers still working in Villaines-les-Rochers in the Loire valley, whose story is told in the chapter on France.

Materials

Cutting willows near
Oath Hill, Somerset
on a bed owned by
PH Coate & Son,
January 1988.
Photo: RJ Whittick

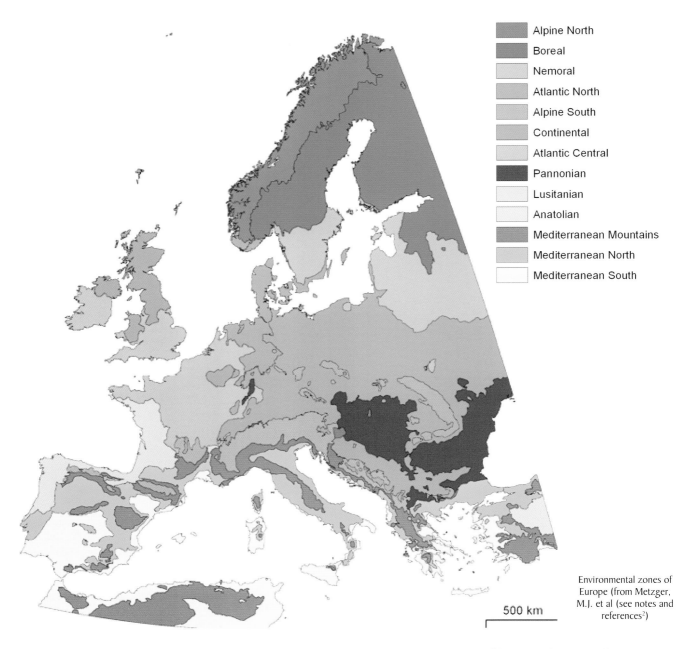

Alpine North
Boreal
Nemoral
Atlantic North
Alpine South
Continental
Atlantic Central
Pannonian
Lusitanian
Anatolian
Mediterranean Mountains
Mediterranean North
Mediterranean South

500 km

Environmental zones of Europe (from Metzger, M.J. et al (see notes and references[2])

Almost all basketry has been created by weaving plant fibres, so the naturally-occurring vegetation might be expected to be the major determinant of the materials originally employed in different regions. These materials need to be pliable to permit any of the basic forms of weaving. They also need to have strength appropriate to the article being made, and preferably to grow as straight pieces sufficiently long to avoid excessive joining, which both slows the work process and may weaken the article.

Some materials conform well to these requirements in their natural form. Thus, one year-old willow rods can be up to 4m in length, almost straight, with a diameter between 2-20mm though normally less in cooler climates, and are extremely supple and pliable when green or after appropriate soaking of dried material. Some creepers, such as cane from SE Asia, clematis in Europe, and certain tree roots (pine, spruce) are even more extreme since they may produce much longer lengths of more or less uniform diameter, although, because of their greater flexibility, they do not hold a shape as well as willow. Many other materials may appear less suitable at first sight, but by appropriate manipulation can be made to conform. Thus, individual stems which are too fine, short and weak, like grass or straw, may be combined together by binding or plaiting to form continuous lengths and then woven. At the other extreme, branches or trunks of trees which obviously have length and strength may be successively split longitudinally until the pieces acquire the necessary pliability for weaving. The splitting may be helped by soaking, boiling, or dry heating.

Climatic regions

Over half a million years the northern part of western Europe and the Alps and Pyrenees were covered with ice masses several times. This period gradually ended some 15,000-7,000 years ago. During these first post-glacial millennia, the path of the moist Atlantic winds shifted northwards with the result that the rainfall which previously watered north Africa and southwest Asia was now deposited in central Europe. This roughly coincides with the start of the Neolithic era and hence the earliest evidence for basketry in Europe. Since that time the pattern of climates has been very broadly as we see it today.

Five or six regional types may be distinguished according to rainfall regimes and winter temperature[1].

- The maritime or oceanic type of the British Isles, and a coastal belt from Norway to the Bay of Biscay: mild, humid, with usually maximum rainfall in autumn
- The arctic of the northern coastlines
- The sub-arctic with a growing season of fewer than 120 days followed by temperatures below freezing for a least six months and mainly summer rain
- Mediterranean with hot dry summers and light winter rains
- The continental, east of Warsaw, with a large range between summer and winter temperatures and rainfall with a summer maximum
- The transitional type which covers the largest part of the whole area and most of central Europe, and is between the maritime and continental climates. In addition, the mountain areas of southern Scandinavia, the Alps, Pyrenees, and Carpathians are colder and have more precipitation than their lower neighbouring regions.

Many variables influence plant growth and development including day length, the amount of solar energy received, the amount of precipitation left over after drainage and evaporation, temperature during the growing season, and the level of mineral plant nutrients in the soil. Biogeographers have developed detailed maps showing the environmental zones of Europe taking into account altitude, slope, latitude, ocean effect, temperature, precipitation and sunshine. The one reproduced here shows 13 environmental zones each with characteristic plant communities[2]. A study of European basketry and its development over time should begin with the plant resources which were available to man before he had today's ability to ship material rapidly from any part of the globe.

In recent times the characteristic vegetation of much of Europe has been broad-leaved deciduous forest which has a dormant season in the winter months. The predominant tree species vary, but include oaks, beech, sweet chestnut, ash and alder. In the more northern regions (Nemoral) this merges first into mixed forest where broad-leaved species, (often birch) are combined with conifers, and then (Boreal) into truly coniferous forests containing pine, spruce and larch. Finally the northernmost regions are tundra, characterised by dwarf birch, willow, pine, juniper and other ground creeping plants.

The south-west (Lusitanean) with heaths and oaks gradually merge into the Mediterranean regions where hot dry summers support cork and holm oaks, pines, olives, fruit plantations, and palm trees on the coasts.

Since altitude has such a pronounced effect on reducing temperature, wherever there are mountains then the vegetation gradually changes up their slopes as though the latitude were farther north, going through mixed, to coniferous forest, to something approaching tundra on the highest ranges. In the regions which are furthest from the western seaboards and the prevailing winds off the Atlantic, climates become more 'continental' with greater extremes of temperature between seasons, and some regions of prairie (long) and steppe (short) grassland (Pannonian) are found in parts of the former Russian republics.

Within a region and within a country, soil types, drainage conditions and altitude caused significant variation in the species that were easily available to the local community. Perhaps the countries which best illustrate this regional variation are Italy, Spain and Portugal. Here there are huge variations in climatic zone caused not only by the north to south distances (800-1000km), but also by the existence of mountain ranges which exaggerate the normal reduction in rainfall from west to east. As a consequence, while oak, chestnut and willow are predominant basket-making materials in the cool, wet coastal regions to the north and west, the hot and dry central and southern areas make much more use of olive wood, bamboo-like reeds, straw, esparto grass and palm leaves.

Modification by man

But, of course, from the earliest times, man's activities have modified the natural vegetation to produce the landscapes which are evident today. The earliest farmers exploited lowland gravel terraces and belts of loess soils by planting food crops and grazing their livestock. They gradually extended their activities into areas of heavier soils and denser forest, cutting, burning, grazing and cultivating so that much of the original tree cover never returned.

Major deforestation occurred in Europe in the Neolithic and early Bronze ages through the use of 'slash and burn' techniques, particularly in the deciduous forests. There was extensive cutting for the timber trade in the eastern Mediterranean lands from the 5th century BC. This, together with fire and animal grazing, had effectively removed the tree cover from regions of Greece by this time. Major phases of clearance also occurred in Europe in the late Middle Ages from the 11th to 13th century, notably through the German colonial drive into the Slav lands of eastern Europe, and in the period from the 16th century to the early 20th century when the populations of Europe increased dramatically and vast areas were cleared for cultivation and for timber[3]. In time, wetlands were drained and water levels controlled in a variety of ways.

The effect of all this forest clearance was to allow many other plant communities, including cultivated crops, to spread and become available for exploitation by man, including their use for basketry. While communities would have relied mainly on the plants growing within a short distance from them, there would have been new ideas and materials brought to their attention by the movement of individuals motivated by trade opportunities, for settling and creating new farms, as well as the major invasions of others bent on conquest.

The most widely used material for basketry, different species of willow, was already well known to the Romans. No doubt its cultivation spread to many parts of that empire, creating a new type of basketry which would have supplemented or replaced the local

Part of Sedgemoor, 1988. The Somerset levels were artificially drained from c1820 and subsequently enclosed to facilitate large-scale willow growing and livestock grazing in summer.
Photo: RJ Whittick

traditions. Similar developments must have occurred many times and in many places throughout history. In some cases, a new material for basketry would have arrived or become much more available as a by-product of some other agricultural development. The widespread use of cereal straw is the most obvious example, but the regular pruning of cultivated hazel and olive trees provided useful rods. Much later, after importation from the New World, the maize crop yielded its papery bracts for weaving into a range of products in some southern countries.

Plant species utilised

It is probably impossible to compile a complete list of all the species that have been employed down the centuries by both professional and amateur basket-makers. Many plants have similar properties and some will have been substituted for a more normal species because of local shortage and abundance, but never recorded nor identified in collections. While detailed examination by specialists can discriminate very accurately between alternatives, there must be many cases where this has not been attempted and

Gustave Métézeau (aged 84) demonstrates how he used to split green oak to make thick slats used as the framework on which white willow rods were tightly woven, 1987.
Photos: R.J.Whittick

so descriptions have remained confused. In the sections below, it has sometimes been necessary to give the genus only, since different species occur in various parts of Europe, and several may have been utilised. More complete lists have been published by others[4].

It is easy for those of us brought up in the British Isles to equate basketry with willow and to assume that every basketmaker would use this material by choice unless it could not be obtained in the area. But when looking backwards into basket history, it is vital to appreciate that wild willow species were just one of the resources available, and that many other plants had superior properties for specific tasks. Even when man had selected willow varieties with improved qualities, there remained the question of the cost of such rods which may have needed to be looked after in dedicated beds. In a simple economy, where time was not money, the basketmaker frequently chose to continue to utilise other species which were free for the gathering from woods and hedges.

Trees

The wood from trees may not immediately seem to be suitable weaving material, but man has proved very inventive in adapting it to his needs. Young, slender, unbranched stems are the simplest to use if they are pliable and of adequate length. Slightly thicker stems which can be easily split down their length may be employed as half- or quarter-round rods. But much thicker wood can also be used if it is first processed into flexible strips. The detailed processes vary with the type of wood and the region but the principles are similar.

The tree is cut down and the unbranched base section of the trunk, up to 10-20cm diameter, is selected. The bark may be removed. The log is then split down its length into two halves, then into quarters and eighths resulting in pieces as long as the original, but with a more or less triangular cross section. The inner, darker heart wood may be separated from the outer paler sapwood by a tangential split down one of the growth rings. Splitting down these rings is continued until there is a series of strips of appropriate width and thickness, using different tools according to the required force

Owen Jones using oak splint to weave the traditional Cumbrian swill, Coniston, Cumbria, 2007

and precision. Splitting may be accomplished simply in green or semi-green wood or with the help of heating or prolonged boiling.

Flat narrow strips consisting of one year's, or even half a year's growth, can be produced for the finest articles, but coarser strips suffice for rougher work. Such strips were known as spale or spelk in England (and splits or splint in the USA where European settlers and native Americans used such material a great deal). I have chosen to use splint in this book. Besides round stems and splint, other material may have to be split out to provide shaped hoops for handles and rims and for ribs.

In order to provide material of the right dimensions for basketmaking (and other woodland crafts), many wooded areas were managed by coppicing: that is, cut every few years close to the ground so that new shoots grow up from the original main stem. A related system is pollarding: cutting some two metres above ground level so that the shoots are not damaged by grazing animals. These procedures provide multiple stems from a single root stock without the need to replant, and the surviving well-developed root system produces very vigorous regrowth of the new stems. Cutting can take place annually in different areas, on a cycle whose length corresponds to the time taken to produce shoots of the required size from that species – from one to perhaps 20 or 30 years.

In time, some woods were machine sawn rather than cleft to produce veneer or thin splint. This was cut, and simply woven and bent to produce chips or punnets particularly used for retailing soft fruit.

Oak (*Quercus spp.*)

Oak splints were obtained from saplings as previously described. They were used both as weft and warp in frame baskets. Another use for the wood, at least in France, was for the wide flat slats around which the round white willow rods were woven (see scuttle work in the techniques chapter). This was found in the classic winnowing fan, but also in back baskets for the grape harvest, dough baskets, and even fire buckets. Some early European settlers in the eastern United States used a third method. They further split the flat strips (of white oak, *Q. alba* and *Q. michauxii*) into rods with a roughly square cross-section and then pulled these through the round holes of a metal die. The resulting round oak rods were used in place of willow rods, mainly in stake and strand work. There is no evidence of this material being employed in Europe[5].

Left: Using a drawshave to smooth a chestnut splint clamped to a simple shaving horse, Mondariz, Galicia, Spain 1995

Right: Jack Rowsell riving an ashpole to provide handles and bands for his Devon splint baskets, 1991.
Photo: Sally Goymer

Sweet Chestnut (*Castanea sativa*)

Occasionally one-year-old shoots were cut and used with the bark on in the same way as brown willow rods. Slightly older stems were used for the rims, handles, and ribs of frame baskets. Stems 5-6cm thick at 3-6 years were split for heavy baskets, or used for hurdles and fence panels since chestnut cleaves easily and has a high proportion of rot-resistant heart wood. In countries bordering the Mediterranean, groves of mature trees were maintained for nut production; and Spain, France, and Italy were major centres for chestnut splint work. By contrast, the areas of chestnut trees in southern England were managed on a coppice system since the nut harvest is unreliable, and straight 12 to 18 year-old stems were mainly split and used for fencing stakes and hurdles.

Ash (*Fraxinus excelsior*)

Ash also has the virtue that it is readily cleft and easily bent. Hence it has frequently been used for basket handles where it wears smooth and does not splinter, as well as for rims and ribs for frame baskets. Cleft ash splints have been used in the same way as oak, either for weaving the entire basket, or as the slats around which white willow rods were woven in English scuttle work.

Hazel (*Corylus avellana* and other spp.)

One-year old hazel stems used as round weaving rods, Canepina, Italy 2001

Hazel seldom grows thick trunks since its habit is to keep producing multiple stems even without coppicing. The wood was therefore frequently employed as handles or rims, or as rough splint weavers used with the bark on; but there are also some beautiful examples of quite fine splintwork. Often several narrow splints were taken off all around a rod leaving the central core which could then be fashioned into a rib, rim, or handle. In regions where hazel nuts are grown as a crop (e.g. Italy), the trees attain considerable size and throw out many new shoots from below ground. These need to be pruned away annually and can be used as round weaving rods.

Willow (*Salix spp.*)

Wild willow trees must have provided basketmakers with some of their material for thousands of years in lowland regions or in wet valleys. Man then learned to cultivate them from Roman times, and thus kept them near to him and improved their quality through selection for his own purposes. The desirable qualities vary according to the work being done; but length, straightness, lack of branching, strength, and elasticity or suppleness are all important for weaving rods, as well as pest and disease resistance.

In England, the most important species were *S. triandra* (Almond-leaved willow) for general purpose work, *S. viminalis* (Osier) which produces stouter rods for heavier baskets and hurdles and *S. purpurea* (Purple willow) with slender rods used for small high-quality basketware. In the Netherlands, Belgium and France, hybrids between the tree willows (*S. alba* and *S. fragilis*) are widely used. It is not possible to describe all the useful willow types here, but sources are given in the references[6].

Most cultivated willows are grown close together in beds and cut annually after leaf fall very near to their point of origin. The stump, or stool, may be at ground level or raised to keep it clear of other vegetation or small animals. The rods are sometimes left for a

second, or even third, year of growth where greater thickness is needed for handles or corner posts in square work. Much thicker branches have been used to make the coarse splints (as with oak, chestnut and hazel) for scuttle work.

Weaving rods may be used in several forms. Fresh 'green' rods can be used, but they shrink when the finished article dries and cause the weaving to loosen. For this reason, most rural basketmakers would allow the rods to partially 'season' (dry) before use. This

drying time varied according to their thickness and whether they were stored indoors or outside. A rough guide was that slender rods up to 1.5m could be used from six to eight weeks after harvesting. They would still be sufficiently pliable to weave while having dried enough to minimise subsequent shrinkage.

Rods cut in the winter and dried with the skin (bark) still on are usually called brown whatever the actual bark colour, and were often used for coarse work or where the article had to sit in water since the bark tannins help to resist decay.

Stems cut in spring just before they come into full leaf can have the bark stripped to produce white rods, but the period during which this can be done is short. More usually (at least in temperate climates) the rods would be cut between autumn leaf-fall and spring, and kept alive by standing them in shallow water pits (15cm deep) before stripping when the buds burst. They are then dried in the open air, tied in bolts according to size, and stored for use or sale.

'Buff' rods are created by boiling in large water vats with the skin on before stripping and drying. The bark tannins stain the inner rod a red-brown colour, and these partially 'cooked' rods are very supple. Boiling can be carried out using fresh green material brought straight from the fields from the autumn, or with dried brown rods at any time of the year[7]. The process seems to have been developed in Britain around 1870 but soon spread throughout Europe.

All forms of willow except green or semi-green have to be soaked before weaving. Brown rods may take from five to twenty days soaking time to render them pliable. Buff or white need only be immersed for a few hours and then allowed to mellow, preferably overnight under a damp cover.

Just as larger trees are split down into strips to make them sufficiently pliable for weaving, so one year-old white or buff willow rods may also be split longitudinally into

two, three or four. This is achieved with a special tool, a cleave. These can then be made into 'skeins' by planing off the pithy centre, (with a shave) but always leaving the outer skin. An even width is achieved by passing the skein between the two cutting edges of another tool called an upright. Both tools can be made in hand-held or bench-mounted forms, or mechanised for hand or electric power. White skeins were used to create the

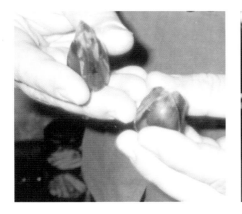

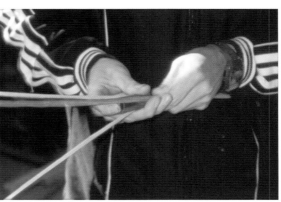

31

Left: Planing off the inner pith to produce a buff skein, Sofia, Bulgaria, 2003

Right: Large-scale production of buff skein, Marginex factory, Gherla, Romania, 1995

very fine quality baskets which were a speciality of northern France and Belgium from the early 17th century and of southern Germany during the late 18th and 19th centuries.

Buff skein has been used for the weavers in many baskets made in eastern European factory workshops. The material is easier to use than whole willow, and makes a cheaper and lighter article. It is also much used in some of these countries as a decorative surface on furniture and shop fittings. It is made from the lower parts of very stout (20mm) one-year rods which can grow rapidly when irrigated during hot summers.

Brown skein (with the skin still on one side) from coarse rods was also commonly used for the weavers on frame baskets made by country people (e.g. in France) for their own use in garden, farm, and market.

Another use for willow skein was as a binding material round the cores of grass or straw used in coiled baskets.

Conifers

Simo Lappi preparing thin pine splint in Finland 2005.
Photo: Anna-Maria Väätäinen

Right: Exposing a root in a Swedish spruce forest.
Photo: Jan Nordahl

Far right: Bundles of prepared branches and roots from Swedish spruce.
Photo: Jonas Hasselrot

In Scandinavia and other northern countries, basketmakers have naturally had to exploit the coniferous species which are often dominant. Pine (*Pinus spp.*) has been split into thin sheets. Spruce (*Picea abies*) branches are formed into ribs for frame baskets, while split juniper (*Juniperus communis*) branches have been popular as weavers in coarse Swedish work. In addition, pine, spruce, and juniper have all been valued for their long surface roots of even diameter which can be used whole or made into skein.

Two coiled mats wrapped in coloured raffia and the grass used for the cores, Castelsardo, Sardinia, 2003

Palm (Chamaerops humulis)

This palm tree grows in several Mediterranean regions, and its leaves have been woven into mats and bags in Spain, Sardinia, Cyprus, and parts of Italy. Raffia is the dried leaf of another palm which is imported as a substitute from Madagascar, dyed in a range of colours, and used as a decorative wrapping around the coils for mats and bowls.

Other trees and shrubs

Many other species have had local importance. These include poplar (*Populus spp.*) and aspen (*Populus tremula*) for thin splint, and lime (*Tilia spp.*) for bast – the fibrous material just underneath the bark which can be used to make cord and net bags and as the wrapping around coiled straw work (see p145). Stems for weaving have been taken from elm (*Ulmus sp.*), birch (*Betula sp.*), acacias and mimosa (*Acacia spp.*), bird cherry (*Prunus avium*), dogwood (*Cornus sanguinea*), alder buckthorn (*Frangula alnus*), *Viburnum spp.*, myrtle (*Myrtus communis*), *Celtis sp.*, chaste tree (*Vitex agnus-cestis*), Spanish broom (*Spartium junceum*), olive (*Olea europaea*), mulberry (*Morus sp.*), *Styrax sp.*, perwinkle (*Vinca major*), and privet (*Ligustrum vulgare*).

Mediterranean palm (Chamaerops humulis) whose leaves are used in coiled work, Castelsardo, Sardinia, 2003

In northern lands, birch trees have also provided their fine roots, but especially their outer bark. This has long been utilised to make containers from folded sheets or woven strips. It is harvested in Finland in late June to early July when it separates easily from the tree trunk, usually in sheets from one section around the circumference. It can also be taken off in spiral strips up the trunk but this is more difficult. The quality differs from tree to tree, and one looks for straight trunks of white bark though it is the inside layers which are mainly used. Bark from the rowan tree (*Sorbus aucuparia*) has been used.

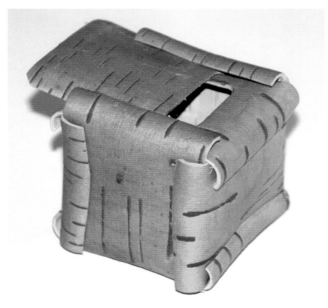

Birch bark box often used to hold shoe pegs, Jonas Hasselrot, Sweden

The rural population has always exploited materials growing wild in hedgerows and waste places. During and after World War II when commercially grown willow was in short supply, there was a movement in Britain to study just which plants were useful as substitutes. This tradition of using hedgerow and garden material is continued by those who derive satisfaction from a wide range of colours and textures, and it is part of the craft's wide diversity today[8].

Frame basket woven in wild clematis on chestnut frame, San Gimignano, Tuscany, Italy, 2000

Creepers and climbers

The long stems of wild clematis (*C. vitalba*) have been collected and used for weaving in frame baskets in Italy and other countries. Hop (*Humulus lupulus*) stems (bines), cultivated or wild grapes (*Vitis sp.*), and honeysuckle (*Lonicera sp.*) have also been utilised in similar ways.

References from Roman times record that the widely occurring blackberry (*Rubus spp.*) provided the binding material for coiled straw work[9]. One year old stems 2m in length were cut and the thorns rubbed off. Sometimes the outer bark was also scraped away while still fresh. The stems were then split into three or four and the inner pith removed to leave thin strips of wood which were dried and stored for later use.

Hanks of imported cane in Stanley Bird's workshop, Great Yarmouth, 1989

Far Eastern cane from several climbing rattan or cane palms has been imported to Europe since the 17th century. Some varieties grow up to 150m while still remaining small in diameter, and are often sold in lengths of 4-10m. It is first processed to remove the spines. The shiny outer covering, when split off, has been used for wrapping and chair seating: the inner 'centre cane' for baskets, particularly by schoolchildren or beginners. Other varieties were used unsplit for fishing and industrial baskets where their durability was valued in conditions of rough use.

Cereal straw

The straw of the four commonly cultivated cereals: rye (*Secale*), wheat (*Triticum*), oats (*Avena*), and barley (*Hordeum*) has been utilised, particularly in drier regions where willow or wetland species were not readily available. Straw was used after the grain had been threshed (but not when it had been smashed by a modern combine harvester). In the most usual method the leaves would be removed, the stems combed straight and drawn out into a continuous bundle or core of constant thickness. This was then both wrapped and linked into the previous coil, usually with a stiff material like skeined willow, or blackberry, or a fibrous string. Many of these articles were small for domestic use, but quite large containers for grain or meal were sometimes made. Straw bunches could also be twined with string (twisted from grass or other plants) and woven into back baskets for carrying heavy loads.

David Chubb, Gloucestershire, demonstrating bee-skep-making from straw and wrapping cane, 1998

Straw plait can be fashioned into baskets by winding out in a spiral from the base to the rim and joining each round with a cord enclosed in the outer edge of the plait. Maize (*Zea mais*) was imported to Europe from South America at the end of the 15th century, and the leaves or bracts enclosing the cob have been used widely in some of the Mediterranean countries where this grain became a staple food crop.

Esparto grass growing on hillside in Andalucia, Spain, 1998

Bundle of dried esparto grass, Andalucia, Spain

Grasses

The stiff stems of marram grass (*Ammophila arenaria*) and bent (*Agrostis sp.*) have been utilised locally in plaiting in Anglesey, Wales, and in the Orkney Isles respectively, but other grasses have supported much larger industries in Mediterranean regions[10]. Esparto grass (*Stipa tenacissima*) and another similar species (*Lygeum spartum*) are widespread in hot dry areas of Spain. The 60cm long leaves are often used in plaited form, but also in stake and strand work. Their use might have originated in N Africa. Esparto has also been utilised in the Netherlands based on imported material. Another species, ropegrass (*Ampelodesmos mauritanicus*) grows in Italy and the south of France, and was used there in plaited and coiled work[11]. Purple moor grass (*Molinia caerulea*) has been used like cereal straw in French coiled work[12].

Maria Raimonda Pinna using fine rush to weave a shallow bowl, San Vero Milis, Sardinia, 2003

Other plants

Many different plants which thrive near or in water - standing, flowing or salt - have been utilised either through their long, narrow, pliable leaves, or their stiffer stems.

Several rushes (*Juncus acutus, J. maritimus* and *J. Bufonis*) with fine rigid stems are made into simple cheese moulds. After drying, reeds (including *Phragmites australis* and *P. communis*), reedmace or cattails (*Typha latifolia* and *T. angustifolia*), and freshwater rush (*Schoenoplectus scirpus*, previously *Scirpus lacustris*) have been used for a whole range of products, but particularly two-

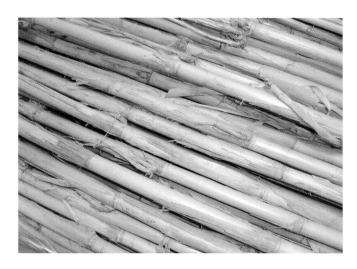

Left: 'Cane' before splitting, Malta.
Photo: Geraldine Jones

Mediterranean cane (Arundo donax) growing wild near Nijar, Andalucia, 1998

handled bags and domestic containers, and for chair seating. In the Netherlands, rush is cultivated as a crop in special beds some 45cm deep in water[13].

The giant reed (*Arundo donax*) is an aggressive coloniser of waste ground, both wet and dry around many Mediterranean coasts though it was originally imported from the Orient. Its bamboo-like stems are split and used for the siding of baskets of all sizes – often in conjunction with willow bases and stakes. Throughout this book I have tried to refer to it as Mediterranean cane or 'cane' to distinguish it from the several sorts of Far Eastern cane which were described earlier.

The asphodel (*Asphodelus microcarpus*) is a member of the lily family which is widespread in Sardinia where it has played an important role in the local production of coiled mats and bowls. The stiff flower stalks, which can grow to 150cm, are dried and split lengthwise to provide a binding or wrapping material with a range of natural colours from buff to dark brown, almost black. The core of the coils can be a bundle of dried seagrass (*Carex sp.*), asphodel leaves, or other grass, or cereal straw.

Asphodel plant growing wild in Sardinia, 2002

Left: Lidded bowl using dried asphodel stems to bind the coils, Bosa, Sardinia

On the coasts of northwest Britain, where tree growth is inhibited by wind and grazing animals, people were sometimes forced to use quite unpromising materials like dock stems (*Rumex acetosa*) for stakes in back baskets and heather stems (*Calluna vulgaris*) for lobster pots. No doubt many other plant species have contributed to local baskets.

Notes and references

1.   Shanahan, E.W. (1964) 'Western and Central Europe - A regional geography'. Macmillan.

2.   Metzger, M.J., Bunce, R.G.H., Jongman, R.H.G., Mücher, C.A. and Watkins, J.W. (2005) 'A Climatic Stratification of the Environment of Europe'. Global Ecol. Biogeogr. **14** 549-563.

3.   Butlin, R.A. (1993) 'Historical Geography'. Arnold p124.

4.   Crawford, M. (2000) 'Plants for Basketry'. Agroforestry Research Trust. Lists over 300 species including 80 willows, with some details of size and uses. Also Braster, B., Parfitt, R., Wynter, S. and Youdale, R. (2001) 'Cultivation and Use of Basket Willows'. Published jointly by the Basketmakers' Association and IACR-Long Ashton Research Station.

5.   Law, R.N. and Taylor, C.W. (1991) 'Appalachian White Oak Basketmaking'. University of Tennessee Press.

6.   See 4 (Braster et al).

7.   Stott, K.G. (1992) 'Willows in the Service of Man'. Proc. Roy. Soc. Edin. **98B** 169-182; and Cousins, R. (2007) 'A Basketful - willow growing and basketmaking in Nottinghamshire and Lincolnshire'. Nottinghamshire County Council and Heritage Lincolnshire, p16.

8.   Basketry based upon wild materials collected from the hedgerow was promoted in England during the 1940s by Mabel Roffey through classes given to members of the Women's Institutes, and then by Nellie Pilcher and Evelyn Legg (see BA NL **97** 17-20 and 25-26). See also Legg, E. (1960) 'Country Baskets', Mills & Boon. Sheila Wynter continued this work and taught Susie Vaughan, whose beautiful book, 'Handmade Baskets from Nature's Colourful Materials' (1994) Search Press, is the obvious guide for today's beginner. A recent welcome addition to the literature is by Bernard Bertrand, 'La Vannerie Sauvage - initiation' (2006) Editions de Terran. The author shows, with the aid of many excellent photographs and figures, how French rural makers traditionally used more than a dozen wild species, often preferring them to cultivated willow because of their special properties, or just because they were free! This too is a wonderful teaching book, together with a DVD.

9.   Frayn, J.M (1979) 'Subsistence Farming in Roman Italy'. Centaur Press, p135.

10. Williams, J.H. (1998) 'The Marram Grass Matters of Anglesey'. BA. NL **45** 0-11 and Strang, S. (1999) 'Plants and People - a visit to Kew Gardens'. BA NL **90** 32-22.

11. Novellino, D. (2006) 'Central Italy (Maranola)'. ICEB 2005: 664-667; and 'Basketry in the Aurunci mountains (Central Italy)' BA NL 119: 25-32, and (2007) BA NL 120: 45-50.

12. See 8. 'La Vannerie Sauvage' p135.

13. Excell, J. (1995) 'A Few Notes on Rush'. BA NL **75** 22.

Techniques

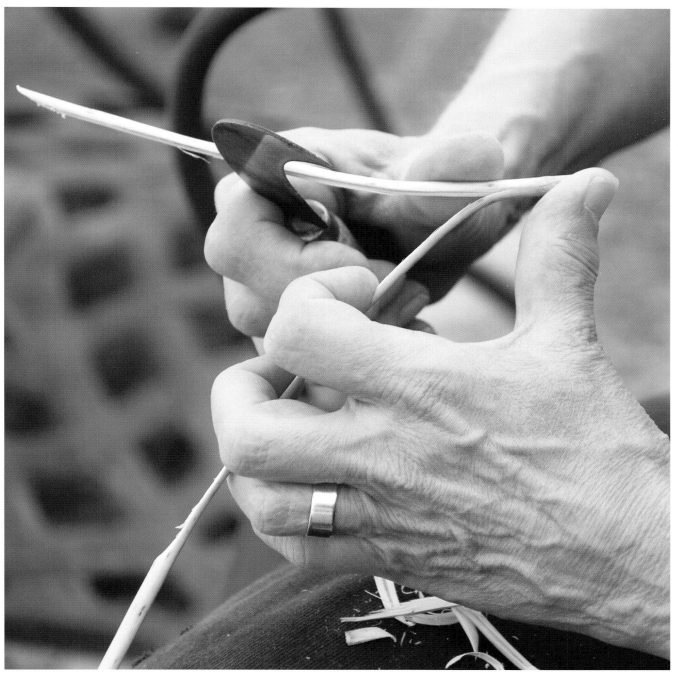

Sally Goymer cutting a tapered end (scallom) on a
willow rod which is then wrapped once around a
thicker rod to join the two at right angles.
Cheltenham, England

Detail of coiled dough basket,
Molinia grass core stitched with
brown willow skein, Lozère, France,
1996

The previous chapter introduced the range of plant fibres used by European makers. What follows is a broad introduction to some of the different methods which were evolved to utilise each fibre. No attempt is made to give instruction on these methods. A selection of instructional books is listed in the notes at the end of this chapter[1]. Some deal with the basic skills of working with cane, willow, rush, straw or hedgerow materials; others with specific regional baskets in an attempt to record their detailed construction before all the traditional makers have ceased to work. In some countries today there are scores of practical basketry courses at all levels. Naturally none of these can take the place of the many hours of repeated practice which were the traditional way of achieving real competence. Nevertheless, we have come a long way from the time when an apprentice like my grandfather had to promise in 1858 'to bind himself to his master for seven years and keep his secrets' in order to learn the art (in his case, of ship's carpenter).

Weaving techniques have been analysed by several authors, and their classifications can become quite technical[2]. They differ in the number and type of elements being used, and the way these relate to each other. For my purposes I only see the need to recognize six main methods which can in turn be sub-divided for greater precision. These are

Coil
Plait
Stake and strand
Loop
Net
Assemble

Naturally, some hybrid articles incorporate more than one of these.

Coil

Coiled baskets are made with a passive element, the core, held in place by an active element, the stitching material. The core may be a single strand like a root or stem, or a bundle of finer strands, for example straw, sedge, rush, grass or leaves. The stitching will usually be done with a thin narrow skein of flexible material commonly prepared from the inner skin of bramble, willow, or hazel stems; or spruce roots; or the split stems or leaves of rush, palm, or (in Sardinia) asphodel. Today lapping cane may be substituted.

Apart from those used to prepare the materials (see previous chapter) the traditional tools are few and simple. Some sort of needle is needed to prepare a gap for the

Lidded workbasket coiled in whole
and skeined spruce root,
Elza Strazdina, Latvia, 1996

stitching. For piercing a straw coil, this was often made from the hollow leg bone of a goose or turkey sharpened at one end; but a similarly sharpened piece of metal tubing or hardwood is adequate. When working with a solid core, the stitching skein passes around two (or more) whole cores rather than piercing the lower one. A bundle coil needs to be kept to an even thickness and a gauge or girth may be used into which the new stems are fed. In Britain this would often have been a section of cow horn with an internal diameter of some 40mm, though thinner coils are found and a metal ring or leather tube can be substituted.

The core is usually a continuous spiral, but in some rows it may be kinked into angles or rounded arches giving an open effect. Exceptions are found in some modern Latvian baskets where successive coils are formed from discrete loops of white willow carefully sized and fitted on top of each other to produce the desired shape.

Coiled work is usually circular or oval (which makes the square corners found in some Scandinavian and Turkish baskets particularly interesting). Many pieces are simple everyday objects: shallow bowls and small containers for household use, sometimes with lids. Others were large storage vessels for cereals, seeds, or other dry goods, and skeps for keeping bee colonies or catching swarms. But the technique was also often employed by women who emphasised aesthetic as well as purely functional aspects and made exquisite items for leisure use. Interesting surface patterns were created by different stitching methods: the proportion of the core which is wrapped, the number of coils spanned by a stitch, and the angle at which a stitch crosses the core.

Celebratory basket in coiled root
work, Norway

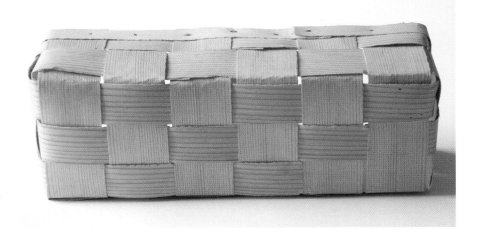

Fruit punnet in thin pine splint, checkweave plait, Krakow, Poland, 1992

Plait

By contrast with coiling, in plaited baskets all elements are active. These are flat or round strips which pass over and under each other at precise angles and are not held together in any other way except at the top edge. The simplest form has two sets of equal width and thickness. One set crosses the other at right angles, over one and under one. Adjacent strips lie close together so that the resultant pattern is like a checkerboard, hence 'check weave'. The angles of the strips can be oblique relative to the base thus giving a diagonal pattern. Twill plaiting has one set of elements passing over and under two or more elements in the other set. This variant can create many and elaborate patterns and also helps to produce a tighter and flatter surface.

Check weave may be used for both base and sides of a basket. The top rim can be finished by folding each vertical strip over and tucking it under the top horizontal strip, or by placing one or two bands around the mouth and lashing (or stapling) them in position. In other cases check weave is confined to the base. Both original sets of base elements then provide just the side stakes while a different material, or a narrower version, is used for the weavers.

Snail basket in esparto plait, Lorca, Spain, 1990

The strips may be unaltered, like flattened rush or cereal straws, or bundles of stems like esparto grass. Alternatively they may be cut from sheet material such as birch bark, or split from logs in the form of thin pine, chestnut, or hazel splint.

Few tools or facilities are needed for weaving the prepared strips apart from knives, and needles for the finer fibres. All materials need to have been thoroughly dried or seasoned before being used for weaving to prevent subsequent shrinkage of the finished article. They may however need to be damped, or even soaked, to restore sufficient flexibility before weaving.

In a quite different method, long lengths of rather narrow plait may be woven and pieces then sewn together perhaps using the same material, or cord, to give the desired size and shape. This technique is found in many Spanish articles in esparto. Narrow straw plait was also sewn up to make hats and bags in several countries. Rush was similarly made up into mattresses and floor mats.

Périgord technique. The brown willow stakes are woven together using a spiral plait, David Drew

It is certainly not obvious to the beginner that plaiting is the primary technique employed in a group of baskets with a very openwork appearance. The iconic French model is known in English as 'the Périgord' since it comes from the Dordogne region. This is an oval bow-handled basket whose bottom and sides are made from a large number of thin brown willow stakes. These seem to be miraculously held together by a plait which starts in the base and spirals around four times before it forms the border. In fact the original stakes and those added after the first spiral do not continue straight to the border. Instead they become incorporated in the next plait, and only reappear as stakes at some distance around[3]. Similar articles can also be found in Italy. This technique or a closely related one is used with bundles of esparto in southern Spain.

Stake and strand

This technique embraces very many baskets made mainly from hardwoods in Europe, and covers a wide range of related methods. They use both active elements and a passive system. All involve the horizontal weaving of long flexible strands (the weft), over relatively inflexible vertical stakes, (the warp). The warp forms the skeleton and shapes each piece. Differences occur mainly in the ways in which this skeleton is built up. Five methods are distinguished here.

Back basket on plank base in hazel splint, Cannero Riviera, Lake Maggiore, Italy, 2000

- **Plank base** – side stakes inserted into holes around the edge of a flat wooden base.

- **Round work** – stakes radiate from a central point in the round base, and then others run more or less parallel up the sides (oval shapes are closely related).

Round tray in several colours of brown willow. Made by Edmond Ghiglione (or his son René) an Italian immigrant working in Biot, near Nice, France, 1989

43

Scuttle work, a large dough basket in white willow on oak slats with hazel rim, Fayl Billot, France, 1981

Right: Square work - a picnic hamper in fine white willow, Mike Smith, Cirencester, England, 1995

Right: Two-handled rush bag, plaited base and twined sides, Y. Hoskovi, Sofia, Bulgaria, 2003

- **Scuttle work** - flat stakes often radiate from the centre, increasing in number and width towards the rim with only narrow gaps between them.

- **Square work** - base stakes run parallel to one side of the square or rectangular base; side stakes more or less parallel from base to border.

- **Twining** - the soft warp elements do not form a rigid skeleton so the weft elements are used in pairs (or more) in a twining weave which grips the base sticks and side stakes firmly and holds them in place.

In these first five methods the top ends of the side stakes are left free until the side weaving is complete.

- **Frame** - stakes (ribs) fixed at both ends early on within a framework which further defines the basket's size and form.

Miniature gwyntell, a frame basket in hazel splint by Dai James, Wales, 1996

Plank base

The maker of a solid based basket needs to have the materials, and some of the tools and skills of both a woodworker and basketmaker. Therefore such a basket could only be made where sawn timber was freely available in addition to branches or roots from hedgerow or coppiced woodland. These combinations have survived in mountainous regions like Scandinavia and the Alps, and robust examples can still be found. The plank base, frequently made from pine, can be cut to any shape. Holes to take the rod or splint stakes are drilled around the edges at an angle to allow the sides to flow out. The stakes may protrude on the underside or be kept flush. One or more U-shaped handles can be inserted in the same way, and their legs also used as stakes. The sides are often woven in wood splint (e.g. hazel). The final row of weaving may be held in place by the folded-over stakes, or by a round of lashing with or without rim bands placed inside and out.

Wood base showing thick ends of stakes, Småland, Sweden. Photo: Jonas Hasselrot

Round work

The methods briefly outlined here for round and square baskets are those commonly found in British work, but variation will be mentioned in regional chapters. In order to make round or oval baskets, professional willow workers usually first weave a separate

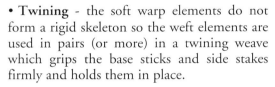
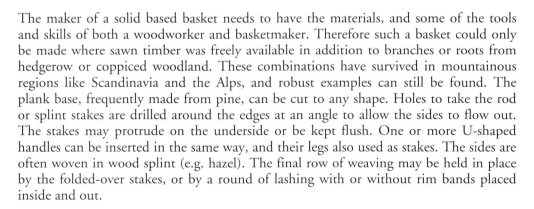

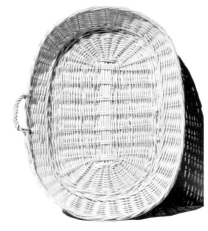

Oval tray for ironed linen in white willow showing the base construction in an oval basket, and one side handle, Spain

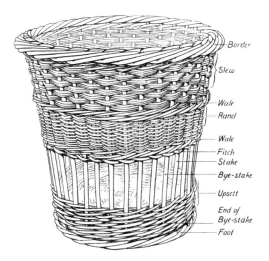

Border
Slew
Wale
Rand
Wale
Fitch
Stake
Bye-stake
Upsett
End of Bye-stake
Foot

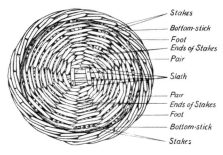

Stakes
Bottom-stick
Foot
Ends of Stakes
Pair
Slath
Pair
Ends of Stakes
Foot
Bottom-stick
Stakes

Engraving of a round basket made by Thomas Okey to illustrate the chief terms used in common basketmaking. Underside view shows base and foot.
Image: The Basketmakers' Association from 'The Art of Basketmaking'.

base with radiating stakes. Several short but stout sticks (e.g. six in two sets of three) are all placed across each other, often by splitting one set in their centres and pushing the other set through. They are tied in this position by weaving a pair of rods in front of and behind each trio in turn for two complete rounds. This is known as tying in the slath. Next, the stick ends in each set are separated and spread out to give the radiating base sticks. The weaving is continued using two fine rods. Additional replacements are added when needed. The base sticks are often held in their position by what is called a 'pairing' stroke. The base is made slightly concave so that the basket will eventually rest on its rim (or on a foot as in the diagram). When the diameter of the base has reached its chosen size, the surplus ends of the base sticks are trimmed off.

The side stakes are then selected (usually two per base stick), sharpened (slyped) at the thick ends, and inserted deep into the weaving at each side of the base sticks. They are bent up 90° in turn. This is called pricking up. They are then held firmly in these upright positions by one or two rounds of a three-strand waling weave. The completion of the sides involves a choice among weaves which differ in their technical characteristics and the patterns they create. When the planned height is reached, the unused ends of the side stakes are woven into a border. This helps to retain them, provides a strong edge to the basket and can enhance its appearance. Finally, one or more handles may be fitted. A single bow handle can be made from one or more thick rods (two- or three-year old willow stems, or older wood from chestnut, ash, or hazel). These are bent to shape with the two ends pointed and forced well down into the side weaving on opposite sides. The ends may be pegged to retain them in place. This handle bow can be left plain, or wrapped by twisting several fine rods around it and weaving their ends into the sides.

An oval basket is little different. It starts with an oval base, created by using one set of longer base sticks and rather more shorter ones which are pierced to receive the longer set. The final effect is to have half of a radial set at each end with two rows of more or less parallel sticks across the longer sides. Small handles at each end are frequently made by first twisting individual rods which partially splits them and makes them rope-like, and this allows them to be tightly curved without kinking.

Scuttle work

This is a method of making long-lasting baskets which are woven so tight that they can retain grain or meal, or even water after soaking. It was always a specialist technique,

Scuttle work. Kneeling inside while rapping down the paired weaving rods between each oak stake when making a winnowing fan, Emilien Métézeau, Villaines-les-Rochers, France, 1991.
Photo: R.J. Whittick

employed by professionals. Both difficult and onerous, in England it required a longer than usual apprenticeship. That it existed in Roman, or even Greek, times is suggested by surviving images, and there are certainly records and objects dating from the 13th and 14th centuries in France and the Netherlands.

The construction usually starts with two or four short splints, crossed at 90° and woven together with a pair of fine white willow rods. These splints or slats are usually hand riven from green or heated wood: oak, ash, chestnut or willow. Longer splints are then shaped and fitted close together so as to almost fill the angles between the original stakes. This procedure continues as the weaving progresses and the basket's circumference expands. Every time the paired weavers cross from front to back, the rapping iron is used to compress the damp rods (hence 'beaten work'). In this technique the work travels from right to left so the iron, in the right hand, is never put down. The weaving is thus kept so tight that the skeleton becomes almost completely covered and no spaces can be seen.

In large circular baskets like the winnowing fan, the maker kneels or crouches inside the work and turns continuously to face the weaving. The rim is finished by placing a thick rod on the edge, bringing the ends of the stakes over it, and tucking them under the last few rows of weaving..

Square work

Inside of picnic hamper in white willow showing square base, Mike Smith, Cirencester, England, 1995

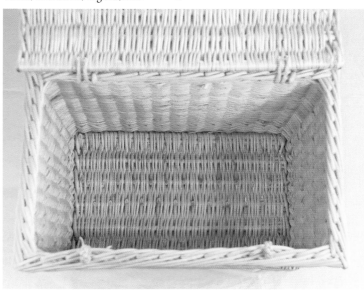

The term 'square work' covers all baskets with right-angled corners, even if they are truly rectangular. Professional willow workers doing square work use a modification of the techniques previously described for round work. Weaving of the separate square base is achieved by selecting a number (perhaps eight) of short but stout sticks, and clamping one end of each so that they are held firmly. This can be done using two boards and sitting on them, or by means of a special screw block. It is common to have two sticks together at each side and the others equally spaced in between. Thinner rods are then woven horizontally back and forth, starting and ending the base with a row of pairing to hold these sticks when released from the clamp. The unwanted ends are trimmed off.

Left: Egg show basket in fitched white willow and cane, Stanley Bird (Basketware) Ltd, Great Yarmouth, England, 1991

Cheese mould in fine twined rush from Cyprus, collected by Iris Hawkes

Side stakes are inserted on all four sides of this square base. Half of them are forced into the ends of the weaving (as in round work), often one by each base stick. The others go into holes made with a bodkin along the lengths of the two outer sticks, or by wrapping their prepared ends once around. This is called scalloming. These stakes are pricked up and upsett, and then the side weaving and border completed as before (except for the extra challenges presented by the four corners).

A related technique found along the western edges of the British Isles involves starting with stout side stakes and inserting them into the ground (or in stony regions into a wooden frame with predrilled holes). The side weaving begins at ground level, proceeds to the required height, and the unused parts of the stakes are bent over and interwoven to form the base of the basket when the stakes are pulled out and inverted. This method is normally used for square work but sometimes also for round. Isolated examples of starting baskets by inserting the side stakes into holes in the ground (or a prepared frame) can also be found in other countries including the extreme northwest peninsulas of Spain and France.

Twined baskets

Twining strokes, where two or more weavers are worked together and change positions as they pass successive stakes, are found in many baskets of the categories already described. Their function is to grip the stakes tightly and hold them in their chosen positions, or just to produce interesting patterns and surface features. But where the warp elements are of a soft material, like rushes or maize bracts, then all of the side weaving may be done by twining after a base has been formed in some other way e.g. plaiting.

There are however a few European examples where twining is essential to the creation of the basket. In these, no separate base is created because the original base stakes run right up the sides to the border and are held throughout by rows of two- or more strand twining, either tightly packed or widely separated. The cheese moulds and related platters and bowls made from fine rush in several Mediterranean countries belong here. So does the kishie, a back basket made from oat straw and grass or rush twine in the Shetland Isles off the Scottish coast. These curiosities are featured in the subsequent chapters.

Mary Butcher, a distinguished English maker, teacher, curator, and author, has observed that many of the weaves in stake and strand work appear worldwide, but that there are small regional or national variations in details of the way in which these are incorporated into the basket, besides ways of inserting the side stakes, upsetting these,

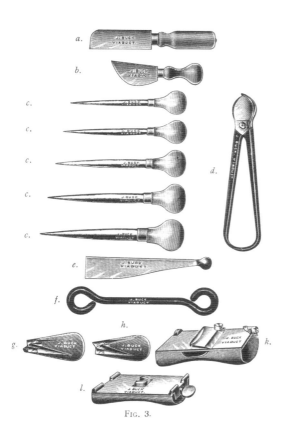

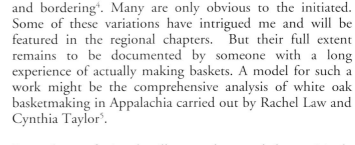

Fig. 3.

and bordering[4]. Many are only obvious to the initiated. Some of these variations have intrigued me and will be featured in the regional chapters. But their full extent remains to be documented by someone with a long experience of actually making baskets. A model for such a work might be the comprehensive analysis of white oak basketmaking in Appalachia carried out by Rachel Law and Cynthia Taylor[5].

Even the professional willow worker needed surprisingly few tools compared, for example, with the cabinet maker or joiner. He used two or three different knives for cutting in various ways (and today secateurs also), bodkins for making holes or gaps in the weaving, a rapping iron to keep the weaving tight, and an iron ring to help bend or straighten rods. Those undertaking fine work would need a cleave (g, h) to split rods lengthways, plus a shave (k) and upright (l) to standardize the thickness and width of the split sections into skeins.

Much of the work has always been carried out while seated on a low chair or directly on the floor with back to the wall[6]. A sloping board or bench over the knees holds the basket during weaving. Round work may be skewered or weighted to the board so that it can be constantly rotated to keep the working area directly facing the maker.

Frame baskets

This sixth category of stake and strand work is characterized by having the stakes fixed at both ends quite early on. These are given the special name of 'ribs', perhaps because they are usually fewer in number and stronger than the stakes in normal round and square work of comparable size and look like ribs when first inserted. In order for this to be possible, one or more additional components must be used to provide a rigid framework. The simplest is a single wooden ring or hoop, in round, half-round, or flat material. This forms the basket rim and provides the anchor points for the ends of the ribs. These arc underneath from one side to the other, and are attached to the rim by a weaving rod, splint, or skein. Their relative lengths control the final shape and size of the basket which is usually fixed before any or much of the weaving takes place. In oval baskets the ribs may either run across the short or the long axis.

A two-piece frame is formed where a strong bottom spine is also fixed, arcing across and underneath the rim hoop. If there is to be a bow handle, then this is usually achieved by

using two hoops at right angles to each other; the top half of the vertical hoop becomes the handle while the bottom half is the spine.

The lashing which attaches the two hoops together at each side often then provides the anchorage for the rib ends which may radiate out from these crossing points. However there are many arrangements of ribs found throughout Europe, and some of these are featured in the chapter on France. In theory they can range between being almost vertical, starting parallel with the spine, and horizontal, at right angles to the spine.

It will be obvious that frame baskets are not made with an initial separate base. The weaving begins on each side under the rim, proceeds backwards and forwards across the ribs, and finishes along the centre of the bottom. The weavers may be round rods, wood splint, or anything in between.

Many rural makers have continued to use this frame technique while for at least two thousand years most professionals have utilised the separate base methods described earlier. The explanation is perhaps that part-time workers exploited materials which they could gather freely from their surroundings. Many of these require considerable preparation before they are ready to use, and even then remain 'unkind' in the sense that they cannot be worked as quickly as cultivated willow rods. For the professional, being paid by the piece, speed is important. By contrast, making a few baskets for himself or for barter in his slack season, the amateur would be more influenced by not having to buy his materials or devote part of his land to growing them. Nevertheless, many smallholders formerly maintained a few willow stools which they cut annually, and used the green or brown rods to make replacement baskets on frames. In addition, there are a few examples of regions which witnessed the expansion of part-time frame basketmaking into a local industry employing scores or hundreds of professional workers. One such was in the Limousin area of France and is featured in that chapter.

Loop

Looping techniques use only a single active weaving strand. A network of interlocking loops is created. String bags are obvious examples, but if the weaving material is sufficiently rigid to make the bag keep its shape, then it seems reasonable to call the article a basket. Lime bast, the soft fibrous layer found just underneath the true bark, has been used in this way in Sweden to make containers for fish. Such baskets have also been looped from a similar cord made by twisting together thin hand-riven splints of spruce wood (see p145).

Mediterranean fish trap being constructed using a netting technique with diagonal stakes of grass, split cane and nylon thread, Malta. Photo: Geraldine Jones

Net

Nets are not usually considered to be baskets but one type, found extensively around the northern shores of the Mediterranean, includes quite rigid three-dimensional round structures which surely qualify. The common design to them all is a foundation of slender stakes in two sets which are inclined some way off the vertical in both directions and therefore cross each other to form a diamond pattern. These stakes may themselves be quite weak, narrow rush stems, or even esparto leaves. In a typical bell-shaped trap, more stakes are introduced as the diameter swells towards the middle, while the number decreases at the narrow top. A third element, often 'cane' splint, is then wound horizontally around the outside. It overlaps the angled stakes wherever these cross, bisecting the diamonds into triangles, and each intersection is firmly knotted with a fine thread. The result is a surprisingly rigid structure.

The technique is most often employed to make fish traps with a narrow inverted neck at one end and a removable cap at the other. Very fine material placed close together is used to catch small fish; much thicker stuff, including myrtle and olive rods, for crustaceans. Sometimes the same method is found in arm baskets and maunds in Spain and Sardinia.

Assemble

These techniques are not the normal weaving methods of basketry. They involve pre-formed pieces which are nevertheless fixed together by lashing, pegging, or nailing to

Below left: Construction of a Devon splint basket by Jack Rowsell, Tiverton, Devon, 1991. Photo: Sally Goymer

Below right: Scale model of basket used to harvest artichokes, assembled by Hubert Sarrazin at La Roche-sur-Yon, Vendée, France. Collected by Sally Goymer 1998

create articles which are quite clearly baskets. A few were
constructed by the cooper's methods: shaped staves fitted closely
together and kept tight by wooden hoops. Several equally robust
models were made for rough farm and garden use. These might
have a solid base and sides to contain small objects, including
grain, or they were slatted to carry larger items or to allow soil to fall through. At the
other extreme we can find plank-sided creations with inset panels of woven splint, or
fretwork, or elaborately painted in bright patterns. These were clearly intended to
announce wealth and sophistication within a rural society. Some of them are featured in
the Nordic chapter.

Notes and references

1. One of the earliest instructional books in English was Okey, T. (1912) 'The Art of
    Basket-making'. Okey was born in 1852 into a family of basketmakers and had himself
    worked as apprentice, journeyman, and master in London for over 40 years. During this
    time he acquired a remarkable virtuosity in modern languages, and a thirst for history
    and literature. Such were his abilities that after a lifetime of basketmaking he was
    appointed, aged 67, to the first Chair of Italian Studies in the University of Cambridge.
    In 1986 the Basketmakers' Association decided that his 1912 volume was so relevant to
    its members that it had the work reprinted. Several useful books appeared during the first
    half of the 20th century, but after these perhaps the most influential in Britain was
    Wright, D. (1959) 'The Complete Book of Baskets and Basketry' which went through
    several editions and publishers, with a 1992 edition by David and Charles. It dealt with
    techniques but also included historical aspects. Another volume dealing with cane and
    willow work was Maynard, B. (1973) 'Modern Basketry from the Start', G. Bell and
    Sons. Since that time there have been more English books including a trio published by
    Dryad Press in 1986: Butcher, M. 'Willow Work'; Elton Barratt, O. 'Rushwork';
    Johnson, K. 'Canework'. Subsequently: Elton Barratt, O. (1990) 'Basket Making',
    Charles Letts; Gabriel, S., and Goymer, S. (1991) 'The Complete Book of Basketry
    Techniques', David and Charles; Basketmakers' Association (2004) 'Basket Borders from
    the Basketmakers' Association', Ed. M. Butcher. The classic French text on willow work
    first written by the professors at the Fayl-Billot school in 1957 is Duchesne, R., Ferrand,
    H. and Thomas, J. 'La Vannerie - l'Osier'. It was reprinted in 1981 by J.-B. Baillière.
    Although never translated into English it has been found useful by many during the past
    half-century. It was translated into Dutch in 1999 as 'Mandenmaken met Wilgenteen'
    and published by Stichting Wilg & Mand. This same Dutch association had previously
    published two useful books which combined instructions for making round and oval
    baskets with some history: Westendorp, A. (1985) 'Het Vlechten van Ronde Manden
    met Teen', and Westendorp, A., van't Hoog, A.D. and Tuinzing, W.D.J. (1985) 'Het
    Vlechten van Ovale Manden met Teen'. Other European general instructional books
    include Verdet-Fierz, B. and R. (1993) 'Willow Basketry', Interweave Press - a beautifully

produced book with masses of black and white illustrations also published in German as 'Anleitung zum Flechten mit Weiden' (1993) Paul Haupt; Madsen, S.H. (1994) 'Flet med Pil', Klematis (Danish); and Barbier, G. and Pichonnet, M. (2003) 'La Vannerie, Rotin et Osier', Dessain et Tolra (French). Other instructional books dealing specifically with techniques in different parts of Europe include: Hogan, J. (2001) 'Basketmaking in Ireland', Wordwell; Fontales, C. (2005) 'Cestería de los Pueblos de Galicia' (2005) IR INDO (Spanish, includes a DVD); Bertrand, B. (2006) 'La Vannerie Sauvage - initiation', Éditions de Terran, (French, includes a DVD); Pichonnet, M. (2006) 'Ces Papés - Memoire et Tradition de la Vannerie en France', Les Brins d'Osier (French). The Basketmakers' Association has a continuing programme of producing instructional videos and DVDs which are available from its sales office.

2. Adovasio, J.M. (1977) 'Basketry Technology - a guide to identification and analysis', Aldine Publishing Co; Seiler-Baldinger, A. (1994) 'Textiles - a classification of techniques' Crawford House Press; and Harvey, U.I. (1975) 'The Techniques of Basketry'. B.T. Batsford. Other classifications are found in the instructional books listed in note 1, and in Butcher, M. (1999) 'Contemporary International Basketmaking', Merrell Holberton.

3. Seidenfaden, E. (1994) 'The Art of Basketmaking: the Perigord technique and tradition.'

4. See 2. Butcher p71.

5. Law, R.N. and Taylor, C.W. (1991) 'Appalachian White Oak Basketmaking - handing down the basket'. University of Tennessee Press.

6. See illustration of Roman mosaic in evolution chapter.

Britain and Ireland

Archie Coates and Les Whiles, his 1935 apprentice, in the workshop of the firm Finch and Son of Gloucester around 1985.
Photo: Philip Sayer

Resources

England, Wales, Scotland, and Ireland were formed from rocks from the whole range of geological periods, and have all been heavily glaciated with the lowland regions being mainly in southeast England and central Ireland. Since no part is more than some 160km from the sea, the climate is milder than in other regions at the same latitude – both because of the insulation effect of the coastal waters and the ease of penetration of the prevailing south westerly winds. Almost all regions have adequate and well-distributed rainfall though with a sharp decline from west to east. This, and the absence of severe (hot or cold) temperatures, means that plant growth occurs over a long season. The natural deciduous woodland cover was extensively cleared from Neolithic times and was reduced to 15% of the land area by the 11th century. Today woodland cover is 8% in England, 14% in Wales, 17% in Scotland, and 8% in Ireland. Hazel, oak and ash were once extensively coppiced and so provided rods for basketry. Willow grew wild in most parts except where soils were too thin or too windswept on the north and west fringes, and willow beds have long been cultivated in river valleys. The lowland arable fields provided rye and wheat straw for coiling and plaiting though oat straw was more common in the highlands. Rushes too were widely available, especially in the eastern coastal areas.

History

The chapter on the evolution of basketmaking sketched out the broad picture for Europe. What was different in these islands? Today's evolutionary scientists have been able to be much more precise about our origins[1]. While there were men and women here as early as 700,000 years ago, today's people can only be traced to those who arrived less than 12,000 years back. Earlier than that these lands had to be re-colonised about every 100,000 years, and successive groups were only here for about 20% of the time before they were swept back into mainland Europe by rapid and violent climate change. The most recent ice age drove out *Homo sapiens* some 13,000 years ago leaving evidence in both Derbyshire and Cheshire. Our ancestors finally arrived in these isles around 11,500 years ago, originating from populations who had survived in the regions nearer to the Mediterranean.

The land would have been bare of trees, and supported reindeer and wild horses. It took a further 2000 years for temperatures to warm up towards the current levels, and a further 1500 years before the early birch woods had given way to hazel and then elm, lime, and oak. The animals then included wild pig, roe and red deer, and aurochs. The returning people were semi-nomadic with winter and summer camps. They left good

Base of Roman basket, base diameter
12.5cm.
Photo: Elizabeth Allnutt

relics in a marshy site near Scarborough which shows that they were skilled in working flint and antlers, and kept dogs. An exciting discovery at Clowanstown, Co. Meath in Ireland was four, largely intact, conical fish baskets preserved in a raised peat bog since late Mesolithic times (5210-4970BC)[3]. At the end of the last ice age the area would have been a small lake used by people who subsisted by fishing, hunting, and foraging there and in the surrounding woodlands. One of the baskets was 112cm long with a diameter of 40cm at the wider end. It was made from 2-8mm thick one- and two-year old rods of alder, birch, and Rosaceae in open work, woven together with a pairing stroke. It may have been used to scoop fish out of the lake or placed within a weir. Farming as a way of life only entered south east Europe through Turkey around 8500 years ago, and took another 1500 years to spread as far as northern France.

Gradually these people killed trees to grow crops and produced food surpluses and the social revolution began. Metal working progressed from copper to bronze and then iron. Pottery, carpentry, and of course basketry were among the crafts which developed. There were active sea lanes all around Britain by the time of the first Roman explorations (55BC). From then on we have written accounts, and these tell us that the tribes had horse-drawn basketry chariots which they deployed skilfully in battle. The Roman occupation (of the lowland regions) after 50AD no doubt brought new skills, but also new requirements as some centres of urban living grew up.

The production of wooden artefacts from Neolithic to Viking times has been specifically studied[4]. Making everyday wooden objects changed from a home-based activity, in which each household possessed many of the skills necessary to produce its own wooden goods, to one where craft specialisation was of increasing importance. Highly-developed crafts such as cooperage, which had at first been utilised to provide status objects for an elite, were reorganised to produce standardised goods on a large scale. This change took place at different times throughout Europe. In much of Britain it occurred under Roman influence during the second and third centuries AD (though it seems likely that there was regression in subsequent centuries). In Ireland there is little evidence for workshop production until the eighth and ninth centuries, and indeed more remote and rural areas in Ireland seem to have been largely unaffected by these changes until as late as the 19th century. The key to the transformation of the woodworking crafts was the growth of urbanism and the development of the market economy. No doubt basketry showed similar changes though it is more difficult to assign definite dates to these.

After 400 years the Romans withdrew, and Saxons, Angles, and Jutes soon invaded followed by Viking raids from the eighth century. The gradual emergence of the manorial system was catalogued in the earlier chapter. We have a good picture of

English society shortly after the Norman conquest in the mid-11th century (though conditions in Wales, Scotland and Ireland are less clear).

Thereafter, while the kingdoms were frequently at war with neighbours, they were never again occupied by invaders. As a result, after 1000 AD in Britain there was a long period of population increase and economic growth up to the mid-15th century (when one third to half of the population died directly or indirectly from the Black Death). But there was then a further 150 years of rebuilding, technological advance and continued development. This growth rested in part on new techniques of cultivation for the food supply (wheeled ploughs) which opened up the rich river valley land, on larger animals (oxen and horses) as power sources, and on a shift from a two-field to a three-field system within the manors allowing a one-third increase in productivity by having less land in fallow[5]. The British Isles certainly had advantages of soils and climate compared with many of the other countries we shall examine in subsequent chapters. But "One can hardly exaggerate the contribution of agricultural improvement to Britain's industrialisation"[6] which in turn had such far-reaching effects on its basketmaking. Post-1500 there was the continued early adoption of new farming techniques many of which were brought by immigrants from the Low Countries. This adoption was made even more effective by the enclosure of the old manorial and open lands in the 18th century. The country was open to receiving those who were excluded from trades in their own lands: Dutch weavers and peasants with knowledge of land drainage in the 16th century; Jews with experience of public and private finance; and Huguenots, merchants, and craftsmen in the 17th century. There were also major gains in land and water transport: turnpike roads, canals, and inns to sleep the users. These were the work of private enterprise which responded to needs rather than being based on prestige or military concerns.

While these material advantages were important, economic historians emphasise three aspects of Britain's culture and institutions which accelerated the country's progress towards industrialisation.

1. Britain was further ahead even than France, the Low Countries, and West Germany in freeing the peasantry from their ties to their manors and seigneurs. By 1500 its land was already mainly farmed by yeomen or free tenants, with the workers (often owners of small plots) hired for cash as needed. Such changes were enormously delayed in most other countries. Indeed, early freedoms were reversed in central and eastern Europe and only regained in the 19th century.

2. Britain did not allow the organisation of its manufacturing to be constrained by the early structures which had emerged in the Middle Ages. Rural craftsmen migrating to the early European towns had taken with them principles, attitudes, and values which had emerged over centuries within the manorial system. When the open fields were of finite size and allocated to each peasant in the form of scattered strips, they had to accept rules which prevented competition and regulated the times of each farming operation. In their new urban environments, they formed corporations or guilds which controlled entry through obligatory apprenticeship and constraints on masterships, limited the number of apprentices in a workshop, prescribed business opening times, upheld standards, and banned the trade-off of quality for cheapness, and so tried to prevent market competition.

    We frequently look back at guild rules with admiration – what laudable intentions! The reality is that markets are driven by greed and ambition. English merchants learned to bypass the restrictions in many ways – in particular by getting additional work done for them at lower cost outside the urban jurisdiction (in suburbs or villages). Even as early as the 13th century they were putting out the tedious and less skilled work to seasonal, female, or young rural workers. But when they did the

doth put himself Apprentice to
Citizen and *BASKET-MAKER* of *London*, to learn his Art; and with
him (after the Manner of an Apprentice) to serve from the Day of the
Date hereof, unto the full End and Term of   Years, from thence
next following, to be fully complete and ended: during which Term, the
said Apprentice his said Master faithfully shall serve, his Secrets keep,
his lawful Commandments every where gladly do. He shall do no Damage
to his said Master, nor see to be done of others, but that he to his Power
shall let, or forthwith give Warning to his said Master of the same. He
shall not waste the Goods of his said Master, nor lend them unlawfully to any. He shall not commit Fornication,
nor contract Matrimony within the said Term. He shall not play at Cards, Dice, Tables, or any other unlaw-
ful Games, whereby his said Master may have any Loss. With his own Goods, or others, during the said Term,
without Licence of his said Master, he shall neither buy nor sell. He shall not haunt Taverns, or Play-houses,
nor absent himself from his said Master's Service Day or Night unlawfully : but in all Things as a faithful
Apprentice he shall behave himself towards his said Master, and all his, during the said Term.   And the
said Master, in Consideration of the Sum of

his said Apprentice, in the same Art which he useth, by the best Means that he can, shall teach and instruct,
or cause to be taught and instructed, finding unto his said Apprentice Meat, Drink, Apparel, Lodging, and
all other Necessaries, according to the Custom of the City of *London*, during the said Term. And for the true
Performance of all and every the said Covenants and Agreements, either of the said Parties bind themselves unto
the other by these Presents.   *In witness* whereof, the Parties above-named to these Indentures interchangeably
have put their Hands and Seals, the   Day of   in the Year of our Lord, 17
and in the   Year, of the Reign of our Sovereign Lord GEORGE III. King of *Great Britain, &c.*

N. B. *This Indenture must bear Date the Day it is executed; and what Money or other Thing is given or contracted for, with the Clerk or Apprentice, must be inserted in Words at Length; and the Duty paid to the Stamp-
Office, if in London, or within the Weekly Bills of Mortality, within One Month after the Execution, and if in the
Country, and out of the said Bills of Mortality, within Two Months, to a Distributor of the Stamps, or his Substitute; otherwise the Indenture will be void, the Master or Mistress forfeit Fifty Pounds, and another Penalty,
and the Apprentice be disabled to follow his Trade, or be made Free.*

same with processes requiring more skill, like weaving, there was a reaction. In Italy, the Low Countries, and Germany the guilds opposed this violently and successfully enforced their rules for several centuries in a variety of ways. England was the one country where 'putting out' had a free field so that "guilds were quickly reduced to ceremonial fraternities"! By the 15th century more than half of the nation's woollen cloth was being made in rural cottages rather than urban workshops. This cost advantage meant that by the 16th century England had changed from a nation exporting its wool, and was well on the way to becoming the premier cloth manufacturing nation of Europe.

3. Thirdly, continental Europe was enmeshed in a web of trade restrictions through river and port tolls, road fees, entrance duties at city gates, and customs barriers with a multiplicity of exemptions and franchises – all maintained by vested interests. The British had largely eliminated theirs in the 15th century, while other countries were much slower to make progress.

As a result of these cultural and institutional differences, Britain developed into an urban, industrial society ahead even of its neighbours with similar natural resources and climates. The effects on its basketmaking would have been several. The decline in numbers of self-sufficient peasant farmers must have reduced the number of traditional baskets made by 'amateurs' specific to their particular districts, and no doubt some of these baskets disappeared. The enormous increase in movement of goods from sources

City of London Indenture document setting out the contract between a master basketmaker and his apprentice (1760-1820). Loaned by Fred Rogers to the Basketmakers' Association

to markets to consumers, plus the steadily growing population, must have greatly multiplied the size of the basketmaking 'industry' and with it the area devoted to growing the professionals' main raw material – willow. There, the range of products made increased greatly to reflect the exact needs of every kind of product and end user. To take but one example: because jars, bottles, and other glassware began to be moved about, we can see from the National List that there was a demand for over 40 different sizes and shapes of partition baskets not to mention 11 sizes of carboy baskets, and another 11 to contain stoneware bottles[7].

We do have a few records of the way new structures emerged to create these changes in volume and variety, but for the most part we can only piece together fragments. One way of approaching this is to take the situation which was surveyed at the beginning of the 20th century and try to look backwards. We are fortunate that investigators from the Agricultural Research Institute at Oxford carried out exhaustive surveys in England and Wales during 1919-1923, although these were mainly confined to the rural sector and did not include city workshops[8]. They described the organisation of willow growing and basketmaking by identifying several groups.

1. Large-scale specialist willow growers. These were found mainly in Somerset and supplied rods both to local furniture makers (three of these employed a total of 170 men), and to a wider market. Their willow beds were worked partly by hired labour, but also by individuals who contracted to look after specific plots for the entire year.

2. In the Trent valley there were growers whose businesses involved selling large quantities of fine-quality rods, particularly to urban workshops throughout the country. At the same time, these growers maintained their own workshops, often in the larger towns where they typically employed from 20 to 100 workers, and in two cases, up to 300. A similar structure existed in a small Lancashire district (Mawdesley in the Ribble valley) though the growers mainly produced one particular willow variety suitable for fine work.

3. A third class consisted of those who were primarily basketmakers but grew their own willows. These were found in country towns and villages in almost every county. The larger ones might employ 50 or more men, and would undertake larger orders for the horticultural industry. Many workshops were much smaller employing family members and using the rods from their 1-3 hectare plots to make a range of products supplying the needs of local farms and households.

4. There were also many rural basketmakers who had some other occupation. Fishermen on the south coast made their own traps, smallholders made what they needed in the winter months, and some thatchers made baskets during wet periods.

What does this tell us about the changes caused by industrialisation and urbanisation in Britain? Clearly the development of large-scale willow growing, where all or part of the output was sold onto rural or urban basketmakers was a direct consequence, as was the emergence of medium- to large-scale workshops. On the other hand, the continued existence of large numbers of smaller makers servicing local and domestic needs suggests little change over the centuries, though it seems likely that the new availability of cultivated willow (from their own plots or bought in) would have reduced the earlier exploitation of alternative materials, and probably the specific shapes and styles that went with them. Certainly there has been a much higher dependence on willow in Britain during recent times than in many less industrialised countries, though this may be partly confounded with the ability to grow good willow in most parts. Straw for bee skeps, split hazel frame baskets in Wales, green elm rods for oyster tendles in Essex, and split oak work in Cumbria, the west Midlands, and east Ireland all provide fascinating

Ian Beaty (far left) demonstrating straw bee skep making, and DG Davies (left) demonstrating the making of a Welsh frame basket at summer meetings of the Basketmakers' Association. Above: Colin Manthorpe from East Anglia, one of the last apprenticed basketmakers demonstrating at the Basketmakers' Association summer meeting, June 2008

examples of traditional baskets which survived, but the overwhelming oeuvre for centuries past has been in willow.

The cultivation of willows in dedicated beds has a long history with rental records at least back to 1240. More than 20 different varieties were collected from several sources and planted in one bed in Bedfordshire in 1795[9]. Nevertheless, France, Germany, and the Low Countries seem to have been rather quicker to increase their areas during the 17th and 18th centuries to cater for the demand for more uniform rods. As a result, Britain's expanding basketry industry relied initially on Dutch imports until disruptions caused by wars encouraged more home production from around 1820[10]. Large-scale drainage in the Somerset levels and their legal enclosure led to widespread plantings there. Other major areas were in the river valleys of the East Midlands, the Ribble valley in Lancashire, and East Anglia. The Irish beds were mainly on the shores of Lough Neagh and the river valleys in Munster. The total British area peaked at some 2800 hectares and was still 2400 hectares in 1925.

Mary Butcher has researched the beginnings of some of the collective workshops in town and country[11]. The earliest surviving records relate to one founded in London in 1661 whose documentation stretches from 1703 until its closure some 250 years later. As we saw earlier, by the 19th century the Basketmakers' Company had ceased to play any practical role in the regulation of the industry and new organisations evolved. The employees formed trade unions in London and some other urban centres. The London Union of Journeymen Basket Makers was established in 1816. Over the years it published lists of basket specifications and the agreed wage rates for each, since most men were employed on piece work (paid per item made rather than by the hour or week). Other lists were produced for Birmingham, Edinburgh and Lancashire, and Cheshire, but they were eventually replaced by the National List in 1956 issued jointly by the then single employers' federation and trade union. This 1956 list contains details of over 50 different types of baskets but almost all could be made in several sizes or qualities so that the total range included more like 1750 items[12].

The system of learning a trade through a long apprenticeship goes back to medieval times and persisted until the 1950s. Thomas Okey was born into a family of London basketmakers in 1852[13]. "My appointed station in life was that of a basketmaker, and straightaway (at the age of 12) I was set to work at the elementary stages as an informal apprentice". At 15 he moved into an unpaved cellar with no heating and lit by tallow candles or rush lights. Weekday working hours for men were 6am to 9pm except Saturdays when they finished at 5pm, but only 12 hours for boys! Okey spent 15 years there. Apprenticeships were originally for seven years. A boy may have learned his trade in three, but because he was always paid less than the journeymen, his master had four

HOP BASKETS, COARSE SLEW

	Bottoms Ins.	Deep Ins.	Top Ins.	Sticks	Stakes	Wages s. d.
½ bushel	9	13	14	5½	19	2 5½
1 bushel	12	15½	17½	5½	21	2 10
2 bushel	15	21	23	6½	25	4 5½

Two rounds of upsetting, no wale under border, two handles on border, one bushel single rod, two bushel double rod.

POTATO HAMPERS

B.S.	Bottom L. Ins.	W. Ins.	D. Ins.	Top L. Ins.	W. Ins.	Stakes		Wages s. d.
7	24	18	20	29	24	35	Loads	7 2
6	20	16	19	26	20	31	2 Measures	5 11½
6	19	15	19	24	18	31	7 Pecks	5 4
6	18	13½	17	23	16	29	Half Loads	4 9½
5	17	13	16	22	16	29	1 cwt.	4 4
5	15	11	15	20	15	27	Measures	3 9½
5	14	10½	14	18	14	25	3 Pecks	3 7
4	13	10	13	17	13	23	½ Measures	3 3

Measurement:—measured at the top of the border, depth to the top of the wale outside. All larger sizes to be 2d. per inch extra.

OVAL CHERRY BASKETS OR PICKERS, LT. RANDED

L. Ins.	W. Ins.	D. Ins.	Top Ins.	Lays	Stakes	Wages s. d.
7	5	8	13½	3	26	3 1
8	5	9	15½	3	30	3 3
9	5	10	17	3	30	3 5½
10	6	11	18½	3	30	3 9½

Two rounds of upsetting, one round of waling, cross handles.

WORCESTER POT HAMPERS—CORNER STICKS

Sticks	L. Ins.	W. Ins.	D. Ins.	Stakes Side	End	Wages s. d.
5	14	10	11	6 and 7	5	3 4½
5	15	10½	12	6 ,, 7	5	3 7
5	18	12	12	7 ,, 8	5	4 5½
5	18	12	13	7 ,, 8	5	4 6½
5	19	13	14	7 ,, 8	5	4 10½
6	21	14	15½	8 ,, 9	6	5 4
7	23	16	16	8 ,, 9	6	5 10½
7	24	17	17	9 ,, 10	7	6 2

The first three sizes to be entitled to two bands on the border all other sizes entitled to four bands.

All sizes entitled to one cane league across, two double rod handles.

Three rounds of upsetting and one round of top waling. Rings 4 for 2d. extra.

Above wages are for uncovered baskets.

Extra for covers on the last three sizes, if required, 1s. 9d. each.

Extract from the National List of basic wage rates in the basket industry in 1956, specifying the dimensions, construction details, and prices to be paid for making each article.
The Basketmakers' Association

years in which to make a profit in return for the wasted materials and time involved in teaching him. Nevertheless, the length of period had to be reduced to keep the system attractive when better paid opportunities became available, and it seems to have been four years by 1900.

These city workshops (125 in London alone in the early 1900s)[14] would have been primarily engaged in satisfying the needs of those who lived and worked in food markets and shops, wine and spirit merchants, railways, post office, hotels and laundries, besides providing trunks and hampers for travellers, and cradles, chairs, and household items for the newly affluent town dwellers. During the 20th century their traditional products were less in demand, and the surviving firms had to respond to many new requests.

We are also fortunate to know the histories of several firms operating in Bedfordshire, Lincolnshire, and Nottinghamshire from the mid 18th century through to their final disappearance in the mid 20th century[15]. Many depended upon the growth of market gardening in the area. Rough brown willow containers were used for harvesting potatoes, onions, Brussels sprouts, peas, beans, and fruit. Huge numbers were needed to send the graded produce by rail to city markets and thence to retailers. Other farm baskets were for broadcasting seed corn, soot or lime on the land. Bakers and butchers took their wares to their customers' houses in large arm or bicycle baskets. Some firms specialised in finer work in white willow and featured items we might not even guess had ever existed. Around 1900 one such workshop manufactured all kinds of laundry baskets including shirt hampers, ironers' trays, and collar baskets. These firms varied in size. No doubt many were quite small family affairs, but one employed 72 workers in 1906 with up to 56 spaces for makers seated on their planks around the walls.

They sometimes employed additional men, travelling journeymen who joined during the summer months. Highly skilled in their own particular branch of the trade, they moved around the country to catch the season for it in different areas. Boiling the rods before stripping leaves them stained from the bark tannins, and seems to have been started in the east Midlands around 1870. These 'buff' rods are more convenient for the maker since they do not require so much soaking before use. They also suit the grower as they allow stripping to be done at any time of the year.

One firm in the south west market town of Gloucester (Finch and Son) was founded around 1909 almost adjoining the cathedral, and survived through several generations into the 1980s[16]. At its peak the business employed 40 workers and made thousands of fruit baskets annually for the local market, oval arm baskets for potato pickers, and delivery baskets for butchers and bakers. During World War I the Government ordered medical panniers, dental chairs, surgical instrument baskets, and mule panniers. Subsequently it made cradles, perambulators, and furniture for families but these too disappeared, and even shopping baskets went out of fashion as people changed towards once-a-week shopping and used their cars.

But it was not just horticulture, industry, and transport which increased their scale and became customers for professional firms. Fishing too grew into a highly organised business, and those employed in it became specialists relying on inputs from other trades. Great Yarmouth on the Norfolk coast was a centre of the herring industry since medieval times. The herring shoals appeared every year in vast numbers, and fleets of small boats followed them around the coast from northern Scotland down to East Anglia taking their catch successively into the nearby ports. Most were not consumed fresh but were processed (split, gutted, washed, and salted) before being preserved as salt

A batch of cane Seine net baskets destined for the fishing fleet, or for builders (used for carrying rubble), awaiting delivery at the workshop of Stanley Bird, Great Yarmouth, 1989

Completing the border of a wet linen basket at Stanley Bird's workshop in 1989, white willow

herring in barrels or smoked in several ways into a variety of products. This work was done by gangs of girls (often Scottish) on shore who travelled gradually south as the season progressed. The herring were carried ashore in one type of basket (the swill), and then other types were used to measure the catch (quarter crans) and to separate each stage of the processing. The shoals collapsed catastrophically in the 1970s. Deep sea trawlers used different baskets for cod and other species, but also needed some for ice and salt. Basket workshops were centred in Yarmouth town employing professionals to turn out large numbers for these fishing trades. They also served the farming fruit and vegetable growers in the region. One of these (Stanley Bird) still employed 40 workers in the 1950s and 1960s.

It is difficult for us in the 21st century to appreciate the scale of the output from these 19th and early 20th century workshops in Britain (but also in the Low Countries). Thomas Okey quoted a 1911 report that some 1200 men were employed in part of Belgium making white willow fruit baskets mainly for the English market[17]. He also knew a single London firm which had imported over 150,000 fruit baskets from across the Channel during the same year. Len Wilcox who worked with his two brothers near Peterborough remembered one contract where a local farmer wanted 2000 potato baskets in six weeks, and the three of them managed to deliver the order on time[18]. One of the last of the Yarmouth apprentices, Terry Bensley, calculated in 2005 that he had personally made some 80,000 baskets in 52 years of working at the trade[19].

Although with careful handling in the home a willow basket can last a lifetime, those used as returnable containers sent from grower to market to retailer and back had much

A load of white willow tomato baskets packed and ready for delivery to the boat in Guernsey. Photo: Carel Toms Collection

shorter lives. Estimates suggest 9-15 round trips which might be over in two years, or up to 10^{20}. Fishing baskets also received rough handling and had short lives. I was born and brought up on the Island of Guernsey whose major industry in the 1950s was still the growing of tomatoes under glass for shipment by boat and train to the wholesale markets in Britain. This had begun in the 1870s and until the 1930s the fruit was packed into oval arm baskets made in white willow with lids and holding 5.5kg. They were made in France then paint marked with the initials of the British salesmen, and hundreds of thousands were stored over winter. When needed, they were delivered to the growers, filled, labelled, the lids tied on, and taken to the harbour for loading and sea transport to ports on the English south coast, unloaded, and sent by rail all over England. The empties were then packed together in fours to save space and returned back up the distribution chain. This small example may illustrate the importance of the basketmaker and the scale of his activities. After World War II these containers were completely replaced by non-returnable wood plank 'baskets' with a wood or metal handle made up on the Island from imported timber.

Above left: Empty tomato baskets imported from France

Above right: Thousands of tomato baskets stacked over winter in fours, 1920s

Above: Delivering empties to the greenhouse

Left: Empty tomato baskets on the Guernsey quayside returned by boat from the English markets, 1890s.
Photos: Carel Toms Collection

The wooden tomato 'basket' used in Guernsey after 1945

By the beginning of the 20th century the basketmaking industry in the British Isles had reached its maximum size, but it was already under pressure from several directions. Imports from the Low Countries competed strongly with the common baskets used for

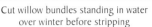

Commercial willow growing on the Somerset Levels 2005. Musgrove Willows, Westonzoyland

Planting a new willow bed in April

Cut willow bundles standing in water over winter before stripping

Bundles of willow sets to be planted

Brown willow bundles

Graded bolts ready for despatch

fruit and vegetables. During World War I many basketmakers were in the armed services and others were diverted to making shell cases and other military requirements. The Dutch increased their share of the British market and this continued afterwards because their products were cheaper but of good quality. The suppliers frequently arranged to store them when not in use – a great service to the English fruit merchants. The Oxford researchers found that "Nearly every kind of basket for which there is any considerable demand in wholesale quantities is now imported"[21].

Further to this competition on price or quality from across the Channel, there was the emergence of new packaging materials that provided non-returnable containers as substitutes for baskets. Nets of coconut fibre, string bags, and wooden boxes or crates began to be used even though these were costing more per journey.

As a consequence the British industry had already contracted sharply during the 1920s. The numbers employed fell from 9400 in 1921 to 7000 during World War II[22]. The period 1939-1957 saw some stability. The wartime emphasis was on making airborne panniers for dropping supplies to overseas troops, and other government contracts continued for some years after the end of hostilities. The decline then became catastrophic. By 1980 there were only around 500 of whom around 200 were disabled or partially sighted[23]. Many of these were employed in dedicated workshops established after the major wars, but they have now all ceased, in part because better paid and less onerous jobs are available for those who can acquire keyboard skills. The resultant fall in demand for willow caused the area grown in Somerset (now the main commercial

Wool skips in cane on wheels or skids at Cotswold Woollen Weavers, Filkins

growing region) to fall from 1200 hectares in the 1920s to only 100 hectares by 1990[24]. Competition from imports from newer sources was certainly one additional reason. Large numbers of domestic articles came in from Eastern Europe and the Far East where wage rates were much lower and there was a need to earn hard currency. But there was also competition for labour from other industries. As the British economy picked up, then low-paid manual work of all types became less attractive. Nevertheless, the primary reason for the industry's decline must be the adoption of new methods of collecting, storing and transporting goods frequently in bulk and using new materials in almost every walk of life. The wooden boxes and crates which were appearing in the 1920s developed later into cardboard containers and plastic crates, and trays were developed to handle foodstuffs and bottled drinks. The postal services and laundries replaced their wicker and cane crates by bags. Bulk crops like potatoes, apples, pears, and plums are picked up by machines and stored in large boxes moved around by fork-lift trucks. Fishing has declined but the surviving boats are larger and use boxes or plastic crates. In spite of these trends some workshops have continued through a variety of strategies which will be considered in the final chapter.

Types of work

The history of basketmaking given in the previous section has already pointed out that the long-established move towards industrial societies and urban living in England had replaced the earlier types of rural basketry by professional workshops and eliminated many of the previous articles. This generalisation applies much less to Wales, to the upland regions of Scotland, and to large parts of rural Ireland. It is in these areas where we might expect to see survivals of such early types. But first we must review the majority output, although mention has already been made of the work of several of the larger firms.

Professional willow

We may sub-divide the output of the many firms of professionals into four kinds according to their buyers, realising that any one firm might produce across the entire range while individual workers sometimes specialised in a very few. Far Eastern cane was used in place of, or in addition to willow where rough use was anticipated.

Farming/Horticulture

The operations which generated the main demand were the initial harvesting of crops and their subsequent despatch to markets. Potato pickers (also used for many other less important crops) were generally round or oval with a single arch handle or finger holes

Left: Potato molley in brown willow

Right: Asparagus gatherer, brown and white willow, cane handle

on each side. The bodies were made in brown, buff or white willow or cane, and the top handle might also be cane. Barrel-shaped baskets in brown and white willow in several sizes were used for peas, but rectangular arm baskets for asparagus. Fruit pickers for apples, pears, cherries, and raspberries were usually round arm baskets in various sizes, but sometimes had a flat side with two slits so that they could be strapped to the waist to leave both hands free.

For transport with return journeys it was important the sizes were constant and that they would stack well when empty, preferably inside each other. The three in most frequent use were pots (open oval in brown rods) holding up to 25kg of apples, sieves (open round fruit baskets in white or brown willow with a half or one bushel (18 or 36 litre) capacity, holding 16 or 32kg of plums, and flats (lidded rectangular in brown willow) used to carry more delicate fruit and salads. All these baskets were needed in their tens (even hundreds) of thousands every year.

Fishing

Producing baskets for the commercial fisheries was naturally concentrated near the coasts where the catches were landed. Containers were needed in the small boats to hold baited lines and gear, and different kinds of fish. Herring were the main catch all down the east coast, and each stage in the processing and curing had specific baskets allocated, usually maunds in open or closed work in willow or cane, either because of their suitability for the different functions, or to clearly mark each phase. One of these, the swill, was a frame basket made in brown willow – a rare example of professionals making this type. But of course these were specialists. Other types, often in cane, were used on the deep sea trawlers.

Industrial

A surprising range of strong containers was used for carrying loose material onto sites (bricks and sand) or loading ships (coal and grain). Initially these were carried on men's shoulders but then larger ones were handled by cranes. In mills and factories, on railway platforms, and in post offices and laundries bulk goods like wool, machinery parts, parcels, letters, and linen were all moved around in a variety of rectangular skips (skeps) and hampers. They were made in thick white willow rods or cane with open work or closed sides frequently bound with leather to reduce wear and often on wheels or runners. For the wholesale meat markets the hampers were made in white rods with lids. On a much smaller scale, retailers needed delivery baskets, often large and oval or rectangular to carry meat, bread, and groceries. These were carried by a strong arch handle or fitted into a framework on a bicycle. In Northern Ireland and Scotland the distilleries used large numbers of oblong-lidded non-returnable containers made

Left: Quarter-cran herring basket, white willow, cane handles

Right: Herring swill in brown willow and cane

cheaply in brown rods to carry yeast. One Northern Ireland firm made 1200 per week with the fastest men completing 40 in a day[25].

Domestic

A wide range of items for use in the home made usually from white or buff rods included arm baskets for shopping, others for linen, waste paper, logs, and pets besides many types of chairs, stools and tables. For pursuing other interests, picnic hampers, fishing seats and creels were made often in buff.

In 1999 I learned that one of the last craftsmen who had served a full apprenticeship in the early 1950s, and then spent almost 50 years 'on the plank' turning out literally thousands of baskets for firms in Great Yarmouth pre-retirement, had a wish. Colin Manthorpe hoped to be able to make one example of each of the types he had turned out during his lifetime to leave as a record of this disappearing craft. He suggested using half the normal dimensions (and hence one eighth final capacity) in order to faithfully reproduce the originals while limiting the total space requirement. Colin was already very well known as a tutor within the Basketmakers' Association and admired for his workmanship. Several types could have been made in a range of sizes, but we decided that a single representative of each would usually be sufficient. We agreed that they could join my collection and he produced 50 different half-scale models within a few weeks. We were fortunate that Colin's repertoire spanned almost the entire range described above in the four sections. He had trained and worked in a coastal firm which served the fishing boats but his trade was also with the agriculture and horticulture of East Anglia and he supplied some industrial and many domestic products.

A related type of work, also only done by professionals, had almost disappeared from England at the time of the Oxford surveys (1919-1923), and it is unclear whether it was ever widely practiced here by comparison with French and German work described in later chapters. It is the tight weaving of white willow rods on a skeleton made of flat wooden strips riven from green ash logs (in France the wood was often oak, in Germany, willow.) In England this was called scuttle work. Two pairs of strips are crossed, and for the larger baskets the maker stands on these while weaving the rods around. He forms a bowl by gradually curving the strips (slats or spales) upward, all the time beating the rods tightly with the rapping iron on top of the previous row to produce a very close texture which can contain grain or meal. As the work proceeds additional strips are shaped and inserted to form the bye-stakes and keep the distances between them even. Finally the rim is formed from a hooped rod and attached to the tops of the stakes.

Basket on bicycle for food deliveries, Willows and Wetlands Visitor Centre

Laundry basket in white willow with leather binding

Flower picker, brown and white willow

Basket to drain and hold crockery and cutlery, white willow. Abbot Hall Art Gallery and Museum, Kendal

Collection of half-scale baskets made by Colin Manthorpe in white, buff and brown willow and cane

Left to right by rows: Signal ball, Lowestoft trawl, Hull trawl, Lowestoft lander
eel trap, Grimsby oval, salt maund, quarter cran, Iceland split
oval cob maund, washing maund, kipper drip maund, pilchard

Fishing

Left to right by rows: Shooting picnic, chair, soiled linen, square log, pet carrier
fishing panier, fishing creel, waste paper, waste paper, wet linen, Norfolk picnic, oval picnic
round dog, oval dog, flower gatherer, market shopper, oval shopper

Domestic

Industrial

Left to right by rows: Cargo tonner, transit hamper, coal wendle
brick basket, cycle carrier, laundry hamper
oval arm, shallow arm, square arm, strum (fire hose filter)

Farming/Horticulture

Left to right by rows: One and half bushel, large pea gatherer
potato picker, Covent Garden bushel sieve
asparagus gatherer, potato molley

Left: Scuttle of brown and white willow on oak slats, MERL, Reading

Right: Southport boat in buff willow with ash handle, spine and central band, MERL, Reading

Below: Base of Southport boat

Scuttle in white and brown willow on slats of ash splint made by Mrs Murby, Leicestershire, 1920. Dryad Collection, Leicestershire Museums

The Oxford researchers describe a large one holding 150 litres (4 bushels) splayed outwards from a small base, besides lesser sizes. Other forms included smaller lop-sided ones for shovelling corn or malt into sacks, 50kg coal scuttles carried on the shoulders to load ships, and oval seedlips used for broadcasting seed or fertiliser by hand on the fields. Apparently farmers were still keen to buy them in the early 20th century, but few were being made because learning the special skills required an extra year's apprenticeship, and the work was reportedly difficult and particularly onerous. Only one or two makers were still active in Yorkshire, Northamptonshire, and Lincolnshire.

This is of course the classic method of making the winnowing fan, known since Greek and Roman times, but it will be mentioned in the French chapter, and a fuller discussion will be provided when I consider German basketry.

One other exception to the generalisation that professionals did not use frame construction techniques was provided by at least one of the firms near Southport in Lancashire[26]. Apparently about 1830 it developed (from earlier local designs) a range in buff willow based on the 'boat' shape – hence the 'Southport boat'. This was an oval basket with rim and handle hoops of ash splint with the ribs running across the short axis. One type had an additional band of splint inserted down the centre of the base from end to end.

Frame baskets

Most of the frame or rib baskets which have survived were used in the rural fringes of Britain and Ireland. Their main uses reflected the normal occupations in those regions. Thus, where arable fields or vegetable gardens were common then 'potato' baskets are seen, though they were in fact made in several sizes and used for many tasks including feeding livestock.

Welsh cyntell in brown willow with wild briar rim hoop by DJ Davies of Cardiff

Welsh cyntell in hazel splint on hazel rim and ribs by Mr Davies of Boncorth

The Welsh variety (*cyntell* or *gwyntell*) was usually made entirely in willow though also in hazel splint with or without the bark. It might have a wild briar (rose), blackthorn, or hazel rim and ribs but willow weavers. The round rim hoop supports two shaped central ribs whose ends protrude slightly. The central few weavers on each side were cut off at the top ribs rather than wrapping twice around the rim, and this provided the two hand holds[27].

Some modern examples show a refinement in workmanship which would seldom have been seen on the farm because they were produced for craft competitions (*eisteddfodds*) D.J. Davies of Cardiff made particularly fine ones with broad ribs, some even

Ulster potato baskets in brown willow near Lough Neagh. Photo: Ulster Folk & Transport Museum

supplemented by pairs of supporting ribs, one each side[28]. The carefully matched weavers begin inside the next-to-the-top rib, cross to the other side, twice around the rim hoop and then finish in the same position below one of the two central ribs. D.J. was a popular teacher and skilled at many Welsh crafts, but he did not normally make baskets for sale. When he died his widow was left with quite a number of these *cyntells*. She decided that they should be made available to people who would appreciate them, and we were able to offer them to members of the Basketmakers' Association who now treasure them.

This same type of 'potato' basket was professionally made in large numbers on the shores of Lough Neagh in Ulster for a brief period from 1914 to 1939. Local brown willow rods were woven onto hoops, originally hazel but later thick willow sticks imported from Holland. The three central ribs were flat lengths of split pine to provide extra strength[29].

Irish sciathóg in brown willow by Alison Fitzgerald. Photo: Joe Hogan

It is of interest that a shallow version of this basic frame type, used in parts of Ireland for straining and serving potatoes is known as the *sciathóg*, itself related to the Irish word for shield (*sciath*). In Joe Hogan's wonderfully comprehensive book 'Basketmaking in Ireland'[30] he speculates that an original flatter version may originally have been used as a breast shield in combat.

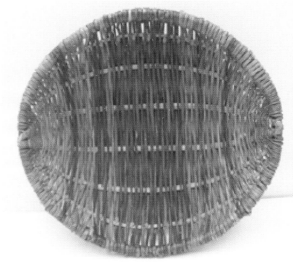

The coastal fishermen had different needs. Apart from their various nets and traps, they set long lines for white fish with baited hooks at intervals and then hauled them in with their catch. These baited lines were carefully arranged, often by wives, in frame baskets whose exact shape varied around the Irish and Scottish coasts[31]. They were more or less oval with

Right: Guernsey fishermen with bait baskets (courges).
Le Tricoteur Museum, Guernsey

Below: Three longline baskets in brown willow

Antrim
Photo: Alison Fitzgerald

Aran by Vincent McCarron.
Photo: Joe Hogan

Aran
Photo: Joe Hogan

Fishing creel (panier à cou).
Sea Museum, Jersey

the ribs shaped to give one broad, deep end and one which is shallow and often narrower. Sometimes the two ends of the rim hoop rod are not joined at the shallow end, so the shape is like a scoop. (An intriguing echo of these shapes is found in the upland regions of north Italy! See the *valetto* in the Italian chapter.)

Other frame baskets were made in the Scottish islands including the wide 'egg' or 'shoe' form which has both a rim hoop and a handle hoop: familiar to us from the way it was developed in white oak splint in the Appalachian mountains of USA. Also the 'hen' or 'gondola' shape which became wildly fashionable in many countries during the 1950s[32]. In this type, the two top-most ribs on each side are themselves often formed into hoops and bound onto the handle hoop with the side weavers forming a hood at each end. It occurs in manuscripts, embroideries, and stained-glass windows during the period between the 12th and 15th centuries. An almost spherical basket (*creelagh*) with a small opening may have been used for gathering locks of wool and containing them for when spinning into yarn[33]. Creels to carry fish were made in various patterns and were often suspended from the neck or shoulder.

Another basket of interest was used to keep sand eels alive in the sea before the Channel Island and coastal fisherman used them as bait for catching whiting or on long lines for skate and other flat fish. They were spindle-shaped rib baskets with the ribs bundled together in a point at both ends, and known in the local patois as a *courge*. In the centre a rectangular opening was kept shut when in use with a cork door. The *courge* was attached to the boat by a line and trailed behind in the water. Much larger versions (hullies) were used as 'store pots' to keep crabs and lobsters alive in the sea before sale by fishermen on the Isle of Wight.

A final relic frame basket survived not in the highland fringes but in the Essex marshes. The oyster tendle was a simple shallow rectangular shape with a handle hoop and rim, and ribs running across the short axis[34]. It was made by the oyster gatherers during the winter period using freshly cut elm rods for hoops and ribs, and also for the weavers. England used to have many elm trees in its hedgerows which spread by sending up suckers from their roots providing slender unbranched rods in their first year. Use of this ancient basket mainly ceased in the 1960s, but one man still went out daily with his in the 1980s[35]. The Basketmakers' Association has recently made an instructional video on its history and making.

Oak splint work

It is arguable whether a proper distinction can be drawn between this type of work and the many other styles of frame baskets described in the previous section, but I am

72

Four Cumbrian swills made by Owen Jones in split oak. Potato basket, cockle basket (with arch handle), scoop, seed hopper (with neck strap)

treating it separately here because the practitioners worked only in this style. It is characterised by having both ribs and weavers made from thin oak strips between 15 and 50mm wide. The ribs (spelks) are some 2-3mm thick and the weavers (taws) only around 1-2mm. Because of this, the weaving can be very close. Such thin material must follow the natural grain of the wood if it is not to crack and must therefore be split (riven) from the logs, rather than sawn. This is achieved by first boiling the straight-grained oak poles and splitting them while still hot. The coppiced poles were about 15cm thick and 17-25 years old.

These baskets known as swills were made in their thousands in several areas of Britain and Ireland where coppiced oak was available. A major centre was in the Furness district of Cumbria, south of England's Lake District after the early iron industry declined in the 19th century, and the demand for oak charcoal was thus reduced[36]. Other centres (where the precise methods and names differed slightly) were in Shropshire, Derbyshire[37] and Co. Wicklow on Ireland's east coast[38]. All the swills start with a round rod of hazel (or oak, ash or rowan) bent into an oval hoop (two pieces overlapping at the joins in Shropshire). The general purpose size (56cm long) then has a central rib placed across the short axis, wrapped around the rim at both ends and tied in with the first weaver. Successive pairs of ribs with pointed ends are then positioned and woven in. The final weavers do not lap the rim but leave a hand hold at each end of the long axis. This type was used widely in Cumbria for picking potatoes and sent north to Scottish farms. It was also used around the world for carrying coal from the jetties onto visiting ships.

Hully or store pot for lobsters, brown willow and cork doors. The Longshoreman's Museum, Ventor, Isle of Wight. Photo: Tom Bichard

Larger ones were made for carrying lighter goods like seed corn and bark for the tanneries or tobacco leaves for snuff. Others, with one almost pointed end were used as scoops for coal or meal, and a few round ones had a hooped hazel top handle and were used by cockle pickers on the estuary sands of Morecambe bay. Small family firms were common with four or five men each making up to 48 baskets in a week. Today Owen Jones works alone in Cumbria, but we are fortunate that he has taught many courses in the technique, and both the Basketmakers' Association and the Museum of English Rural Life at Reading have produced DVDs documenting both his preparation of material and the weaving[39]. A related type of work is done in France with chestnut wood, and in Poland.

Similar baskets were still being made late in the 20th century by a few itinerant makers in Cumbria using hazel and willow rather than oak[40]. The rims were two whole rods spliced to form the hoop, the ribs were of riven hazel or willow. Most of the weavers were semi-green willow rods, often gathered from the wild, but the two central ones might be riven hazel.

Irish creels mostly in brown willow made and photographed by Joe Hogan

Above from left to right:

Mayo type of hinged-bottom creel (pardóg)

Connemara type

Tuam type pardóg in hazel

Bottom view of Mayo creel with hinged base and retaining stick

Longford type foddering creel for carrying hay

Creels

This type of basketry was characteristic of the northern and western fringes of the British Isles, particularly Ireland and the Scottish islands. Joe Hogan's full account[41] is the basis for this brief review. Its distinguishing feature is the method of inserting the stakes into the ground (or, where there is little soil, into holes in a wooden frame) and weaving around these to form the sides. In order that this weaving cannot slip off the stakes when once they have been removed from the ground and inverted, a special weave known as the mouthwale is used for the first round near the ground. This then forms the border. When the sides are complete, the base is usually woven from the top halves of the stakes before the creel is inverted. The creel was widely used as a human back-basket for carrying all sorts of loads, often up to 65 kg. It was retained by a rope passed over the arms or shoulders so as to leave both arms free. Pairs of creels were also used as panniers on pack animals. Originally these were ponies in Ireland, but after the early 1800s the impoverishment of the peasantry and rise in population led to their replacement by donkeys. These carried seaweed up from the beaches, brought turf home from the bogs, and loads to and from markets. On some types (*pardóg*) a separate base is made, hinged onto one side and retained by a removable stick. This enables the base to be opened and the creel's contents dropped while the basket remains upright on each side of the donkey.

Creels were mostly made from willow (*S. viminalis*) but also from hazel. They were usually rectangular and made narrower at the mouth if the load was to be dropped through the bottom. Naturally there were regional variations. In Ulster and Scotland the sides and bases were more rounded[42]. Taller more open-sided variants carried hay. Seaweed creels with fairly open bottoms were carried on one shoulder by women on the Aran Islands while their men-folk cut the kelp in deep water with long-handled sickles. The rotting kelp was used to create soil and fertilise their poor fields. In other areas, large creel-like baskets were made to fit on a two-pole slide to drag loads of turf behind a horse in place of a wheeled cart.

Fish traps

Wherever there is water in rivers, lakes and estuaries, or on rocky shores, there is human food in the form of fish or crustaceans. Our ancestors studied their habits and designed ways to catch them often in the form of basket traps.

Eels are some of the most mysterious fish since they only breed across the Atlantic deep down in the Sargasso Sea. The young hatch and then after three years gradually return to rivers all along the coasts of Western Europe. After several years of growing in

Eel traps mounted on a weir on the Thames at Reading.
Photo: 'Berkshire of 100 years ago' and Berkshire Library and Museum Service

streams, canals, ditches, and even isolated ponds, the adult fish were caught in the rivers on their way downstream. The traps were tube-shaped baskets whose precise form differed between regions and countries and according to how they were intended to be placed: in weirs, with nets, or lying on the stream bed. Most incorporated a mechanism which allowed the eel to enter by pushing through a hole between a number of rods, either to seek some bait or a quiet dark place in which to consume it. Its exit was then prevented since the sharply pointed rods had sprung back and closed the hole, or because the diameter was too narrow for it to turn around. Some are made with a quite narrow bore and close woven. Others are much larger with relatively openwork sides. Mary Butcher has studied different types made in the Fens (where commercial trapping still goes on), in Yarmouth, Lancashire, and Gloucestershire, and compared them with others made on the west coast of France and the river Loire[43].

Irish eel trap with hinged lid in brown willow.
Photo: Joe Hogan

In the Fens a man might set around 20 traps in the river bottom, each around 120cm long and woven in split willow or cane, placing them in the evening baited with earthworms and lifting them early next morning[44]. Like most traps, they were often made by the men who used them though they were included in the lists of some professional firms. Before rivers had become too polluted there were several workshops in Oxford city where eel traps (and crayfish creels) were made from brown willow rods for the Thames fishermen. These supplied the residents before the railways came bringing cheap sea fish inland.

Also on the Thames, batteries of large compound traps were mounted on frames so that they could be lowered into the water to form a weir. More than 2m long, the large openwork mouths fed through into a closely woven section via the 'non-return valve'. Another smaller section was mounted on this at right angles to allow access to the catch.

Various fish traps in brown willow and hazel, Welsh Folk Museum, St Fagans

A related trap, the salmon putt, was also constructed from three separate baskets: the two larger ones tapered to fit into the mouth of the next. The first was some 1.5m long in openwork (willow or hazel rods). The second 35cm, and third 15 cm were both closely woven in willow. These putts were set out as a single row weir, containing up to 120, and facing upstream to trap the salmon and sea trout as the tide brought them down the estuary[45].

The salmon putcher was a simpler construction in the form of an openwork funnel into which the large fish swims and is unable to reverse out. It was made of stout willow or

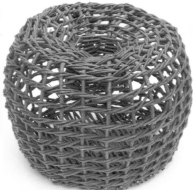

Above from left to right:

Ulster type (hazel)

Connemara type (willow)

Kerry style (similar to those used in Cornwall and Brittany, willow)

hazel rods split into two, about 2m long and 70cm diameter at the mouth. They were mounted on timber rails built out into the Severn estuary at right angles to the shore during the open season from April to August. Three or four rows high, they might contain 800 separate traps which were covered at high tide and then exposed again when the water receded. In the mid-19th century there were more than 13,000 of these baskets along the estuary, but by the 1990s there were only two or three installations still in use[46].

The most familiar traps are the pots made to catch crabs and lobsters. Again, their precise pattern varies around the coasts, and Joe Hogan's book describes several types from parts of Ireland[47]. Green or brown willow rods were most common, but sometimes hazel rods, and even heather stems, were used. The mouth was usually started by inserting the stake rods into holes drilled into a wooden block. After weaving these together, the stakes are arched over 180° and down to form the sides. In parts of Ireland the block was dispensed with and the stakes just pushed into the ground (as for the creels described earlier). The side of the pot was woven after removing the stakes from the block (or ground). These stakes are then bent a further 90°, and the base completed either by weaving them across each other or binding them together with extra rods in a circular weave. The pots were baited with fish or crab meat and weighted

Heather pot

A row of salmon putchers on the Severn at Littleton-on-Avon made of willow rods and worked by Dave Bennett in 1993.
Photo: Paul Felix

76

Cecil Quick of Lyme Regis
making lobster pots from brown
willow rods, 1984.
Photo: RJ Whittick

down with stones to keep them on the sea bed with a rope and float attached. The fisherman could then recognise the location of his own traps, haul them to the surface, and inspect them daily.

Smaller whelk pots were sometimes made with a wooden side door to ease removal of the shellfish. The whelks were used as bait when long-line fishing[48].

Specific items

It is quite impossible to feature all the different baskets which have been made in Britain and Ireland over the centuries. In this section (and in subsequent chapters) a personal selection has been made usually from those types of work not already covered, or because they seem particularly characteristic of the region.

Wood plank 'baskets'

These of course contradict the normal definition of a basket as a woven object, but may substitute for them. The woods around Herstmonceux in Sussex have supported a local industry for centuries, even back to the Domesday book, producing light but strong shallow oval trugs for garden and farm use. Ash or chestnut is used for the handle and rim hoops. The body is made from wide strips of willow which are split as thin as possible from the log, and then shaped thinner and narrower at each end where they are

Above left: Sussex trug, chestnut or ash handle and rim hoops, willow planking

Above right: Devon splint baskets by Jack Rowsell in elm base, fir sides, and ash bands. Photo: Sally Goymer

Irish potato straining basket (skib) in brown willow, made and photographed by Joe Hogan

nailed to the rim – like a clinker built boat. They are still made today in many sizes by a few workshops[49].

The Devon splint basket, by contrast, has all but disappeared since World War II. Fortunately its construction has been written up with a good photographic record including the tools and jigs used, and examples can be found in several museums[50]. Most had an arch handle and were used for general tasks like potato or apple picking. They came in five sizes, from 7-20kg. A larger maund would carry livestock feed. The oval base was shaped from an elm plank. The sides are essentially shaped staves, as in a barrel, cut from Scots Pine or Douglas Fir, and nailed at their narrow bottom ends to the edge of the base. The handle and top band are prepared in advance by fitting them around jigs and clamping them to gain the correct size and shape. They are fitted after the end staves have been nailed in place and the remaining staves are fitted and secured. These were very strong containers with a long life. Another variant leaves gaps between the staves to let soil fall through.

The skib

This basket, once widespread in Ireland, reflected the hardships of peasant life where the holdings were too small and infertile, and the climate too wet, to provide grain and flour for the family so that potatoes were the staple food[51]. These were simply boiled in a metal pot and the contents poured into the skib. It served both as a strainer and serving dish. It is in brown willow and begins with three or four pairs of stakes spread apart from each other to give a grid-like centre to the base. These are not bound together as normal, but instead the pairing weave begins at the grid edge and continues to the rim. The basket is commonly around 45cm diameter with low sides about 8cm high. Joe Hogan has written extensively about the skib and given full instructions on how to make the regional variants.

Peat kishie

The Shetland Isles (nearer to Oslo than Edinburgh) are too windswept and heavily grazed by livestock to grow trees, even willow. Nevertheless, the smallholders (crofters) needed to carry manure or seaweed onto their tiny fields, carry potatoes back, and make the journey home from the peat bogs with high loads of precious fuel for the hearth. So the men made back baskets using straw from the local black oat (*Avena strigosa*) and a cord which they twisted from field rush (*Juncus effusus*) or bent grass. Sometimes they were used as panniers on pack animals, but more usually were carried by men and women. The method used is twining where the warp is a bunch of straw and the two weavers used in a pairing stroke, are the rush or grass cord (or imported twine). Once again, knowledge of this relic basket had almost disappeared, but one of the last remaining makers has recently taught courses and the Scottish Basketmakers' Circle has recorded the techniques and history on video[52].

Coracles

Different kinds of wicker-framed small boats, originally covered in animal hide, have been used as transport around our coasts, and for fishing the rivers for millennia[53]. They varied in size and shape (oval or boat-shaped) and the amount of weaving in the hull. The river versions were very light (14-18kg), and because of their small draught could work in shallow water. Some used only round rods of willow, others were made with thicker stems of split willow, hazel or ash, and sawn laths in more modern times. The hide covers have now been replaced by canvas or calico covered with tar.

Those found on the river Spey in Scotland are more easily recognised as baskets, closely woven in split willow with the stakes finally lashed onto a hazel rim (gunwhale)[54]. In 1970 other types were still used in small numbers on three Welsh rivers, but in the 1860s there were over 300 on the river Teifi alone. The Welsh versions (though all different) are more skeletal structures made of laths. Some types have several rows of weaving at the rim and a woven floor mat. The fishermen work in pairs: two coracles drift downstream with the salmon net between them.

The Boyne *currach*, the only river coracle that was still in use in Ireland in the 20th century, was built like the creel. Hazel rods were inserted in the ground and the mouth wale woven before bringing these ribs across to form the base and then inverting the whole skeleton. The intersections were tied securely before the hide was fitted[55].

All types had a plank seat, though the Boyne type carried a second man who knelt and used the paddle when fishing while the seated man manipulated the net. This ancient

Left Rush frail, MERL, Reading

Right: Rush frail and carrying stick, Swinford Museum, Filkins, Oxfordshire

method of fishing ceased in Ireland in the 1940s, but may still be seen in Wales and a coracle society strives to keep the traditions alive.

Frail

Many items were once made of rush in the wet lowland areas of the British Isles, but just one has been selected here. The frail was an oval lidded bag made from plaited strips sewn together and fitted with top handles which continue under the base. It was used by farm workers to carry their mid-day meal to the fields and can be traced back at least to the 12th century[56]. Other sizes and patterns carried workmen's small tools. In coastal areas they were made of marram grass which grows on the sand dunes[57].

Strawberry pottles

Strawberry pottle in willow splint. MERL, Reading

This curiosity is included as an example of the cheap non-returnable containers used for centuries to package soft fruits. Records back to the 16th century prove the early use of these conical baskets made from willow chip and holding around half a pint (250ml), and they were still around in the mid-19th century[58]. After filling, they were carried in a larger head basket and hawked in the streets of London. Cream was sold from a jug. In 1849 it is reported that 600,000 pottles of strawberries were sold in the three main London produce markets[59].

Notes and references

1. Stringer, C. (2006) 'Homo Britannicus - the incredible story of human life in Britain'. Allen Lane; and Sykes, B. (2006) 'Blood of the Isles - exploring the genetic roots of our tribal history'. Bantam Press.
2. Allnutt, E.R.T. (1991) 'Roman Basketry from Carlisle'. BA NL **58** 12-14.
3. FitzGerald, M. (2007) 'Revolutionising Our Understanding of Prehistoric Basketry' Seanda 2: 49-51 (www.nra.ie/archaeology).
4. Earwood, C. (1993) 'Domestic Wooden Artefacts in Britain and Ireland from Neolithic to Viking Times'. Exeter University Press.
5. Landes, D.S. (1998) 'The Wealth and Poverty of Nations'. Little, Brown and Company p41.
6. See 5, p214.
7. The Basketmakers' List (1989) Originally published as the National List of basic wage rates in the basket industry in 1956. Reprinted by the Basketmakers' Association, p32.
8. Fitzrandolph, H.E. and Doriel Hay, M. (1926) 'The Rural Industries of England and Wales II: Osier growing and basketry and some rural factories'. OUP. Republished 1977 by EP Publishing Ltd.
9. Bagshawe, T.W. (1981) 'Basket Making in Bedfordshire'. Luton Museum and Art

Gallery.

10. Stott, K.G. (1992) 'Willows in the Service of Man'. Proc. R. Soc. Edin. **98B** 169-182.
11. Butcher, M. (1999) 'The Origins of Contemporary Basketmaking' in Contemporary International Basketmaking, Merrell.
12. See 7.
13. Okey, T. (1930) 'A Basketful of Memories'. J.M. Dent.
14. See 11 p13.
15. See 9 and also Cousins, R. (2007) 'A Basketful - willow growing and basket making in Nottinghamshire and Lincolnshire', Nottinghamshire County Council and Heritage Lincolnshire.
16. Coates, A. (1981) Transcript of taped interview by Chris Morris. Gloucester Folk Museum.
17. Okey, T. (1912) 'An Introduction to the Art of Basketmaking'. Pitman. Reproduced 1986 by the Basketmakers' Association.
18. Nene Park Trust (1992) Extract from 'Working Willows' reproduced in BA NL **60** 19-21.
19. Scott, P. (2005) 'Coffin-making with Terry Bensley'. BA NL **115** 30.
20. See 8 p67.
21. See 8 p73.
22. Stott, K.G. (1960) 'A Review of the British Basket-Willow-Growing Industry'. Ann. Rep. Long Ashton Res. Sta. 155-166.
23. See 10.
24. See 10 p170.
25. Smyth, P. (1991) 'Osier Culture and Basketmaking: a study of the basketmaking craft in south-west County Antrim'. The Universities Press (Belfast) Ltd.
26. Wright, D. (1977) 'The Complete Book of Baskets and Basketry'. Charles Scribner's Sons (subsequent edition 1992 by David and Charles).
27. Campbell, H. (1996) 'Welsh Frame Baskets'. BA NL **79** 10-11.
28. Davies, D.J. (1999) 'A Lifelong Affair with Willow'. BA NL **88** 5-8.
29. See 25.
30. Hogan, J. (2001) 'Basketmaking in Ireland.' Wordwell. p71.
31. See 30 p111 and 25 p164.
32. See 16 and 26 p119.
33. See 26 p123.
34. See 26 p151.
35. Elton Barratt, O. (1985) 'Regional Baskets - the oyster tendle'. BA NL **32** 7-10.
36. Fitzrandolph, H. and Doriel, Hay, M. (1926) 'The Rural Industries of England and Wales I: Timber and underwood industries and some village workshops'. OUP. Republished 1997 by E.P. Publishing Ltd, p96.
37. Barratt, M. (1983) 'Oak Swill Basketmaking in the Lake District'. Rollinson, W. (1998) 'Making Swill Baskets'. Smith Settle. Bury, A (1991) 'Wyre Forest Oak Whiskets'. BA NL**58** 18-19.
38. See 30 p77.
39. Owen Jones making a Cumbrian oak swill. Two DVDs (Preparing the material, Weaving the swill), the Basketmakers' Association (2006); and Brigden, R. (2008) 'The Swill Basket Maker' in Rural Crafts Today, a film project at the Museum of English Rural Life 2006-2008.
40. Fuller, S. (1998) 'Cumberland Swills'. BA NL **85** 38-41.
41. See 30 pp17-65.
42. Strang, S. (2003) 'Creel Workshop May 2003'. BA NL **106** 28-32.
43. Butcher M. (1997) 'Eel traps without eels' in Obscure Objects of Desire, Ed. Harrod, T., Proc. Crafts Council Conference. 230-238.
44. Luxford, N. (2000) 'A Working Life on the Great Ouse' S.B. Publications.
45. Geraint Jenkins, J. (1974) 'Nets and coracles'. Ch. 3, Putchers, Putts and Basket Traps. David & Charles.
46. Goymer, S. (1993) 'Putchers.' BA NL **64** 13-15.
47. See 30 ch6.
48. Killip, M. (1980) 'The Osier Garden'. J. Manx Museum **8** 89 22-24.
49. Sage, A. (2005) 'Re the Sussex Trug'. BA NL **113** 43-33.
50. Betts, J. (1992-3) 'The Devon Splint Basket'. Folk Life **31** 44-48; Goymer, S. (1991) 'The Devon Splint Basket'. BA NL **58** 16-17; Burns, H. (2004) 'Devon Stave Baskets'. BA NL **109** 33-34.
51. See 30 ch3.

52.   Scottish Basketmakers' Circle (2003) 'Kishie making with Lowrie Copland'. (Video with transcript).
53.   See 45.
54.   Badge, P. (1989) 'The Rebirth of a Spey Curragh'. BA NL **50** 22-23.
55.   See 30 ch4.
56.   See 26 p112.
57.   Strang, S. (1999) 'Plants and people – a visit to Kew Gardens'. BA NL **90** 32-33.
58.   See 26 p165.
59.   Behennah, D. (1989) 'Strawberry pottles and punnets'. BA NL **48** 2-5.

Multi-tier poultry
carrier.
Photo:
Nederlands
Openluchtmuseum
Arnhem

Bolts of graded willow, De Wissen museum, Stokkem, Belgium

Resources

The main land area covered in this chapter surrounds the Scheldt-Meuse-Rhine delta and has long been known as the Low Countries. It encompasses the present day kingdom of The Netherlands and the NW lowland part of Belgium. The whole region is relatively flat, much of it below sea level, and consisted of marshes and lagoons behind the coastal sand dunes. The soils were based on materials left behind by ice, rivers, and the sea, in the form of clay, peat, and sand. Much of the natural vegetation was water-tolerant plants, or moorland, with scanty tree growth, but the area today is largely man-made through massive drainage and soil mixing projects.

The region of France north of the river Somme can also be included, particularly the area on the Belgian border known as the Thiérache. Not only did the political border move during history, but the fine basketry developed there based upon skeined (split) willow was also characteristic of Halle south west of Brussels, and it is treated here rather than included in the chapter on France.

The climate is maritime with mild winters and cool summers that favour grass growth and hence grazing livestock, particularly cattle. It has a long sea coast facing the North Sea and the English Channel so fishing has always been important. Easy transport by water, either on the sea, or using the extensive system of inland waterways, had encouraged trade long before the advent of good roads.

History

The first four or five centuries AD experienced the imposition and then the loss of Roman culture followed by the emergence of the feudal system. During the 9th to the 14th centuries, while agriculture remained the main occupation, the peasantry was freed quite early from obligations to give labour service to the landowners, and strong cities with concentrations of industry and trade developed around the rivers and coast. The commercialisation of agriculture led to The Netherlands becoming the mainspring of European agricultural improvement from the 16th century. This revolution in farming involved reclaiming land from the sea, drainage, woodland clearance, land enclosure, crop rotation, early mechanisation, and other developments. The resultant improved productivity meant that a much smaller workforce was needed in food production so, already by the 17th century, half the population lived in towns and cities – the highest proportion in Europe – with Gent becoming the second largest city in western Europe (after Paris). This of course not only freed up people to become specialist craft workers, it also created demand for their products from large numbers of citizens who no longer

Rectangular market basket with two hinged lids in skeined willow. Musée de la Vie Rurale et Forestière, Saint-Michel en Thiérache, France

had the materials, skill, or inclination to make their own baskets. The huge increase in manufacturing, and thus transport, caused new types of baskets to be developed. These ranged all the way from coarse containers used to move bulk materials by water, to the finest luxury products for those whose business success had given them and their families wealth and leisure. Furthermore, the region early on became important for products from other lands, up river or overseas, to be processed and re-exported, and by 1550 there was an important merchant fleet. Even those who remained on the land now grew a greater variety of crops and farmed larger areas so that their needs for specialised basketry items increased.

With few local sources of wood, but an ideal climate for growing willow, it was natural for basketry in the region to be almost entirely based on this material, at first wild but then cultivated. Large-scale willow beds were planted both along and within the river banks and on clay soils in the freshwater tidal delta areas. They had an additional function in helping to build up the land level on estates during regular inundation by flood water. They were looked after by superintendents, and provided winter work for local men with the annual crops of rods being sold by auction (a practice which lasted until the 1950s). While the coarser articles used brown (unpeeled) rods, white willow was needed for all the finer work, and school children were given holidays in May to help with the family activity of stripping or peeling. Workshops were situated on or near a canal so that willow rods could be brought by boat, and also soaked before use.

Statue of girl stripping willow rods, Stokkem, Belgium

A consequence of the urbanisation of basketmakers, as with other craft workers, was the creation of guilds. The earliest known was founded in Dordrecht in 1367. As elsewhere, these had the objectives of binding allied workers together for their common interests and for the wider interests of their town or city, and in the northern Netherlands they also gained political influence.

No fewer than 26 different basketry guilds have been documented for the Netherlands[1]. Each normally encompassed masters producing all types of basketry, though there was sometimes a division between workers in brown or in white willow. In a few cases, the basketmakers shared a single guild with another complementary craft: in Zierikzee (Zeeland) with thatchers, perhaps the same men alternated between summer thatching and winter willow weaving; in Flanders with fruiterers; in Maastricht with fishermen; and in other parts with besom (broom) makers. In Halle (in the Brabant region of today's Belgium) there were two separate groups, each with its own entry requirements. The skeined-willow candidate had to produce a five-sided cheese basket, a rectangular layette basket and a rectangular market basket with two hinged lids. These were evaluated by existing guild members before the decision was made to admit the new candidate and confer the esteemed title of 'Master'.

Window screen portrayed in 'The Ass in the School '1556 Pieter Bruegel.
Staatliche Museen Preussischer Kulturbesitz, Berlin

Reproduction window screen made by Arie van t'Hoog

In Alkmaar the 1684 ordinance lays down that workers in brown rods had to make two types of eelputcher (trap), a fish storage basket, and a square candle basket. Workers using white willow had to submit a cradle, a layette basket, and a window screen (to exclude birds or rubbish), well illustrated in Bruegel's 1556 engraving 'The Ass in the School'. The winnowing-fan makers naturally had to produce a fan.

The guild system controlled the craft in towns for several centuries and thus serviced the needs of the majority of the population. True, the Reformation (late 16th century) brought enormous changes since guilds in the northern republic (today's Netherlands) had to shift from their Catholic foundations to the new Calvinist structures. After the middle of the 18th century hardly any new members joined, in line with the general European movement to greater individual liberty (culminating in the French Revolution of 1789), and the guild system came to an end in The Netherlands in 1798.

During the second half of the 19th century, large workshops grew up to supply commercial fisheries, agriculture, and many different industries. Increased volumes of traded products required huge numbers of containers which were often moved by rail or water and then returned empty for re-use. They were sold both locally and in other countries nearby. Dutch workshops competed very successfully with their English counterparts for the supply of baskets to English fruit-growing regions and continued to be the dominant source through the first half of the 20th century.

Left: Fisherman's creel in fine skeined willow.
Musée de la Vie Rurale et Forestière, Saint-Michel en Thiérache

Right: Carrier for cat or dog in fine skeined willow. Offered by Harrods, London in 1929 in four sizes.
Musée de la Vie Rurale et Forestière, Saint-Michel en Thiérache

Very few basketmaking workshops could survive the Second World War and the subsequent competition from new packaging methods, and they entered a terminal decline. Nevertheless, in 1956 there were still some 1350 hectares of willow cut for basketmaking (and for ties used in horticulture, thatching and dyke construction) and around 2000 basketmakers – mostly old. Large quantities of rods (brown, white and buff) were still being exported.

Of course, not all basketry was produced first by the guilds and later by the new large workshops. Some small farmers had always made for their own needs and for their neighbours. Mia Pot interviewed Jan Telgenkamp in 1978 when he was already over 70. He had some two dozen willows, pollarded at about 50cm above ground to keep the rods out of the grass. He cut these between December and January and used them 'green' (without drying) to make 10 to 20 baskets. These were mainly stake and strand maunds for potato harvesting with two small side handles, but he also made half-spherical frame baskets using thicker stems (hazel or mountain ash – Sorbus) for the handle and rim hoops and the large ribs. He had learned from his father, and needed only a knife, secateurs, pincers and an 18cm home-made oak bodkin. Such farmers with this additional skill must have existed everywhere, and no doubt traded or bartered their products with neighbours proficient in other activities.

The Thiérache is the region in the north of France close to the Belgian border whose traditions of willow growing and basketmaking can be traced to the 14th century. In the 16th century fruit growers in the Meuse area were exporting through Boulogne to England in baskets purchased in these valleys (Thon and Oise). In the mid 17th century there seems to have been an intake of unemployed linen and hemp weavers, and it was perhaps their influence which developed the tradition of *vannerie fine* using fine white willow rods or skein. The region developed a reputation for the elegance and sophistication of its work and was therefore well placed to expand when the demand for basketry exploded and production changed from family based enterprises towards an industrial scale. Several large firms established themselves in the area creating factories to colour, varnish and decorate the products (fit hinges, legs, locks, linings, straw or raffia plaits and ornaments) coming from the basketmakers both home-based, and in workshops. Not surprisingly, this rapid growth of the industry employing 5500 workers in some 22-25 villages at the end of the 19th century meant that willow had to be imported from other regions.

A holding company 'La Vannerie Française' was created by mergers in 1919. It had premises in Britain, Belgium and Germany. Such businesses struggled between the two wars, and had to compete with the output from prisons, orphanages and workshops set up for the war wounded, but survived by continuously providing new models to cater

General purpose farm baskets (maunds) in three sizes in brown willow.
Stadsmuseum IJsselstein

Cherry picking basket with crooked stick for hanging from branch.
Stadsmuseum IJsselstein

Frame basket with green willow weavers made by Jan Telgenkamp in 1978 when aged over 70.
Photo: Mia Pot

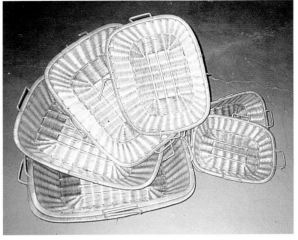

for changing fashion. In 1939, the region offered over 1000 models in several sizes, or more than 5000 overall, from only a few cubic centimetres to over one cubic metre. They produced a lot of buff rods (boiled and then peeled) for items preferred in the British market.

There was considerable specialisation among villages, a phenomenon seen also in the villages of N Bavaria in Germany. One or two produced practically all models, but others mainly produced fishing creels, picnic hampers, rectangular shoppers, containers for fresh vegetables, covered market baskets, skeined shoppers, bottle covers, and bird nests. One village (Gercy) even specialised in frame baskets – but still finely made.

Exports were important and were encouraged by international exhibitions and travelling sales staff, and facilitated by offices and storage facilities overseas. By the 1960s Italian and Spanish baskets competed for the French market in fine basketry as well as imports from Asia. Far Eastern exporters learned to copy their new models within six months and have them retailed in Europe at less than the French production cost. La Vannerie Française finally ceased production in 1971[2].

In 1906, economic depression in a region of poor soils in the northeast (Noordwolde, Friesland) stimulated a local clergyman and doctor to travel to Lichtenfels in Germany and bring back a teacher to instruct the children in a variety of woodcrafts. Their basketry thus absorbed influences from Germany but also from other places. New materials were imported, like esparto grass from Spain, and used in conjunction with more traditional fibres. Finished baskets came in from the Dutch East Indies and these in turn influenced work in the school. After World War II, these workshops coped with a big demand for well-designed cane chairs, and then moved on to heavier furniture. The National Vlechtmuseum opened in Noordwolde in 2002[3].

The valley of the river Meuse (Maas) was an important willow-growing region and the village of Stokkem, near Maastricht (but today in Belgium) once had a thriving basketry industry. Early products featured round brown willow maunds for transporting iron ore, chalk, and coke into the iron-smelting ovens. Other items included openwork designs for laundry, bread and patisserie, and large numbers of round lidded containers for butter.

A school founded in 1923 offered a three-year training in both basket and cane furniture making. This continued until the 1970s. The low wages paid to willow and cane workers encouraged them to quit the industry and find alternative employment in the nearby coal mines. The industry ceased and might have been soon forgotten. Fortunately, the community decided to use money from the gravel extraction industry

Stone carving on house in Alkmaar
c1650.
Photo: Mia Pot

(which replaced the willow beds) to fund a modern education centre to illustrate many aspects of the river's ecology. 'De Wissen' (willow) houses excellent exhibits on willow growing and basketmaking in the village and beyond, and shows the variety of wares offered by an itinerant merchant who cycled through the villages attending markets until the 1960s[4]. In the village itself, several delightful sculptures remind everyone of the once-common activities of stripping and weaving willow.

There are two useful sources of information about historic baskets from these regions – long after the original articles have perished. First, drawings, prints, and paintings from the highly skilled artists supported in the 17th century by the profits from Holland's trade, and by court and church patronage in the south. Rubens painted a winter landscape around 1620 with a very clear representation of a winnowing fan[5]. Many others recorded domestic scenes with cradles and layette baskets, or markets displaying produce in a wide variety of woven containers.

A lesser known source is the large number of stone carvings (*gevelstenen*) on the fronts of 17th and 18th century houses in The Netherlands and Flanders. Some of these houses were owned by the skippers of boats which traded in the items depicted (peat, nails, tobacco), but in other cases the carvings may have been advertisements for shops (e.g. a grain fan outside a bakery, a girl carrying both poultry and eggs[6]).

The Dutch organisation Wilg & Mand (Willow and Basket) was formed in 1980 to help to preserve the craft, and attracted some 600 donors who supported a variety of activities including a newsletter, meetings, courses, and book publishing. Its historical group is building an archive and acquiring a collection, part of which is on display at the Stadsmuseum, IJsselstein.

Types of work

Professional willow work

In a region where agriculture was commercialised very early, where urbanisation was well advanced by the 17th century, and where the sea coast, rivers, and canals fostered fishing, and both inland and export trade, it is not surprising that a large professional basketmaking industry existed. Its historical development was sketched in the previous section, but what were the characteristic products?

We might expect that individual fishermen would have made their own traps for fresh- and sea-water prey as the remaining older men did in the 20th century, but in the 17th

Reconstruction of workshop
producing fishing baskets.
Visserijmuseum, Vlaardingen

89

Nursemaid feeding baby seated in
a bakermat by Esaias Boursse,
Amsterdam 17C

Bakermat in white willow by
Arie van t'Hoog

century, even eelputchers were professionally
made by guild members. Sea-going vessels
needed a large variety of simple maunds, each
adapted to its specific function: holding bait,
tackle, catch, and ice. They varied in size,
number of handles, whether close or open work
sides and bases, round or oval, and were
produced in (mainly) brown willow in coastal workshops. When oriental cane became
available, it was sometimes substituted for the willow weavers, though stakes often
continued to be the thicker willow rods. There is a good selection on display in the
fishing museum at Vlaardingen (Visserijmuseum).

Baskets for use in harvesting, transporting and marketing agricultural and horticultural
crops were also made in large numbers, and we have already noted that Dutch
professionals competed successfully in supplying a range of fruit baskets to Britain. But
particular mention should be made of the white willow work for household use. Cots,
cradles and laundry baskets in several designs were similar to those found elsewhere
(though particularly well made). Hooded chairs were made in large numbers for use on
North Sea and Baltic beaches[7], while two other articles were more specific to this
region.

The *bakermat* may have originally been a flat mat. It later acquired low sides, higher at
the back than the foot end, and often lower on one side[8]. Its function was to provide a
measure of comfort for the nursemaid (*baker*) sitting with feet outstretched near the
open fire, feeding or attending to the baby. It would have kept her off the cold floor
with the high side stopping some of the draught from the doorway. A small handle at
one end would allow it to be hung from a wall when not in use. It was usually made
with close weaving in white willow in a stake and strand construction, but sometimes in
open work. This basket was found throughout the western areas until the 18th century,
and illustrations by Rembrandt, Dou, van Ostade, van Mieris and Boursse show several
17th century variations[9]. Mia Pot and Arie van t'Hoog decided that my collection
should display a *bakermat*. Arie who had spent years making traditional Dutch baskets
and documenting the methods, made one in white willow, and they very kindly
presented it to me in 2001.

Clothes airer with internal heater.
National Vlechtmuseum,
Noordwolde

The clothes airer was perhaps particularly needed in a damp climate. Many surviving
examples consist of a round maund, close or open woven, with a raised canopy of open
rods on which damp clothes could be hung. A small brazier would be placed inside the
base to provide the necessary heat to dry or 'air' the clothes.

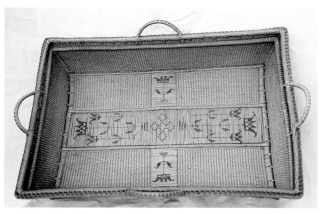

Antique fine willow skeinwork decorated in red and green silk binding c1720-40. Four-handled layette basket. All photos: E Hartkamp-Jonxis

Openwork layette basket

Fine willow and skeinwork

As befits a prosperous and increasingly urban society, the craftsmen of Halle (SW of Brussels) and the Thiérache along the Belgian-French border developed some of the finest basketry work ever seen in Europe at least as early as the 17th century. The work utilised fine white willow rods, both whole and split into skein. Not only does the preparation of the skeins take time and skill, but weaving with such fine elements also means that many hours are absorbed by quite a small basket, and it is naturally less robust than articles made with whole rods. Hence the technique was usually reserved for small articles which inevitably sold for relatively high prices and would be used with much more care than common basket work. Typical products were layette baskets (for baby linen), others to be used on the table with bread or fruit, placemats, and dolls' furniture. Mia Pot described a particularly luxurious set of articles that included larger

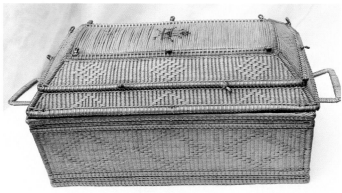

Container for drinking glass bearing the name HAL (French for Halle, Belgium)

Lidded layette basket

Below from left to right:

Inside detail

Underside of base reinforced by wooden slats

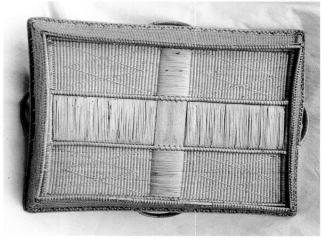

pieces like a cot, as well as protective cases for a goblet and a glass tumbler and billiard balls. Some of these, from Halle, were additionally decorated in red and green silk binding, and must have been made for wealthy patrons around 1720-1740.

These and others were assembled for an exhibition in IJsselstein in 1998 and although the pieces are now dispersed again to their sources in several countries, the publication preserves an excellent record of these beautiful examples of the basketmaker's craft[10].

I was privileged to see, handle, and photograph some of these extraordinary pieces in August 2000 in The Hague. They belong to the family of Mrs Hartkamp Jonxis, curator of textiles at the Rijksmuseum, Amsterdam and have been lovingly preserved down the centuries. Mary Butcher and Michael Thierschmann described their experiences in 1995 when commissioned to make copies of very similar baskets for Hampton Court Palace near London: "Fine skeinwork is like spinning straw into gold"[11].

Needlework basket in fine willow skein inherited by Mia Pot and repaired by Michael Thierschmann

In a 16th century household, linen and the linen chest were some of a housewife's most precious possessions, and the contents of a layette basket were part of it. The basket, like the cradle, was probably ordered by a reasonably prosperous family only once, for a firstborn child. Mia Pot and Arie van't Hoog suggest that such items were not part of a basketmaker's daily output, but were masterpieces in which he could show off his craftsmanship and take time to add decorative finishings. They researched four examples included as details in altarpieces by Flemish master-painters working in the late 15th and early 16th centuries, and deduced that all the baskets came from workshops in Antwerp and Bruges. All four are oval with tapering sides, and have lids which close over the top sides. The lid has a central handle, two hinges on one side, and a fastening on the other. Most had decorations in colour. While much of the work is in fine white whole-willow rods, there is also skein-wrapping in places[12]. Few such items will have survived to this day, but luckily there are more recent examples of ladies' sewing baskets which may have evolved from them, sometimes entirely in fine skeinwork.

Specific items of interest

Back baskets

Back baskets were a common method of carrying heavy loads on long journeys, or in hilly and mountainous regions – but these countries are small and flat! Nevertheless, there do seem to be rather more examples from this region than in nearby, and not so flat, Britain, even if fewer than in Germany (see chapter). The answer may be related to the difficulty of using wheeled transport across sand dunes or from boat to shore.

A flat-sided oval basket in a blocked pattern of brown and white willow with a strong foot, was made in Alkmaar for carrying fish or beachcombing. Sometimes ordinary round fish maunds would be slung on the back using simple shoulder rope. Many houses were warmed by peat fires, and the fuel was brought by canal boats and then man-handled in coarse maunds balanced on the shoulders or strapped on the back.

But Dutch craftsmen also devised willow back-baskets sub-divided into several layers. Some were used to transport poultry (with net decks) and a similar open-work version was made for small pottery items. A double-decked white willow basket on a

Pair of oval handbaskets for fish carried by shoulder yoke, 1928. Photo: van Pluis, Musselkanaal

'The prodigal son' Jeroen Bosch
(1450-1516).
Museum Boijmans van
Beuningen, Rotterdam

boarded base carried butter to market with a removable shelf which fitted neatly onto a raised line of weaving.

An alternative method of carrying heavy loads was to use a wooden shoulder yoke with hanging ropes hooked onto stout-handled baskets. In this way, a strong person could use their hands to steady the loads while their shoulders bore the weight.

Poultry baskets

This distinctive bell-shaped design has a round (or occasionally oval) base, and the lower third may have close weaving up from the base. The open-work stakes are then drawn sharply in before finally returning to the vertical to form a neck, and there is a hinged top which may be close or open work. This allows the birds to be inspected through at least the middle section and to be removed under control through the relatively small neck. The flat base allowed the light load to be carried on the head, or on the arm, using a side strap. Careful inspection of detailed engravings and paintings by the Bruegels and Beuckelaer from the 1560s show the same design[13]. I was delighted to see them still in use when I visited the Dutch open-air museum in Arnhem in 2000 where the poultry fanciers happened to be staging a show.

Poultry carrier, brown and white
willow seen at breeders' show
2000, Arnhem

Notes and references

1. In assembling this chapter I have been greatly helped by the tireless work of Mrs GM Pot-van Regteren Altena from Schoorl, near Alkmaar in the Netherlands, known to all her friends as Mia. Trained in calligraphy, she had a family and friends with interests spanning art history, weaving, pottery, medicine and biology. Her wide knowledge has not only pointed me to pictorial representations of articles from the past 400 years, but she personally searched the archives and documented many aspects of the craft in her country. She published over 60 contributions in the Dutch Wilg & Mand (Willow and Basket) from its beginning in 1981 and also sent regular material to the Basketmakers' Association newsletter. But more than that, she introduced me to relevant people and museums, and spent hours translating and discussing many aspects for my education. In consequence, I have been able to present a more detailed historical account for this region than I have so far found possible in most other countries.
2. 'Vannerie & Manufactures - la toute fine vannerie de Thiérache'. (1994) Museé de la Vie

Detail from 'The numbering at Bethlehem' Pieter Bruegel c1565. Musées Royeaux des Beaux-Art, Brussels

Rurale et Forestière. Editions Saint Michel. 143pp.

3. Barnhoorn, T. (2001) 'Opening Museum in Noordwolde'. Vlechten **2** 28-30; Hofman, E. (2003) 'Noordwolde, Basketry Village of the Netherlands'. BA NL **107** 33-34.

4. Belemans, R. (1996) 'Met Korven wonnen Hunne Kost' (An Illustrated History of the Region and Museum). Bezoekerscentrum De Wissen, Stokkem, 74pp.

5. Peter Paul Rubens (1620) Winter. The Queen's Collection.

6. Pot-van Regteren Altena, G.M. (1993) Stone tablets (gevelstenen) on houses in the Netherlands. BA NL **102** 21-23; and Ferro, F. (1994) 'Hoe Steenhouwers Manden Hakten'. Wilg & Mand 17-22, 44-48.

7. Pot-van Regteren Altena, G.M. (1996) 'Hooded Wickerwork Chairs'. BA NL **78** 8-9.

8. Pot-van Regteren Altena, G.M. (1994) 'The Bakermat'. BA NL **69** 22-24.

9. Rembrandt (1640-41) Bedroom with Saskia in bed. Rijksmuseum, Amsterdam; Gerrit Dou (1613-1675) Rest on the flight to Egypt. Private Collection; Adriaen van Ostade (1610-1684) Drawing in State Print Room. Rijksmuseum, Amsterdam; Willem van Mieris, panel in Rijksbureau for Art History Documentation, The Hague; Esaias Boursse, 17th century Amsterdam.

10. Pot-van Regteren Altena, G.M. (1998) 'Een Mandeken van Fine Teenen'. Stichting Wilg & Mand 24pp.

11. Butcher, M. and Thierschmann, M. (1995) 'Hampton Court Willow Skeinwork'. BA NL **74** 27-29.

12. Pot-van Regteren Altena, G.M. and van t'Hoog, A. (2004) 'Four 16th Century Flemish Layette Baskets'. BA NL **111** 30-35.

13. Bruegel, P. (1566) 'The numbering at Bethlehem'. Musées Royaux des Beaux-Arts, Brussels; and Booth, D. (2007) 'Bruegel, Baskets and Chooks'. BA NL **121** 18-19.

Statue of basketmaker, Stokkem, Belgium

France

Christophe Romand tying newly-dried
white willow rods into bolts,
Villaines-les-Rochers, June 1988.
Photo: R.J. Whittick

Glass demi-johns covered in white willow, Vallabrègues museum, 1997

Resources

France is favourably situated in a climatic zone between the maritime and Mediterranean, and has a generally westward slope. This promotes equable temperatures and well-distributed rainfall, but with a high component of sunshine and summer heat. Temperate forests, mainly deciduous except at the upper levels of tree growth, were once extensive and still occupy 30% of the land area and much more in some parts.

There are different geographic regions each of which is several times the size of other European countries like Belgium or The Netherlands. The Paris basin, equivalent in size to the whole of England, is predominantly limestone and chalk, and its soils have long been fully cultivated. The north west corner has a different geology and milder climate leading to livestock farming and coastal fishing. By contrast, the Massif Central is an eroded plateau with generally poor soils, while the south west is more favoured and supports a wide range of crops including vines. Early settlement on the Mediterranean coast and Eastern Pyrenees removed the forests. Subsequent erosion left thin soils which supported drought resistant vegetation. The crops were grapes, olives, chestnuts, wheat or irrigated crops.

The smaller regions to the east include the French Alps, Alsace and the Vosges mountains, and French Flanders up to the Belgian border. The Agricultural Revolution had its origin in technical improvements in Flanders, and these then spread throughout the most favoured regions of Europe. Paris emerged early as the dominant centre, and the north east naturally grew its population relative to the remainder.

Most regions could grow willow, and it has emerged as the major material used by French basketmakers. But in the forested areas larger tree species, especially hazel and chestnut, were put to good use by farmers or fishermen for their own needs. Even full-time professionals used them in some areas. Straw was also widely available as were coniferous trees in the alpine regions. Mediterranean cane grows in the south.

History

As with other countries bordering on the Mediterranean, France received Phoenician and Greek settlers around 3000 years ago, followed by Romans, and some parts must therefore have been exposed to their sophisticated basketry techniques based upon both wild and cultivated willows. No doubt these survived in places after the decline of Roman rule, and since Paris has long been an important city there may well have been urban workshops there throughout its history. But most baskets continued to be made out of local materials by families for their own use. The makers were involved mainly in small-scale farming with crops and livestock, sometimes supplemented by fishing from rivers, lakes, and sea coasts, This survived until at least the 19th century.

We are fortunate that France not only has a large and long-lasting basketry tradition, but that its scholars have done some thorough research. A great deal of information now exists on the materials used, the products, the lives of the makers, and the organisations involved at various times during their history. These authors have produced records of professional makers from all over the French countryside, not merely from Paris and other urban centres.

In the Pays d'Arles near the mouth of the Rhone in the far South, the *banastiers* were included in 1247 among those having been conferred the privilege of establishing a brotherhood of craftsmen. This Provençal word refers to large oval close-sided baskets mainly used for the harvest and transport of fruit and vegetables. By 1269 there were around 100 such brotherhoods listed as existing in Paris, and there was a 'rue de Vannerie' and a 'rue de l'Oseriae' (willow beds) in the city. From 1292 the first written records of individual basketmakers occur in the register of taxes. Even at this time the craftsmen were subdivided into different groups according to the type of work they produced: *paneliniers* who made *paniers*; *corbeliniers* – *corbeilles,* or large open baskets; and *vanetiers* who worked with willow on wood slats to produce the complex *van* or winnowing fan.

In 1350 they created their coat of arms (three scallop shells or winnowing fans). Their corporation was recognised in 1467, the 46th in order of the trades, and their statutes confirmed. These laid down the duration of apprenticeship (three years) and limited a master to two apprentices. A further two years were required as a journeyman (*compagnon-ouvrier*) and recognition as a master involved the submission of a test-piece and a money payment. Masters' sons were excused the test. The Museum of Compagnonnage in Tours holds several of these surviving masterpieces from the early 19th century.

These corporations (for example that founded in Orléans in 1409) were similar to the guilds in other countries. They required regular attendance at church services and meetings, maintenance of strict codes of conduct within the 'brotherhood', and provided a degree of mutual insurance for masters and their families who needed

Right: Grape harvesting basket (hotte) carried on the back, which used to be made by the vanetiers or cloturiers in white willow rods woven onto oak slats. Museum at Château de Troussay

Traditional rectangular frame basket in chestnut and willow used for transporting goods, Musée des Vallée Cévenoles, St Jean du Gard

support. Their function was to maintain standards, share out the available work among all masters, and prevent competition from outside. The statutes were revised in 1561 when the apprenticeship was lengthened to four years (to maintain his dependence on his master) and the trade divided afresh into three groupings:

mandriers who worked in white or brown willow and produced closed (or fully woven) work where the flexible weavers created a full body on the stakes or skeleton.

faissiers who produced 'open' work where the stakes are not completely woven over. This work also included the covering of glass bottles and jars.

cloturiers who made fans, back baskets for grapes (*hottes*) or those for holding dough, animal feed or even water by reason of the very close-fitting weaving of white willow rods on the wooden slat foundation or skeleton.

As the population grew, more people adopted an urban life (especially in Paris) and more agricultural and industrial products needed to be transported, even exported to England and other countries. It became obvious that the old system of corporations controlling the work in each urban centre was unsuitable for these changing conditions, and in 1776 a government edict suppressed them and declared the professions free. After suppression, apprenticeships in the cities were controlled by the *Associations Compagnonniques* which survived the Revolution (1789) and reorganised from the early 1800s. Many basketmakers plied their trades in workshops under a *patron*.

Openwork grape tray in white willow, ENOV, Fayl-Billot

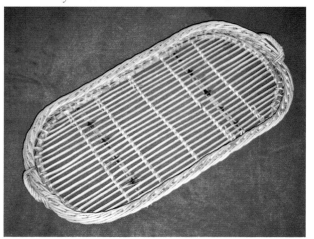

The strong economic expansion in the 19th century, based on increasing agricultural productivity, growth of industries, greater urbanisation and foreign trade, all caused an increase in demand for traditional baskets for harvesting and transport, but at the same time created a need for new types of containers for long-distance transport by rail, river, or sea. This was the era when industrial methods were beginning to be applied to all ancient trades and basketmaking did not escape. The Paris workshops could no longer cope, so in order to supply large orders to the towns, new organisations and workshops or factories were created in several regions where conditions were suitable for growing willow. Existing areas with a history of growing and utilising their own material had obvious advantages and expanded their production, but some new regions also emerged.

Two shopping baskets in fine white willow.
Far left: la mandelette ronde.
Left: le marlier,
Villaines-les-Rochers

The initial development was for some progressive makers to move into wholesaling the products of several workshops where these still consisted of a family and perhaps a small number of paid employees. But then entrepreneurs, either from within or without the industry, built large specialist facilities in the regions. These might store the raw material for distribution to families who still worked at home, or for use in workshops on site. They would provide facilities for finished work to be received weekly from outworkers, inspected, sorted and finished. Such finishing might include varnishing or painting, lining with fabrics and the addition of trimmings. Consignments would then be made up from stores to be despatched by rail to distant, even export markets. Some would go to produce wholesalers who supplied their growers, or their fish and shellfish suppliers; others to the large new retail shops in the cities.

This phase of expansion was at its maximum during the period 1870—1910. It involved huge changes from the previous way of life of a rural or even urban basketmaker. Competition could be fierce with downward pressure on price. Many different individuals were in the supply chain, and all needed to earn a reward. As in so many other industries at the time, it was the ordinary maker and his family who were in the weakest position and who often suffered from very long hours of manual work but lived in poverty. The First World War, the subsequent economic depression lasting almost to the Second World War, and the increasing development of new packaging materials and systems produced continuous change in the basketmaking industry. The individual enterprises became larger and fewer, and women moved into making baskets rather than merely performing related tasks like stripping willow rods[1]. The Government brought in new laws to try to protect the workers, but all the time the demand for these traditional products was reducing while the imports of cheaply produced articles increased from countries with lower wage rates in southern and eastern Europe and then the Far East. Some of the large enterprises survived in greatly reduced form until the 1960s or 1970s, or moved into furniture-making based upon imported cane. Cooperatives were formed in areas where these large firms were not operating and two have successfully survived to this day. But the story of 20th century basketmaking in France has been a more or less continuous decline. Today there may be fewer then 200 professionals still active, a mere handful compared with 40,000 a century ago.

Villaines-les-Rochers (below left) and Fayl-Billot (below) both pride themselves as centres of French basketmaking today, and use basket street furniture to advertise the craft

Typical frame basket in chestnut splint (panière) made in many sizes in Limousin in the late 19th century for the transport of food and other products

Types of work

Professional basketry (mainly willow)

France's different regions have, not surprisingly, given rise to quite different professional industries. Five of these have been selected for more detailed attention here. A sixth (the Thiérache) specialised in fine willow work and has been included in the chapter on the Low Countries since its history is closely tied up with that region.

1.   Limousin

Limoges is in the Department of the Haute-Vienne to the west of the Massif Central and north of the Dordogne. The land lies generally above 300m and slopes to the west with mixed arable and cattle farming interspersed with chestnut woods. The rural population traditionally looked after its own needs for basketry, and most families could make simple articles from straw (dough baskets and containers for dried food besides bee hives, seedlips, flat trays, egg baskets and bottle covers), or from split chestnut wood. A valuable study published in 1967 by Maurice Robert describes how one community in the village of Mas-Gauthier, close to Limoges, developed from being almost entirely small-scale farmers in 1831 to 50% basketmakers by 1886, and this proportion remained until the 1930s[2]. For most of this time they worked entirely in chestnut wood and made a single type of frame basket – large rectangular containers with a rim and longitudinal ribs, woven with chestnut splint and without added handles. They were made in a variety of sizes, 30-110cm long, 30-60cm wide, according to their use. This temporary national demand for a traditional local product was associated with the increased transport of food and manufactured products. Many went to canning factories or abattoirs and meat processors, plant nurseries and florists.

The chestnut trees were coppiced every 6-10 years in the winter months when they reached 3-7cm diameter at the base. Stems were trimmed of side branches and placed in large water-filled pits until needed. They were then split to make rims, ribs and weavers (0.5–1.5mm thick, 1-3cm wide). At the height of this industry (1900-1920) each maker would weave around four per day, or 1000 per year, and the village turned out 3-400 per day. They were sent all over France until chilled food transport and lighter, cheaper containers for other goods destroyed their market by the 1930s. By 1962 there were only 11 basketmakers still active in the village, with an average age of 64. All had learned their trade from their fathers. Most had worked in small workshops in their own houses, though there had been some larger groupings, up to 14 working in one shop in 1907. But even in that shop, unlike some other communities, there had never been any association or cooperative. They all worked as independent makers, so in some

ways they represented an intermediate type of organisation between the family and the urban structures which evolved in other regions. The industry was killed by new technology, not by exhausting its raw material, since regular coppicing of chestnut, hazel or willow is an excellent example of the sustainability which is so frequently advocated today. Fortunately some work in split chestnut is still exhibited at the Basketmakers' Fair in Issigeac, near Bergerac, held annually in July[3].

In the Limousin area some men worked in hazel rather than chestnut, but few other types of basket were made commercially. Chestnut furniture had a short period of fashion, and willow was used briefly to make fruit sieves for export to England around 1910–1920.

This first example of a professional industry is very different from those found elsewhere in that it harnessed the traditional methods of peasant farmers making baskets using the frame or rib technique.

2.   Le Petit Morin

The next region to be considered, near Brie 75km east of Paris, had no tradition of professional basketmaking. With its clay soils it was better suited to dairy farming though some areas of loess (wind-blown soils) produced good crops. The industry developed in up to a dozen villages strung along the valley of the Petit Morin.

The growth of Paris in the first half of the19[th] century multiplied the demands for baskets of all sorts. The Parisian workshops, with 10-15 workers under a *patron* were in the new districts surrounding the centre, but could no longer satisfy the growing demand, and so developments took place in some of the neighbouring provinces. The first makers appeared in 1830 in the Brie area. A factory was established in 1863, and the company started to cultivate its own willow and employed 60 workers. Some of these came from the families of workers whose own trade (e.g. sabot making) was in decline. Around 1888 a school to train workers was opened by a Paris-based merchant and continued until 1914. In total around 280 workers were employed in the factory and in some 15 other workshops.

Their main products were articles in brown and white willow for handling produce for the new covered markets, for travel and for the surrounding rural world – for butchers, florists, laundries, bakers and patissiers, and wine growers. Trunks for removals were a speciality, some of them very large, made in several workshops employing up to 20

Local fruit displayed in a model van,
Vallabrègues, 1997

workers. As demand for these items reduced other products replaced them – furniture, household articles.

In 1898 an organisation was formed, half way between a buying cooperative and a union. It aimed to purchase supplies in bulk, fix sale prices to the merchants, and harmonise rates of pay, but members found it hard to honour the agreed prices in a declining market and conflicts arose between militant workers and their employers. This modest industry grew up, flourished, and disappeared completely within the 100 years from the mid 19th to mid-20th century. At the time of the 1994 study, after four generations only one maker remained active[4].

3.   Vallabrègues

A quite different picture emerges from the 1980 study by Charles Galtier of the history of the industry in the village of Vallabrègues, situated on the banks of the Rhône between Avignon and Arles just 80km from the Mediterranean[5]. An alluvial plain on the delta where a tributary river enters the Rhône, including several islands, provided good growing conditions for willow, wild and cultivated in a region which would otherwise have a Mediterranean climate with hot, dry summers. There were also areas of 'cane' (*Arundo donax*).

The basketmaking trade based on local willow must have had an extremely long history since there was an approved 'brotherhood' as early as 1247. The total inhabitants of the village were never more than 2000. Agriculture developed rapidly in the last quarter of the 19th century, especially market gardening and fruit growing using irrigation, and there was a need to transport the produce by rail to urban markets. In addition, the needs of the growing chemical and pharmaceutical industries to move their products encouraged the growth of a professional industry. This employed over 350 makers at the turn of the century. Just as the new types of agricultural production needed a forwarder between themselves and the urban markets, so the individual basketmakers needed a wholesaler/merchant – who then opened a 'factory'. But whether the craftsmen worked at home using their own material, or in a workshop provided by the merchant, they continued to be paid by the piece. As in other regions, this number declined rather rapidly after 1920, but in 1965 there were still 75, and they and the chair makers still made up one quarter of the active professionals in the village. Galtier's study revealed how, even though they lived together in the village, farmers and basketmakers formed two communities with different and opposite calendars of activity. In an analysis of 319 marriages, farmers' daughters rarely married basketmakers while some 70% of basketmakers married daughters of basketmakers.

Lidded basket in willow and split 'cane', Vallabrègues museum

Modern reconstruction of a cabane which housed several Vallabrègues families working in the willow beds on island`s in the Rhône from November to May, with cladding in split 'cane'. Photo: Comité des Fêtes de Vallabrègues

A special feature of the industry was the way that around half the village population, men, women, and children, went to live among the low lying willow beds from November 1st to early May, to harvest and strip the rods. They lived in rough huts made of 'cane', large enough for several families to sleep, eat, and work and were organised by *patrons* who provided the huts and basic rations and paid them for their output. Some of the men continued to weave baskets during this period while their wives helped to strip the new crop, but the main basketmaking took place back in the village from May through to the end of October. This system persisted until the early part of the 20th century. It then began to break down (absence of men during World War I), and finally ended in 1951.

This village industry produced a wide range of articles in many styles and sizes, but almost all round or oval in stake and strand, all willow or with 'cane 'siding. The 'cane' was cultivated at the field edges and also harvested from mid-December to mid-March. The stems were stripped of leaves, then split longitudinally into four. These splits needed soaking for 24 hours before being used as weavers on willow stakes. Round baskets were made with one large or two small handles for picking fruit, olives, cherries, wine grapes; special ones used white willow for dessert grapes. Others were for holding fishing lines with hooks, for shellfish, plants in pots, and cylindrical cheeses. 'Cane' siding was employed for transporting pharmaceutical products (150,000/year for one Paris company alone) with a range of sizes to contain glass bottles for wine, oil, and acids. Strong containers were needed for soil, sand or stones for ships' ballast. Oval baskets with large handles were made for butchers and abattoirs or with two small handles for washing and linen.

The characteristic fruit and vegetable transporter was the *banaste*. It was oblong, begun as an oval base, but with flattened sides and made in willow. There was a small handle at each end and it frequently had two long batons attached to the sides which projected far enough for the full basket to be carried by two men in tandem. An alternative was to have two extra side handles so that two men could walk abreast. It was made in special sizes for each crop (apricots, peaches, haricot beans, tomatoes, peppers, aubergines, and asparagus). For strawberries, the same shape was made in open work.

Another product was the *bresset*, also oblong in willow with a 'cane' lid made in 'thousands of dozens' for fishermen and merchants, and similar ones for transporting eels to markets in the Low Countries.

Full-sized and miniature banastes in white willow, the typical product of Vallabrègues, 1997

Linen chest in white willow, Musée de la Vannerie, Cadenet, Vaucluse

It is of interest that most of their output was of related kinds. Much was based on the long strong willow rods produced locally and well suited to such large containers, without the use of moulds. They hardly produced any square work until after 1911 although the village of Cadenet, only 70km to the east in Vaucluse, had workshops which specialised in such articles. During the period of industry decline, the second and third quarters of the 20th century, some of the remaining firms tried to survive by moving into other work including baskets for the urban consumer: shoppers, trays, handbags, fancy pieces for the home, and furniture made of imported cane. This work was not so price sensitive and needed both less material and less time than the traditional containers on which the industry had been built. But it had to be based on finer, purchased willow which increased costs. State intervention that reduced working hours and imposed social security taxes also raised costs. Competition from eastern Europe and the Far East finally killed the industry off completely before the end of the century.

While the last basketmaker ceased working in 1980, the village has fortunately maintained an important presence in the French scene. A museum was opened in 1990 which, besides displaying typical products from the past, reproduces the huts which the families occupied, and shows something of their way of life while among the willow beds. Every year during the second week in August a festival is held which re-enacts the return of the population to the village in horse drawn carts, including baskets piled high. Many of the village houses are decorated with the basketry articles once sold to the wholesale

Street scene decorated with banastes during the annual Fête de Vallabrègues, 1997

Example of scuttle work in white willow on oak slats(basket for holding dough or feeding livestock) from Haute-Marne, 1981

markets. Large numbers of stalls display and sell baskets from all over France and neighbouring countries over the weekend. Our visit brought to life all that we had read in Galtier's historical account. If you can stand the August heat, then attending the *Fête de la Vannerie* at Vallabrègues is a wonderful way of taking in these local traditions while also seeing work from many other regions. And if commercial basketmaking died out here in the last century, the local hospitality is still alive and well.

4.   Haute Marne

This rural area of eastern France on the SE edge of the Paris basin is the same latitude as Tours in the west. The village most associated with basketry is Fayl-Billot, some 30km east of Langres.

There is some evidence that professional basketmaking may have begun here only around 1688, perhaps initiated by hermits who sold their products in the village[6]. The number of workers increased only slowly at first: from 12 around 1700 to 30 in 1815. At about this time the previous production of narrow oval bags in plaited straw (*cabas*), back-baskets (*hottes*), winnowing fans, and other products in willow on oak slats was widened with the emergence of *mandeliers* who made maunds (*mannes*) and other close-woven willow articles, and of *faiseurs* who made lighter open-work products. These elegant fitched baskets in fine white willow have long been their characteristic products. The range was further increased in the 19th century in order to serve not only the various tradesmen, but also the urban population. This trend was hastened by the development of the railway network and the number of basket makers increased rapidly to 60 in 1830 and more than 200 in 1860. At the end of the 19th century almost all these makers grew their own willow. By 1892 there were close on 600 workers with 500 hectares of willow beds. These beds are today positioned mainly on the tops of the low hills rather than in the valleys since local *S. fragilis* varieties tend to grow too soft and pithy on low land[7].

Grape gathering basket (hotte) in white willow at the cooperative, Bussières-les-Belmont, Haute-Marne, 1996

Around 1880, competition for their traditional output became severe, both from prison workshops and imports from Germany, Belgium and Italy. The trade had been taught by fathers to sons and had remained very specialised, but at this time they decided they needed to widen their skills and diversify their products away from the usual articles. They asked the local council to open a school to instruct the young in willow growing and basketmaking. It took 20 years to progress but finally became a reality in 1907. A range of buildings to accommodate 60 students was completed between 1908 and 1927, though additional facilities have since been provided. At that time there were many disabled ex-soldiers after the Franco-Prussian war who took up basketry.

Elegant openwork arm basket in white willow, ENOV, Fayl-Billot, Haute-Marne

Teachers were employed from other areas in France specialising in different fields of basketwork in order to centralise instruction in all the traditions of the country. In spite of some opposition from local craftsmen, many new types of basketry (and later chair seating and cane furniture) expanded in the region under the school's influence, with the high point reached after World War I.

A survey in 1929 revealed over 800 basketmakers and 130 cane workers, with over 1300 willow growers cultivating around 800 hectares. In total several thousand people lived directly from these trades. But, as has been noted in other regions, this prosperity was brutally stopped by the worldwide slump in the 1930s and the reduced demand for products from traditional basketmaking.

In 1942 some of the remaining makers formed a cooperative in a nearby village, Bussières-les-Belmont, which still survives as one of the two main organisations producing basketry in France – some 50 makers were active in 1988.

The school École Nationale d'Osiériculture et de Vannerie de Fayl-Billot is now an agricultural college with options in horticulture as well as willow growing, various types of basketry and cane furniture. In 1996 it offered two- or three-year courses for senior school pupils as well as one-year paid training for ten 18-year olds, follow-on (refresher) courses for experienced makers, and leisure activity courses for mature students. About half of the professional students were male, who mainly opted for the course in heavier work in willow. Both they and the female students mostly succeeded in entering the profession after their diplomas, some remaining in the surrounding villages and selling through wholesalers or the local cooperative. Others moved to work in the other cooperative at Villaines-les-Rochers.

The school has a collection of over 80 varieties of willow from different areas in France and overseas, started in 1914. It has been active in developing and popularising optimum cultural methods for basketmaking willows, particularly as both cutting and stripping have been mechanised, as well as the identification of high-yielding varieties suitable for different types of work.

Fine work in white willow by members of the cooperative at Bussières-les-Belmont, Haute-Marne, 1996 - bird cage and livestock carriers

Fayl-Billot, together with the Association for the Promotion of Basketry in the region which brings together all the interested sectors in the trade, has been a powerful force in maintaining and promoting the highest standards and quality of French work. The Association has been able to provide subsidies for young craft workers to get established, and to encourage willow planting.

Three views of Villaines-les-Rochers showing cave workshops and willow rods drying outside houses, 1990/1

There is a permanent exhibition at the school, and the cooperative has a showroom with excellent examples of its work, almost all in white willow. Our visits to these two centres always remind us of the wide range of articles which were once the mainstay of hundreds of local families, but also of the continuing high levels of craft skills which live on through the professors and working craftspeople of the surrounding villages.

5. Touraine

The village of Villaines-les-Rochers is 30km south west of Tours in undulating country with streams flowing into the River Indre and thence the Loire. The well-watered fertile soils are alluvial or wind-blown loess, good for the cultivation of willow, but there are also outcrops of calcareous rocks. In 1850, of the 1150 inhabitants, 950 actually lived in caves carved out of the soft rock. Villaines had skilled basketmakers many centuries ago. In 1563 there was a baptism at which the father, Jean Rossard, recorded his profession as *vannier* though he probably also grew willows and vines and had a small farm. Their cave workshops, at a constant 14°C and 60–80% humidity were ideal for working with willow.

Nevertheless this area seems to have suffered dreadfully from the effects of competition and low prices earlier than others, and in 1849 their worker priest Jean-Laurent Chicoisne persuaded 82 of the craftworkers (heads of families) to form a Basketmakers' Society in order to fight against the merchant wholesalers. These numbers grew to 112 in 1855, 139 in 1879 and 150 by 1900. The new Society participated in expositions, and sold into the major cities. It had the advantage of being able to fulfil large orders for specialist work, including for the army. The craftsmen also created a scheme for mutual insurance of members and their families. In 1930 the Society was reconstituted as a

The showroom of the basketmaking cooperative at Villaines-les-Rochers, 1985

modern cooperative: the Société Coopérative Agricole de Vannerie. The village is a community of basketmakers whose members always grew their own willow. They each required around 0.5 to 0.6hectare. Cutting the rods in winter took one or two weeks, then sorting into bundles of the same length and standing in water took 3-6 weeks; stripping in May, and drying before bundling a further 2-4 weeks. Hence 6-12 weeks were used, plus time to keep the growing rods free from weeds and insect or fungal pests. The remaining 9-10 months would be available for making baskets, besides tending their garden and vines.

Above: Selection of dough-proving baskets for sale in 2007 (white willow lined with cloth), Cooperative showroom, Villaines-les-Rochers

Above right: Covered basket for taking dairy produce to market, white willow, Villaines-les-Rochers, 1982

Right: Old dough-proving basket in scuttlework, Musée de la Vannerie, Villaines-les-Rochers

Below: The author's children in front of willow beds holding baskets collected from Fayl-Billot, Haute-Marne, 1981

Using the dough-proving basket when baking a loaf

The Cooperative has had to continually adapt in order to cope with changing conditions. Around 1950 a large part of its output had been long dough baskets for holding the baguette before it went into the oven, but new baking methods largely made these obsolete. A course was organised to stimulate the search for new products and as a result there was a move into furniture and decorative articles – combining willow with glass, wood, cane, wrought iron, and formica. But even these products soon came under pressure from imports and the enterprise was again in trouble: in 1960 only five young makers were following their parents. In 1975 the Cooperative opened its doors to outsiders for the first time. In the next five years more than 50 craftsmen, many trained at the National School in Fayl Billot, came into the village and worked in one of the six new collective workshops. Also since 1983 a basketmaking apprenticeship scheme has been available and has produced one or two newly qualified workers each year. As a result the average age was reduced from 60 years in 1968 to 40 years in 1996, and 35 today. It now represents some 60 makers, of whom half grow their own willow, with a further 10 employed in administration and the large display shop. Their annual output from this one village is at least one third of the total for the whole of France.

I have been visiting and buying from the cooperatives here and in Haute Marne since 1979 and several times my young children had to squeeze into our car and sit among and under the baskets for the long drives back to England. Many are the loaves which have been baked during almost 30 years using their *bannetons*, white willow dough baskets lined with linen, in various shapes and sizes. Using these, and then inverting the risen loaf onto the oven shelf, ensures the maximum amount of crust.

Not all of the craftsmen in Villaines are members of the Cooperative. The Métézeau family has remained independent and continues to make and sell a wide range of baskets from its members' workshops. Étienne, of the youngest working generation, currently makes and teaches courses. His retired father Maurice, and uncles Émilien and Joël are all master craftsmen. Their late father Gustave (see p26) was a Compagnon of the craft guild and honoured in 1949 as one of the *Meilleurs Ouvriers de France*. He could trace the craft back at least four more generations to 1748.

Maurice included the local variety of eel-trap in his repertoire, and Étienne continues to make a wide range of traditional articles while introducing new weaves and new colours in his brown willow work – which contrasts with the predominantly white willow output from the Cooperative.

Above Large grape-harvesting basket in white willow,
Émilien Métézeau, Villaines-les-Rochers, 1997

Émilien Métézeau completing a winnowing fan in white willow on oak slats in 1991, probably the first one made in Villaines-les-Rochers for 70 years.
Photo: R.J. Whittick

Right: Layette basket in fine white willow, Émilien Métézeau, Villaines-les-Rochers, 1990

Émilien first made me an *hotte*, the strong back basket traditionally used when harvesting the ripe grapes for wine making. He subsequently agreed to produce a *van* or winnowing fan – perhaps the first to be made in the village for at least 70 years. I later acquired some *bannetons* made by him using this same time-consuming technique, white willow rods woven tightly on a framework of flat oak (or acacia) splint. When apprenticed to his father, Émilien had been forced to spend long periods practising this method, so that normal willow work would subsequently seem easy by contrast! As several of the best craft workers in Europe have become well known in recent years and received requests to demonstrate in other countries, Émilien has taught the technique to courses in Denmark.

Guy Barbier and Michèle Pichonnet, in their delightful homage to Guy's many teachers, have recorded in words and pictures the work of Gaston Guy from the Jura who made five or six dozen *vans* annually in his youth. The demand for these lasted until around 1950, but he continued making smaller round baskets in the same way for dough or for carrying feed to animals. He learned the technique from his father from the age of 18 and remained loyal to it throughout his working life, eventually teaching Guy[8].

1

2

3

4

5

6

7

8

9

10

11

12

Frame baskets

1. Peeled hazel splint on hazel frame (panier à sardines) 1983

2. Brown willow on hazel frame, Cantal, 1979

3. Brown willow skein on hazel frame, Lozère, 1982

4. Brown willow on hazel frame (child's gondola) by Guy Barbier, 1996

5. Brown willow on hazel frame, two rim hoops coming together at handle, Bordeaux, 2007

6. Peeled hazel splint on hazel frame, Lozère, 1982

7. Chestnut splint, Limousin, 1983

8. Brown willow on cane hoop and willow ribs (panier à cassis), Haute-Marne, 1981

9. Pine root skein on chestnut frame, Hatue-Savoie, 1996

10. Clematis, Musée de la Vannerie, Villaines-les-Rochers

11. Hazel skein on hazel frame, Lozère, 1982

12. Hazel splint on hazel frame (cageole) by Bernard Bertrand, Haute-Garonne

Frame baskets

In addition to the highest quality professional willow work so characteristic of France, and still produced near Fayl-Billot and in Villaines-les-Rochers, I decided to feature the amazing variety of shapes and materials used by part-time makers in their frame baskets. The majority are medium-sized with a single arch handle, and used for holding almost anything in the daily lives of country people. Of course there are other shapes and sizes including the flat oval baskets with side spaces like those already described from Limousin, but here I concentrate on ordinary multi-purpose baskets.

These baskets have a skeleton, most of which is created at the outset, that controls their final appearance (see techniques chapter). Usually two strong hoops cross at right angles and are lashed together where they intersect. One forms the rim, the other provides both the handle and the bottom spine. The lashings made from weavers often provide a distinct decoration, but also determine how the ribs can be inserted and retained. The carefully shaped pairs of ribs may all be inserted first and then the side weaving fills in the gaps from these points through to the central spine. In other patterns, successive pairs of ribs may be inserted throughout the weaving process. The order in which they are added, the angles they make with the spine, and their relative lengths, all produce the final shape of the basket. (This has been well analysed and illustrated by Rachel Law and Cynthia Taylor in their book on Appalachian white oak basketmaking[9].)

Throughout France the materials used and the positioning of the framework components vary greatly, and enable the expert to assign the many examples to their regions of origin. The wood for the handle and rim hoops may be chestnut, hazel or ash used as round rods, half-round, or shaved flat with or without the bark. The rim hoop can be bent round, oval, or more or less rectangular. The ribs use similar material but it will normally be split and shaped. They can be formed to create round or flat bottoms, or allow the two halves to sag below the central spine. The sides may be straight or curved.

The weavers are frequently brown or semi-green willow rods, round or split. But they may also be chestnut, hazel or spruce root split into wide or narrow splint; or buckthorn, viburnum, wild clematis, honeysuckle, broom, or even bramble. Sometimes there are bands of different weavers which produce patterns from their colours and textures. The closeness of the weave may reflect the intended use: loose (or even without weavers), to hold discrete items or to allow soil from root vegetables to fall through; or tight, from thin wide chestnut splint to prevent leakage when holding grain.

A fascinating local variety *cageole du Comminges* is found in Haute Garonne and used for picking fruit from tall trees. The vertical hoop (handle and spine) is strongly oval. Its bottom edge rests in the fork of a branched stem whose two side arms are brought up to the rim hoop to form a third component of the frame. Ribs are then added (5 or 6 into each quarter) with their tips fixed into the lashing around the fork and their top ends attached to the rim hoop. The weaving starts at the base and goes right around. The ribs protrude slightly above the rim after the side weaving has been completed (in hazel splint). The conical basket thus made can be hung from a branch or anchored in the ground so leaving both hands free[10]. A similar type occurs in Croatia (see p226).

Specific items of interest

The huge range of basketry items contained in the collections of the Musée National des Arts et Traditions Populaires in Paris (unfortunately almost all in the stores) reveals

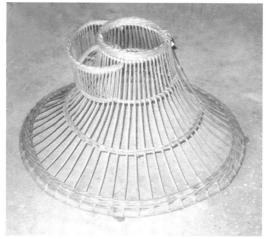

Above from left to right:

Baby minder in coiled straw by
Ian Beaty

Baby walker in willow,
Musée de la Vannerie,
Villaines-les-Rochers, 1991

Bread carrier in white willow,
Villaines-les-Rochers, 1985

examples of articles repeated in many other parts of Europe. Those described here have been selected from the many which could be featured.

Baby minder (*Porte-enfant*)

This simple construction was sometimes made in coiled straw, but also in white willow rods. The principle is a narrow tube, in which the child is stood up to its armpits. It is given stability either by a greatly widened base, or by long splayed wooden legs. The 19th century nursemaid could thus keep several very young children restrained![11] A slightly older child could learn to take its first steps in the walker.

Bread carrier (for *flutes*, *ficelles* or *baguettes*)

When the country moved away from its more traditional, round, wholemeal loaves (*boules*) or other regional shapes and took to eating the freshly-baked, long, airy, white loaves that the world now thinks of as French bread, not only did it need new long proving baskets (*bannetons*), but also carrying baskets to accommodate these fragile new shapes. This carrier in white willow doubled both for delivery and for displaying long loaves within the shop.

Sparrow trap

How often does it happen that those born and brought up in a tradition remain within it all their lives, even while demand for it slowly dies? But an outsider, once initiated, may continue exploring and taking from multiple traditions. No one fits this better than Guy Barbier who started life working on engineering projects. Almost 30 years ago he watched a craftsman complete a basket, bought it, and decided to change career. He tried to learn from those working in Villaines-les-Rochers, but could not afford a long unpaid apprenticeship while rearing his first child. So he worked on his own, at first in cane, but then in willow and other woods. Ever since he has added to his skills by seeking out old basketmakers (*les papés*) and learning their specific skills and designs – around 100 over the years. Furthermore, he has collaborated with academic historians and archaeologists, recreating the types of basketry discernible from preserved remains, mosaics, stone statuary, and carvings. He does not claim to have acquired the same level of skill with specific baskets as those who have spent a lifetime producing a more limited range, but his output straddles many styles. His workshop *Les Brins d'Osier* is in Le Pont-Chrétien in the centre of France, due east of Poitiers. Less than a fifth of his sales are from

Guy Barbier and Michèle
Pichonnet outside Guy's
workshop 'Les Brins d'Osier',
Le Pont-Chrètien, Indre, 2000

115

Above left: Sparrow trap in brown willow by Guy Barbier, 1997

Above right: Sparrow trap in brown willow (Périgord weave), Vallabrègues museum

Right: Cheese safe in chestnut splint and brown willow by Guy Barbier, Musée des Vallées Cévenoles, St-Jean-du-Gard

Below: Cheese safe in white willow, Musée Rural des Arts Populaires, Laduz, Yonne

home, the remainder occur at shows where he demonstrates. During all his travels his partner Michèle Pichonnet has recorded his contacts in words and pictures while Guy has acquired new skills and knowledge of the craft and made many friends. Their affectionate tribute to *les papés* was published in 2006 with an amazing photographic record of materials and techniques, and stories to go with them[12].

One of Guy's many recreations of traditional objects is the bird-trap made in collaboration with Louis Popovitch, from near Vallabrègues. Up until the early 20th century, such traps would have been used to catch sparrows and other small birds to add a little meat to an otherwise vegetable soup. Like many fish traps, the basket is built around a narrow inverted tunnel which the birds would negotiate in pursuit of some grain visible from outside, and would eventually be taken out by a small hinged gate in the side.

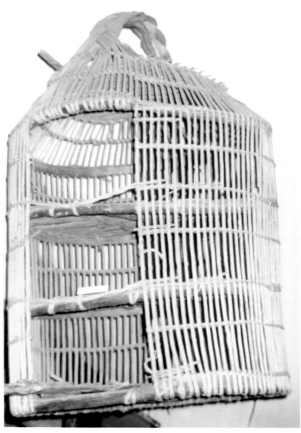

The Périgord weave, a type of plait, used in an arm basket by Norbert Fauré, Villaines-les-Rochers. Photo: Joe Hogan

Cheese safe

Guy Barbier was working with the museum at St Jean du Gard in the Cévennes due east of Avignon in southern France when he was asked to make a copy of an old cheese safe. The material is split chestnut. It would hang at a convenient height, out of the reach of animals, and closed by a door to keep out flies. It has three shelves and would receive the small fresh goat cheeses to ripen on straw before consumption or sale. When we saw it in 1996, it was looking very smart and new, but already doing its job.

Guy has surely done more than any basketmaker in his time to keep the old French traditions alive by documenting so many techniques before they disappeared with the last original craftsmen and has now been honoured as one of the *Meilleurs Ouvriers de France*.

Périgord

This unique openwork basket first caught my eye in 1984 when I purchased one in Paris. It is neither a frame basket nor in conventional stake and strand, and is constructed without the normal base (see techniques chapter). The side stakes originate as a carefully balanced series in the base held together by a continuous spiral plait from there to the rim. Usually made by country people in the Dordogne and Lot, it may have been brought over from Africa by the Moors and then adopted by gypsies. The *bouyricoun* (its patois name) can be quite delicate in fine rods, or much more robust. Its strange construction has fascinated several of the north European basketmakers who now travel freely between countries and who have risen to the challenge of learning the technique and teaching courses, and today we even have an instruction book and DVD[13].

Notes and references

1.   The Basketry Museum at Villaines-les-Rochers mounted an exhibition in 2001/2 devoted to the role of women in basketmaking and gave it a social dimension through an ethnographic study published in 2002 as 'Des Vanneries et des Femmes' Cahier No 1 du Musée de la Vannerie, Éditions des Compagnons du Terroir.
2.   Robert, M. (1967) 'La Vannerie en Limousin'. Société d'Ethnographie du Limousin de la Marche et des régions voisines, Limoges.
3.   Adams, A. (2005) '12me Foire aux Paniers et la Vannerie, Issigeac, 17th July 2005'. BA NL **115** 14-15.
4.   Association La Chanterelle (1994) 'Les Vanniers du Petit Morin et Alentour en Brie'. Eds. AMATTEIS.

5. Galtier, C. (1980) 'Entre Provence et Languedoc: Les Vanniers de Vallabrègues'. Centre Alpin et Rhodanien d'Ethnologie, Grenoble.
6. Anquetil, J. (1979) 'La Vannerie'. Dessain et Tolra/Chêne p88.
7. Heseltine, A. (1982) 'Fayl-Billot, France'. BA NL **21** 6-9.
8. Pichonnet, M (2006) 'Ces Papés .. Mémoire et Tradition de la Vannerie en France'. Les Brins d'Osier.
9. Law, R.N. and Taylor, C. W. (1991) 'Appalachian White Oak Basketmaking - handing down the basket'. University of Tennessee Press.
10. Bertrand, B. (2006) 'La Vannerie Sauvage - initiation'. Editions de Terran (with DVD).
11. There is a charming 19th century painting of a nursemaid looking after no fewer than five small babies in such straw baskets, plus a toddler, by J.P. Haag *La gardeuse d'enfants en Normandie* in the Musée municipal de Louviers. It is reproduced as the frontispiece in 'La Vannerie Française' the catalogue of the basketry collections in the Musée National des Arts et Traditions Populaires, Paris.
12. See 8.
13. Siedenfaden, E. (2004) 'The Art of Basketmaking: the Périgord technique and tradition'. www.vissinggaard.dk.
14. Coste, B. (2002) 'Les Tresses de Bois - la tradition vivante du panier dans le Massif Central'. Editions du Laquet. This useful little book deals with traditions in the central areas of this large country. In particular it lists addresses in Auvergne, Limousin, Languedoc-Roussillon, Midi-Pyrénées, and Rhône-Alpes where basketry can be seen and purchased.

Spain and Portugal

Antonio Campelo of Mondariz,
Galicia with some chestnut splint
baskets he makes in retirement

Much of Spain is short of water: poor grassland surviving on eroded soils in Andalucia

Resources

This large compact landmass is an area of contrasts and one of transition between Europe and Africa. Northern regions of Spain, particularly Galicia, Asturias, and the Basque Country, enjoy a largely Atlantic climate with relatively high rainfall. The centre is mainly a high plateau, around 1000m, with mountain ranges at the edges and little in the way of coastal plains. This creates high pressure systems leading to hot summers with high evaporation and cold winters. The long Mediterranean coast is quite arid except where irrigated.

Such a varied geography has produced a great diversity in natural vegetation and crops. Almost every region has grown cereals, especially wheat and rye. Even if yields are not high, straw has been available. The less mountainous parts of the north have more in common with regions of Britain and Ireland than with the rest of Spain. It comes as no surprise then that split wood basketry based upon oak, chestnut, and hazel is a particularly strong feature. Willow is not as widespread as in countries with more rainfall, although there are actually more varieties of wild willow used in basketry in some areas than in northern Europe. These exhibit very different colours and textures. Cultivated willow was centred on Cuenca in central Spain where the terrain and altitude favour the production of good quality rods.

People living near lakes, river valleys, and coastal marshes have utilised many different rushes and reeds. The 'cane' (*Arundo donax*) found throughout the Mediterranean lands has been exploited in the south. In Andalucia and Aragon one or two species of drought-resistant grass known generally as *esparto* have been important basketry materials. Palm leaves were available along the southern coasts.

History

The first chapter summarised several features of the Mediterranean region which favoured the early development of civilizations. The Phoenicians, Greeks, Carthaginians, and Romans all left their traces on the earlier Iberian peoples in the south, though less so on the Celts in the north. Metal working skills were well developed when Phoenician traders arrived (1100 BC) and these attracted subsequent invaders on a more permanent basis. In addition, the Romans exploited the agricultural potential at least in the south. They in turn were over-run by Germanic tribes from the 4th century and then North Africans (Moors) from the 8th to 14th centuries. During this period, Spain became prosperous with Cordoba perhaps the largest and wealthiest city in western Europe though the country was still divided among independent kingdoms

until the 18th century. But as the Christian peoples gradually regained control of the entire peninsula, over a period of some 750 years, they failed to capitalize on this promising start. In fact, successive monarchs managed to delay the replacement of the old feudal system until the 19th century through a series of policies – some of then deliberate. These discouraged the emergence of corporations, so that craftsmen continued to work alone. They hounded out those who were not Catholics, particularly those with Jewish or Moslem ancestors. And in spite of establishing overseas empires from the 15th century, which brought enormous riches from gold, silver, spices, sugar, slaves, and other products, this trade only made monarchs and nobles wealthy while suppressing the development of home industry and agriculture. This overseas bounty was used up in trying to maintain a monopoly of the high seas, importing grain, and unsuccessfully waging war against almost every other European nation.

Even in the first half of the 20th century, much of Spain and Portugal remained poor and undeveloped with high illiteracy, famines in the 1940s, and large-scale emigration. Conditions finally began to improve in the 1950s with aid from the USA and the growth of tourism, and after 1986 when both countries joined the EU.

The long-continued lack of prosperity in rural and urban sectors no doubt reduced the demand for professional basketmakers by comparison with many other European countries which needed to move vast quantities of goods into and out of cities. When travelling around these two countries towards the end of the 20th century, it was still possible to see many types of baskets for sale and in use, particularly by market traders. While a few of these and others in museums show a high degree of craftsmanship, there seems to have been a devastating decline of local basketry standards in recent years. Many of those on offer may have been made by people well past retirement age.

It is therefore ironic, but most fortunate, that the basketry traditions of both countries have been so comprehensively studied and documented by local authors. Bignia Kuoni had a background in textile weaving and realised that there was much unexplored territory in the weaving of baskets. Her research, supported by a two-year scholarship from a Swiss bank, culminated in 'Cesteria Tradicional Ibérica' in 1981[1]. This is a serious academic study, lavishly illustrated, and one of the best single volume accounts devoted to the craft in any European country. In addition, Maria Elisa Sánchez Sanz was asked in 1981 to produce a book on traditional Spanish basketry. She was inspired by Kuoni's study and spent eight years interviewing some 500 people, recording the results in a 12-volume work. Her 1994 doctoral thesis 'Cesteria Tradicional Aragonesa' is the summary of the larger work and deals with all aspects of the crafts in one north east province, Aragon, which runs up to the French border[2]. I have drawn freely on these two volumes to supplement my own extensive travels through both countries.

Above left: Fine white willow bowl in Madeira weave, or pulled work, with decoration. Perhaps gypsy work, Porto 1995

Right: An old culeiro which has been repaired with new basal splints

More recently (2005) Carlos Fontales has produced a new account of techniques used by Galician makers which aims to instruct as well as inform[3].

As in most other countries, basketmaking was historically a very lowly occupation. This was mainly because so many people could weave and plait, and investment in elaborate tools was not necessary. Even worse, the craft was associated with gypsies and beggars who stole the raw materials! That said, one group of makers, the *esparteros* were recognized from the Middle Ages as practitioners of a trade in the cities. Eighteenth century documents from Catalonia refer to the craft guilds of *esparteros* in Barcelona (1716) and Valencia (1738) embracing sandal makers, rope makers, and basketmakers. In Aragon too, there are records of a structure involving apprenticeship which taught not only practical skills but craft traditions, codes of honour, and professional secrets leading eventually to approval as a new Master; but the guilds lost their importance at the beginning of the 19th century.

The organisation of the craft in the 20th century could be classified according to the workers involved. Gypsies did casual and seasonal agricultural work and at other times produced characteristic articles in fine willow throughout the peninsula. In regions with little basketmaking tradition, both men and women were considered proficient, but in established willow areas the Roma were not rated so highly. Where they had ceased travelling they usually settled in separate localities and sold in nearby villages and towns.

Most peasant farmers or farm workers made their own baskets during the winter, just as they produced many of their other needs. Many 'professional' basketmakers existed but also continued to work their land. Others offered their labour into agriculture, horticulture, charcoal burning, or the building trades to supplement their earnings. In Catalonia they were often barbers or musicians. Their busy season (for basketry) was before the crop harvest (grapes or olives). In some areas like Galicia in the northwest they would tour in groups of two to four, offering their services to the estate owners. They would make and repair wooden or willow baskets and receive bed and board at the farms.

In the larger towns and cities the full-time basketmaker would often work on his own and combine his workshop with a shop to sell both his own output, items of furniture, and imported articles. Other workers were wholly employed making complete articles or just doing one process in a workshop or at home. In addition, basketry was featured in some workshops for the blind and in prisons. However, there were pockets of 'industrial' production. Some large workshops were dedicated exclusively to the provision of baskets for the fishing industry based, for example, in Vigo, Galicia. Other

Carretero in willow by Francisco, Trives, Galicia showing the typical features of many splint baskets, including maker's mark branded near base

Chestnut coppice

centres covered wine flasks or used 'cane' to make woven screens, drying racks for fruit, fencing, and interior partitions and ceilings as well as baskets. Concentrations of workers in esparto, palm leaf, and fine willow could be found - the latter supported whole villages in Valencia and Alicante. Woven willow furniture continued to be made until recent times in Salamanca.

Types of work

Willow, 'cane' and straw work can all be found in Spain and Portugal, and several specific examples are featured in the next section. But I find that the distinctive work in these countries has often been done in other materials, and it is these which are emphasized here.

Wood splint

The wetter areas which support tree growth have given rise to a variety of related, but different, basketry traditions. All are based upon strips cleaved or separated from logs or branches. The main tree species utilised were chestnut, hazel, oak, ash, willow, mimosa, alder buckthorn, and dogwood. The splints could be obtained in several ways. Larger logs would be cleaved into four or more triangular sections and these then split along the growth rings. Smaller stems, especially hazel, might have several strips peeled off tangentially leaving the central core which could be used for hoops or ribs. Thin stuff could be split down into three or four (like willow rods) with a cleave, and planed or scraped with a knife to produce one flat and one convex surface on the skein.

Simple farm basket in chestnut splint

In most splint baskets, the base strips are usually quite wide, 2-8cm, and are often crossed by similar strips (check weave) to form tight square or rectangular bases. Both sets of splints are then upturned to form the side stakes. The side weavers are almost always narrower and may be of a different wood. The sides terminate at the rim, frequently round or oval, and these shapes are achieved by creating gaps between the original stakes and inserting additional (bye) stakes, pointed below, to keep the weaving tight. The rim may be created from one or more rods bent into the required hoop shape, and the ends of the side stakes are bent over this and tucked under the final rows of weaving (outside or inside). Alternatively these side stakes are trimmed level and the rim hoops are lashed onto them using a length of wrapping weaver which pierces the side stakes. In other cases both methods are employed.

Right: Basque country basket with two side handles in chestnut splint 1988

Harvesting grapes in the Douro region of Portugal using the cesto vindimeiro carried high on the back supported by the hand and forehead band

One of the simplest forms is a maund, made for general farm or garden use out of chestnut splint with a square base and more or less round top, and a rim made from a stout round rod with the bark left on. The side handles are created by cutting two side stakes slightly short of the rim. It is made in the Basque regions[4].

Chestnut and willow were also the preferred woods for the peasant farmers in western Galicia and the Douro region of north Portugal who produced a range of coarse farm baskets, often without handles, which were carried high on the back. The base could be rested on a soft shoulder pad retained in place by a straw or fabric band around the forehead. These tall baskets, up to 90cm high, were steadied either by clutching a small handle half-way down the front, or by holding a stick hooked over the front rim.

While the classic *culeiro* and *cesto vindimeiro* were employed to carry grapes out of the sloping vineyards in these regions, they and similar shapes were also used for many other tasks like displaying produce in markets, potato harvesting, or even carrying manure from stable to field.

Right Old cesto vindimeiro now used as a rubbish bin, Valença do Minho, Portugal, 1995

Below : Group of traditional wood (willow) splint baskets by retired maker Francisco, Trives, SE Galicia, 2002.
Photo: Anna Champeney

Anna Champeney, an English craft researcher, found a collection of these baskets in an ironmonger's shop in 2002, the output of a single maker, Francisco. Born in 1923, he had worked his small farm in Ourense province (Galicia) in summer, and travelled around in winter making and repairing baskets on local farms and selling in markets. This collection was all in willow splint, though Francisco also worked with willow rods. The smaller items were used for seed sowing, fruit picking, and gathering chestnuts. Anna found that such articles were now neglected since cheaper plastic containers, sacks, and bulk handling methods had replaced them. But more than this, the villagers had

turned their backs on baskets and other traditional craft products as symbols of a miserable, poverty-stricken past – which had driven so many of their relatives to emigrate.

Mondariz, another small Galician town inland from Vigo, was famous for its basketmakers who were its largest working group, and has in recent years held an annual festival. Even up to the start of World War II, young men served an apprenticeship for several years to become full-time makers. Sons followed fathers in the craft. Others combined farming and part-time basketry.

In 1995 at the 6th Festa de Cesterios in Mondariz, two of the surviving makers, Antonio Campelo Trigo (born 1920) and José (Pepé) Rivas Martinez (born 1935) were offering small-scale versions of the much larger baskets they had made when they were younger. Anna encouraged my wife and me to attend, and these pensioners were clearly delighted to show us their craft. Antonio had been an itinerant maker during part of each year. His son demonstrated the traditional ways of splitting chestnut stems and planing the clamped splint to the required thickness with a draw knife. Pepé, who had learned from his father in the 1940s, had only worked part-time at the craft since the early 1980s when he returned to farming and beekeeping. In these miniatures he used narrow, 5mm alder buckthorn splint as weavers on wider chestnut stakes. In addition to arm baskets and bowls, he covered wine bottles in the same material which displays an attractive golden colour.

The techniques employed for these covered bottles are clearly related to the methods once used to create a range of vessels for serving wine in Galicia - the *jarras* or *xerras*. These jugs were made with a capacity from a quarter litre right up to the 16litre *ola*. The elegant 20th century models were made on multi-piece wooden moulds which could be withdrawn when the weaving was finished. The widths of the flat elm or chestnut ribs were varied along their lengths to permit the shape to flow out from the base, and again at the rim. The skein weavers were tightly packed and then sealed with pine resin to produce a watertight vessel. Funnels to help fill the jugs from casks were made in the same way. Today it seems that willow is substituted to produce copies for tourists[5].

Oak splint items were still on sale in 1993 in the typical Galician country market in Betanzos near La Coruna. Thick strips produced such strong baskets that the farmer, bending down to plant potatoes from it, could rest his weight on its handle. A much more elegant version, also purchased there, would not shame a sophisticated town housewife. Still in oak, the splint has been carefully smoothed and the design lightened and made less deep to carry purchases home or display them on the table.

Right: A very strong type of arm basket in chestnut with skeined 'cane' weavers, Barcelos, NW Portugal

Far right: Bottom view of a very fine maund in thin mimosa splint from Ponte de Lima, Portugal

Above from left to right:
Small arm basket in thin mimosa splint from
Chaves, Portugal, 2002.
Photo: Anna Champeney

Rough oak splint potato basket, Betanzos, Galicia, 1993

Elegant oak splint shopping basket, Betanzos, Galicia, 1993

Below left: Shallow canastra collected in Porto, often carried on the head

Right: Canastra probably in willow splint by Manuel Antonio dos Anjos Ferreira from Coimbra region of Portugal

A quite different construction found in the Pyrenees is being continued by Lluis Grau who formerly worked in Catalonia but now makes and teaches in Galicia. This is the oval frame basket known as the *bres*. The skeleton starts with a round rim rod in unpeeled hazel with a second rod forming the spine, or central rib. This utilises the heartwood core of a stem after four splints had been taken from its outer surface. Its two ends project above the rim and serve as handles. The pairs of side ribs are inserted horizontally, parallel with the rim hoop, with their ends overlapping and resting inside the spine[6]. A very similar basket from the French Pyrenees was illustrated on p49.

Moving south in Portugal there are still country markets displaying regional baskets in their hundreds. The Thursday market at Barcelos was characterized by wood splint work. In one example, the 4-5cm chestnut splints which form the square base are supplemented on the sides by even wider shaped inserts at each corner to allow the sides to flow out into a circle of twice the diameter of the base before coming back into a little towards the rim. The side weavers are in 7-8mm skeined 'cane'. Many other shapes were displayed using the same techniques and materials.

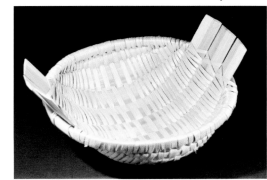

Left: Crude arm basket in chestnut splint, Evora, Portugal

Right: Arm basket (mego) in hazel splint, Los Ancares.
Photo: Anna Champeney

More sophisticated work was on sale in Ponte de Lima in 1993. The basic principles are the same, with the square base of the maund changing to a round opening with the addition of a single extra side stake at each corner. The whole construction is almost as tight as a winnowing fan though it is made of very thin splint, perhaps mimosa wood. The same wood, with a fine, straight grain, and an attractive sheen, was used in a small arm basket made in Chaves in 2002.

Between Porto and Lisbon in the Coimbra region are found other examples. These *canastras* are distinguished by some of the base splints curving up to finish projecting well beyond the rim band. Manuel Antonio dos Anjos Ferreria recently sold pretty bowls, probably in mimosa splint, while a much larger version was purchased in Porto in 1995. It is designed to be carried on the head and used to display bread, fish, or other foods.

A cruder, more rural style was for sale from the city of Evora further south. Thicker splint had been cleft from chestnut and made into a range of baskets to service both traditional and more modern living. A small arm basket has its handle created by continuing two or three of the base splints up one side and then arching them over to join their opposite numbers within a crude lashing. In a variant of the old donkey transport system, the same material is woven into a pair of panniers which fit either side of the rear wheel of a small motor cycle.

Lluis Grau recording and measuring baskets on display in the family-run palloza museum, Casa do Sesto, Piornedo, Los Ancares.
Photo: Anna Champeney

There must be other types of wood splint baskets still to be found and brought to the attention of people outside the peninsula. The (British) Basketmakers' Association recently funded Lluis Grau to study some particularly fine hazel splint work found in the mountainous area of Los Ancares where the northern Spanish regions of Galicia, Asturias, and Castile-Léon meet[7]. The tightness of the finished article is achieved both by careful preparation of the materials and by working in reverse (from right to left) so that the right hand can always hold the metal tool used to beat the weaver close to the preceding round. This is similar to the scuttle work technique, with willow rods, described in the techniques chapter. It is hoped that the fairs

and exhibitions being held in Catalonia, Tenerife, and Galicia will help to foster an interest in such traditional baskets while there are still a few craftsmen able to demonstrate them, even if most of the rural population is still in denial of their value.

Esparto

Along parts of the Spanish Mediterranean coast the arid hillsides, long ago denuded of their original tree cover and soil, carry a secondary vegetation – a wiry grass surviving among the stony surface material (see p36). Its natural habitat was the Algerian plateau, but it spread along this most southerly coast of Europe (Andalucia) and in the Ebro valley in Aragon. The Spaniards call it *atocha* (*Stipa tenuissima* or *Macrochloa t.*) while a coarser version is *albardine* (*Lygeum spartum*). This may look an unpromising material upon which to base a basketry culture, but the local people have done just that.

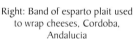

Above left: Bundle of esparto grass, Nijar, Andalucia

Right: Band of esparto plait used to wrap cheeses, Cordoba, Andalucia

The linear leaves are open and flat when green, but rolled up and thin when dry, and are called *esparto*. They are attached to the base by a short 'claw' and are harvested by careful pulling, rather than cutting, so as not to break them and retain the claw. Tied at the base into bundles, they are left on the hillside to dry for 20-30 days.

Further processing (soaking, pounding and combing) can be used to extract the fibres for spinning and weaving into sacking, or twisting into chair-seating cord, ropes, or harness. Sandals were made from the cords as well as clogs with wooden soles.

The longest leaves, around 55cm long and 1-2mm diameter, are used for basketry, normally by plaiting long lengths of multi-way flat braids which are then sewn edge to edge with twine to create the required shapes. In general the plaiting was women's work, often done communally in the street while men did the sewing-up indoors. The large-scale industry ceased around 1975, destroyed both by reduced demand and by levelling and destruction of some of the grasslands to make ways for intensive vegetable production in irrigated poly-tunnels.

One of the simplest articles is a 17-strand braid, 8cm wide and 130 cm long with each strand composed of 6 leaves. It then continues for a further metre as a much narrower three-strand braid. It was used in cheese making where it would be wrapped around in a spiral forming a cylindrical mould to contain the soft sheep's-milk curd. The braid was removed after the curd had set sufficiently and the cheese ripened on a flat shelf but still bearing the embossed pattern of the esparto leaves. Other cheeses used to show the natural imprints of their rush or broom-twig moulds and today's Manchego displays a pattern on its waxed surface which imitates these.

Left: Arm basket in esparto with simple plait handle, Nijar, Andalucia

Above: Lidded pannier basket in esparto plait to carry water jars on a donkey or mule, collected in Barcelona

A more complex braided basket is the pair of double panniers carried each side of a donkey or mule. Each one has two circular depressions to contain ceramic water pots and a lid which folds down over them both. Can there be any more vivid illustration of the value of water in this parched region than the existence of such a basket to regularly carry small quantities over long distances?

In 1998, when strolling around the hill village of Nijar east of Almeria in Andalucia (better known for its pottery), we found a wide variety of other braided forms including flat matting and roll-up window blinds.

A second weaving technique used with esparto is a type of plaiting which looks rather like coiling since the 'coils' are continually joined to the preceding row by additional leaves during the plaiting process. No extraneous sewing material is used. This can either result in a close-sided texture for an arm basket, or the much more open weave found in a double-pointed bag (which expands as it is filled with shellfish or a live chicken).

It seems extraordinary to use the thin esparto leaves in a third way: the stake and strand method so commonly employed in willow round work. But examples of arm baskets from Nijar show that some workers did indeed treat the individual leaves as single weavers. The base of one was begun with four flat bundles, each of seven or eight leaves which form the base stakes. Single leaves are then woven across these to form a rectangular slath. The projecting leaves are grouped into eight bundles on each long side, and 16 at each end. The oval base was then completed with 16

Window blinds in esparto plait, Nijar, Andalucia

Left: Expandable bag to hold fish, shellfish or perhaps even a live chicken, in esparto, Nijar, Andalucia

Left: Esparto arm basket woven in the stake and strand method, Nijar, Andalucia

Right: Arm basket in esparto showing the method of making the base and creating the handles from one length of plait, Nijar, Andalucia

rounds of three-rod waling, and the same weave continued right up the sides – for a further 65 rounds. The border, made from the stake ends, is an outward facing plait. The handle is formed from a single long braid placed against the stake bundles on one side, taken across over the top, down to the base, up to the rim, down again, and then back again to the first side.

This is an amazing example of utilising a free resource and putting little value on the hours of work involved while using considerable skill to turn it into an article for daily use. Kuoni tells us that when gypsies used esparto they typically used this stake and strand method[8].

A related industry, using a different grass (*Ampelodesmos mauritanicus*) is featured in the Italian chapter.

Specific items

Animals as food

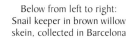

Below from left to right: Snail keeper in brown willow skein, collected in Barcelona

Snail keeper in brown willow rods, attached cover, collected in Barcelona

Rabbit and chicken basket in brown willow, with rope border and sides in skeined 'cane', wire netting cover, collected in Barcelona

The food customs of ordinary people naturally lead to specialised containers. Where snails are appreciated as a protein food, they need to be collected and then held without feed for some days while they purge themselves before being consumed. The holding baskets were usually barrel-shaped, tapering to a neck with a removable lid which prevented live snails from escaping. I collected two examples outside Barcelona, both in brown willow, either whole rods or split; but in the far south they were made from plaited esparto sewn into a similar shape.

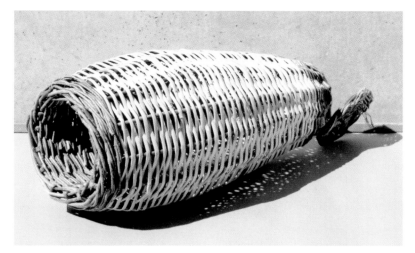

Above left: Eel trap in brown willow with skeined 'cane' siding, collected in Barcelona

Ferret basket in white willow by Lluis Grau from Catalonia, now working in Galicia

Reared on garden surplus, tame rabbits are much eaten, even today. They and various poultry are brought to market in shallow baskets with see-through lids so that customers can select before purchase while the livestock remain safely constrained. These lids were originally in open-work willow[9], more recent examples have utilised wire netting on a frame.

Fishing, hunting and trapping were all country pursuits. Hunting wild rabbits could involve the use of ferrets to chase them out of their burrows into carefully placed nets, and these fierce little creatures would be carried to and from the warrens in their own baskets. One in twisted willow rods was given to me by Lluis Grau, a skilled maker from Catalonia.

Finally, the eel trap is a brown willow structure since the bark helps the submerged rods resist rotting for some time, but the siding is in split 'cane'.

Careful examination of some of these willow baskets reveals interesting variations. Some round or oval examples have a base quite unlike the radiating stick method described in the techniques chapter. A pair of rods is first shaped and tied into a circle which defines the perimeter. Two bundles of rods are placed across this, to serve as base sticks and eventually side stakes. The base weaving is then completed back and forth over these, leaving some weavers protruding beyond the perimeter on each side. These and the base sticks are then pricked up to provide the side stakes. There are good illustrations of this Catalan base in the references[10].

A related technique is used in Galician square bases. Pairs of long base sticks are simply laid out and held in place under the maker's knees while other rods are woven across them to complete the base. The side stakes are formed by upsetting the ends of the base sticks and a proportion of the base weavers[11].

In a fascinating echo of the Irish technique for constructing the creel (see p74), makers living in the Atlantic peninsula of Barbanza, west of Santiago de Compostela, start their baskets by inserting side stakes into holes in a frame. The sides are woven upside down and the free ends of the stakes then turned across to become base stakes. After the base is completed, the opposite ends of the stakes are withdrawn from the frame and woven into a border[12]. In Muros (Galicia) there is a basket with the same design and construction as the Irish creel[13].

Four fire fans made in different ways.

Clockwise from above left:
Chesnut splint with alder buckthorn weavers by José Rivas (Pepé)

Chestnut splint, N Portugal

Alder buckthorn weavers on chestnut splint, Mondariz

Esparto plait and twine, Valencia, Andalucia

Fire fans

Another characteristic product of these countries is the small fan used to help start the domestic fire or to revive a charcoal brazier when roasting chestnuts at home or for sale on the streets. Several different solutions have been seen. Pepé (from Mondariz) takes a round chestnut branch, splits it two thirds down its length into three, turns the central splint through 90^0, inserts six triangular splints in-between, and weaves them together with dogwood skein, tucking the top ends down to retain the upper rows of weaving.

Another solution from Portugal is to cleave the branch into more splints (eight), turning all through 90^0 and splitting the central six so as to spread the fan even wider before weaving them to retain the shape. A third method from Mondariz was to shave both sides of the branch to produce only a single central splint. A round rod is inserted through the handle and bent like a horseshoe to create the outside edge. Three shaped splints are positioned each side of the central one, and the whole set is woven together with alder buckthorn splint. Finally, one from Andalucia is made from one piece of braided esparto curled into a circle with the two ends combined into a short handle. Four ways of constructing such a simple tool; how many more variants are hiding within apparently similar versions of a more complex basket?

Ironed linen

This large oval basket, 50 x 70cm, is almost flat – just a large oval base with low inclined sides. It is used to carry laundry after it has been ironed and folded. A plain

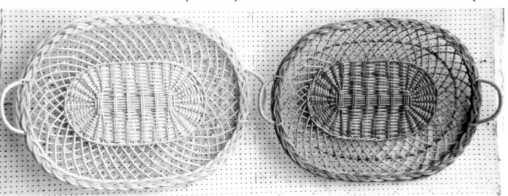

Two decorative trays for ironed linen in white and buff willow seen in Nijar, Andalucia

Arm basket in olive rods and cork base by Feliciano Pérex from Cortelazor, Huelia province. Photo: J.M. Ramiro Guitierrez

version I bought in Sant Cugat near Barcelona was made in white willow rods but varnished, and has now taken on an almost gold colour after many years of use (see p45). In between times it can be hung conveniently on the wall. Much more decorative examples have the side stakes curved out into tracery patterns and a plaited border. These were seen on sale in Andalucia.

Cork base

The south east regions of Spain, close to the Portuguese border, have large areas of oak trees (*Quercus suber*) dispersed thinly across natural pastures. These trees are utilised by harvesting the outer layers of tree bark, or cork, and by fattening herds of native Iberian pigs (which produce the highest-priced cured ham) on the acorns. It is natural that some of the cork should have been utilised in basketry and I recently came across a lovely example[14]. Olive stems are cut in autumn and used while still partly fresh. A round cork base is made with a dozen holes around the perimeter to take the side stakes in pairs (which are cut at a node to retain them). More olive stems are used to weave the sides and rope border, while the arch handle is twisted from a further 16 rods.

Notes and references

1.   Kuoni, B. (1981) 'Cestería Tradicional Ibérica', Ediciones del Serval. Long out of print but now republished with sponsorship of the Catalan Basketmakers' Association.
2.   Sánchez Sanz, M.A. (1994) 'Cestería Tradicional Aragonesa y Oficios Afines'. Gobierno de Aragon.
3.   Fontales, C. (2005) 'Cestería de los Pueblos de Galicia'. IR INDO Edicións (with DVD). A beautifully illustrated modern work with detailed instructions and updated list of museum collections. There are useful chapters on straw, rush, and willow work in Galicia which have not been featured here. See also Méndez Garcia, R.M. and Sáenz-Chas Diaz, M.B. (1993) 'A Cestería'. Museo do Pobo Galego. A useful little booklet on Galician traditional work.
4.   Filmer, R. (1988) 'Jesus, a Basketmaker in Basque Country'. BA NL **44** 7-9; and Bury, A. (1988) 'Basque Country Baskets'. BA NL **47** **5-7**.
5.   Champeney, A. (2003) 'The Jugs of Ulla' . BA NL **104** 43-45; and a section in Carlos Fontales' book, see 3 p150-154.
6.   Lawrence, S. (2005) 'Splitwood Basketry Course'. BA NL **115** 18-21.
7.   Grau, L. (2008a) 'Split Wood Basketry of Los Ancares'. Report to the Basketmakers' Association 24pp.
8.   See 1 ch 13.
9.   Goymer, S. (2003) 'V Fira del Cistell'. BA NL **104** 41-42.
10.   See 1 p210 and 9 p42.
11.   See 3 p79-91.

12.   See 3 p94-99.
13.   Grau, L. (2008b) Personal communication.
14.   Ramiro Gutiérrez, J. M., González-Tejero, M.R. and Sánchez Rojas, C.P. (2006) 'Spain (Huelva province)'. ICEB 2005 671-672.

The Nordic Lands

Large coiled root celebratory
basket from Sunnfjord and two
painted wooden types from
Hordaland, Norway.
Photo: Ann-Marie Olsen

Resources

The three most northerly countries, Norway, Sweden, and Finland are united by sharing a region where a harsh climate and generally poor soils made life very difficult for its inhabitants over several millennia. Denmark and southern Sweden fared better on both counts, but their histories were intimately bound up with their northern neighbours. The present appearance of all four countries is the creation of the last ice age. The northern three were scoured by glaciers (though Norway and Sweden still have extensive mountain ranges) and have not had sufficient time, with their short growing seasons, to build up replacement soils through the normal weathering processes. Denmark on the other hand, at close to sea level, was the recipient of much of the material eroded from further north, and has fertile boulder clay and sands which have been further improved by man.

Their current climates change in both the north-south and east-west directions. Denmark is cool and temperate, not unlike eastern England, though drier with colder winters. The Norwegian coast is humid and relatively equable, but Lapland is sub-arctic. The highland range running up Norway and Sweden forms a barrier so that moving east it is drier and colder – semi-continental. Southern Finland is surrounded by the Baltic sea which is much less saline than the open oceans and therefore freezes for much of the winter and fails to provide the warming effect of other seas.

As a consequence, the far north is too cold even for coniferous forest and supports only stunted birch scrub. Spruce and pine forest covers much of the three northern countries with mixed woodlands only in their southern regions. These woods have largely been cleared for agriculture: barley, rye, wheat, oats, potatoes, and pastures for grazing and hay. Denmark (and the southern tip of Sweden) can grow these cereals, as in England, but in recent times has concentrated on dairying from grassland, and pigs and poultry based on imported feed and dairy byproducts. The plant resources available for basketry thus included straw, willow, hazel, ash, aspen, rowan, lime, birch, bird cherry, black alder, juniper, pine, and spruce with their importance varying between countries.

History

Only the coastal areas were attractive for settlement when man first started farming (and even today Finland farms under 10 percent of its land while Norway's total is nearer three percent). These early inhabitants would have exploited the seas and forests and become skilled boat builders and navigators. The Danes share a common cultural heritage with their northern neighbours, but with over 70 percent of their land able to

be farmed they became the most populous and wealthy. This did not stop them from participating in the Viking expeditions between 800 and 1000AD (in Britain all the Viking raiders and settlers were called Danes). During this period, the Swedes ventured through the Baltic to Russia and the Middle East. Danes and Norwegians went as far as Iceland, the Faroes, Greenland, Eastern Britain, and Normandy. These raids, trades, and settlements brought initial wealth, but their inherent agricultural disadvantages held them back. Other settlements were based on timber exports. Finland became part of Sweden for 500 years until the early 19th century, and then part of Russia for a further century losing its eastern part when it gained independence. Norway became a Danish province between the mid-16th and early 19th centuries, and then Sweden took over until 1905.

It is therefore not surprising that large numbers of people left Norway and Sweden from the mid 19th century to seek better lands in north America. Mineral resources were available, but many of these were not easily exploited until other technologies had been developed. From the 19th century Scandinavia started to industrialise, later than the European leaders, but has since developed quickly.

The relevance of this to basketry is that the absence of large urban centres early on would have kept the craft mainly confined to peasant farmers and fishermen. The relative lateness of industrialisation meant that there was no great surge into large workshop production, and by the time that inland transport became well developed other types of packaging were replacing baskets. Hence the Scandinavian basketry types described here are mainly the products of individuals making for their own needs. The long periods of common history have also resulted in a sharing of many styles, though the extreme differences in environment from northern tundra to lowland Denmark inevitably left their mark.

Nevertheless, there have been some considerable concentrations of basketry activity, and two of these are described in the next section. There were also small-scale willow-based industries in Helsinki and Turku where masters from Germany and Sweden taught. Rushes do not seem to have been widely exploited, with exceptions near Kokkola in west Finland, and the Randers fjord in northwest Jutland in Denmark where both plaiting and coiling techniques were used for mats, bags, and shoes.

During World War II people had to make baskets owing to a shortage of alternatives (e.g. leather goods), but afterwards in Finland at least, the craft became associated with 'peasant life'. 'Birch bark culture' is now a derogatory reference to those former times.

Coaling an engine with juniper
baskets. Museum in
Dalecarlia, Sweden.
Photo: Kurt Möller

Types of work[1]

Juniper splint

Juniper was valued for being tough and resistant to decay. It was used extensively for
the rougher types of baskets, for example gathering potatoes on the farm, or holding
fish on the boats or shore, instead of the brown willow rods that are often used in
milder climates.

A common 'juniper basket' was a general purpose maund with two simple handles at
the top of the rim. The base is started with a 'frame' of two crossed splints. 'Ribs' are
progressively inserted in each quadrant as a single splint weaver binds them in. They are
then pricked up and (an odd number) are carried up as side stakes right to the rim.
After the sides are woven, the ends of the stakes are bent down to form a simple border
and two small handles are attached. This technique may be thought of as midway
between a frame basket based upon crossing hoops and the professional willow worker's
method of starting with a separate base before inserting the side stakes. It will be met
again across the Baltic in Poland.

After about 1850 this humble basket began to be produced in volume by Swedish
workers. Apart from its use on farms and at the coast, there arose an increased demand
from the railway companies which were constructing the new transport system. To
enable quick coaling of the steam engines, large numbers of 50 litre baskets were filled
with coal and stacked on raised platforms along the tracks. At the turn of the century
hundreds of thousands of such juniper baskets were sold for this purpose each year.

Left: Wide pine splint basket,
Lindseth, Vefsn Bygdemuseum, Norway.
Photo JH Munksgaard

Right: Plaited back basket of Finnish type,
pine splint and twisted birch rod straps,
Dalecarlia, Sweden.
Photo: Jonas Hasselrot

Frame baskets in juniper were also very common with or without arch handles, and used for many purposes like gathering eggs or potatoes, and washing and storing clothes. One such basket was made especially for carrying charcoal when moving it into sleighs for transport from the forests and again at the ironworks. It was shaped like a giant scoop about one metre long. It was filled by placing on the ground and raking the charcoal in from the low side and was then lifted by two men. A similar basket was made for the iron furnaces of northwest England using split oak from coppiced woods (see chapter on Britain and Ireland).

Charcoal scoop in willow,
Uppland, Sweden
Photo: Jonas Hasselrot

Thin wood splint

In heavily wooded countries it is natural that the inhabitants utilised the products of forest trees and not merely coppice. Carefully selected short pine logs were repeatedly cleaved using only an axe, a knife, and a mallet. The resulting hand-riven splints were strong even when as thin as 1-2mm since they followed the grain closely.

In Norway and Sweden wide splint was simply bent into a flat cylindrical form, joined and fitted with a base and handle. Narrower splints of 30-50mm were used to make lightweight containers by plaiting, either straight or diagonal. The straight version is a little easier to weave and seems to have originated in Finland. It was brought into Sweden in the 17th and 18th centuries, so Swedish examples are mainly found at the former Finnish settlements. No lashing or nailing is required to complete the basket, the vertical splints bend over and tuck into the penultimate horizontal row, alternately inside and outside the rim. Sometimes a pair of rope-like straps is fitted, made from the twisted stem of a tall young birch sapling, so that the basket may be carried on the back. It may also be reinforced along the rim with a similar rope.

Diagonal plaiting may have evolved in Sweden in the 19th century using Finnish techniques previously employed with birch bark strips. The hand-riven splints were eventually replaced by the products of planing – at first, hand planes, but later machines. Less than perfect wood could be used, and aspen was often substituted for the traditional pine. The baskets were completed by lashing or nailing a pair of thicker splints each side of the top edge to form a rim.

Diagonally plaited pine splint
basket of Swedish type.
Västergötland, Sweden.
Photo: Jonas Hasselrot

In two provinces, Dalecarlia in the north and Scania in the south, production of these baskets became quite an industry, and they were widely exported. In the early years of the 20th century Swedes were travelling to Russia, Germany, Denmark, England and USA to sell them, and sometimes they settled down to make them on the spot. Several firms were established in Denmark in the 1890s to avoid the taxes levied on imported goods[2].

Right: Twill plaited pine splint with wood base, Västergötland, Sweden

Far right: Plaited and painted splint, Hälsingland, Sweden.
Photos: Jonas Hasselrot

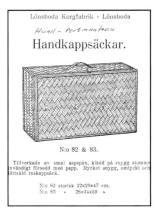

Lönsboda Korgfabrik · Lönsboda

Hand - Portmanteau

Handkappsäckar.

N:o 82 & 83.

Tillverkade av smal aspspån, klädd på snygg stomme, invändigt försedd med papp. Mycket snygg, omtyckt och lättsåld reskappsäck.

N:o 82 storlek 22x29x47 cm.
N:o 83   »   26x34x59 »

Above and right: Illustrations from Lönsboda punnet factory, 1935 catalogue, Sweden

Below: Plaited aspen splint, cane handles, poker-work decoration, Småland, Sweden.
Photo: Jonas Hasselrot

Lönsboda Korgfabrik · Lönsboda

Punnets for fruit and berry

Frukt- & Bärkorgar.

Med grepe.

N:o 12—16.

N:o 12 Rymd 1 liter
» 13   »   2 »
» 13/b »   3 »
» 14/a »   4 »
» 14/b »   5 »
» 14/c »   6 »
» 15   »   9 »
» 16   »   15 »

N:o 16 är försedd med 2:ne band under bottnen, levereras såväl 5 i sats som var för sig, endast vita.

Most people outside Scandinavia are only familiar with fruit and berry punnets made of wood splint, but the material was used to make a much wider range of baskets. The Punnet Museum in Lönsboda in the far south of Sweden is housed in premises of the former factory. Some 150 different types were manufactured for over 100 years from about 1840 in almost every home in the town, but by 1992 only three workers remained active. The firm's 1935 catalogue lists fruit and berry punnets in 10 sizes from 1 to 30 litre capacity. But it also illustrates baskets for logs, soiled clothes and laundry, waste paper, shopping and market display, for cats and needlework; besides cases, trunks, handbags and dolls' prams.

Also, in Scania province in southern Sweden they evolved twill plaiting with splints, where one element crosses two or more others. This method makes it easier to push the splints together to form a tight wall as there are no conflicts in the crossings as with plain (check) weave. The side of the basket was made separately as a slightly conical cylinder. This was then nailed to a plank base through a wrapping splint and a border of two splints was nailed around the rim.

It is perhaps surprising to us today to realise the scale of this manufacturing – though admittedly it involved little real craftsmanship. Four firms in Denmark (some originally from Sweden) between them sold at least a million baskets there in 1950.

The smooth surface of the splints invites decoration. In the north and especially in Norway the outside of fine baskets was often painted all over and then decorated with patterns. In the south baskets might be finished with flowers in poker-work or watercolours, particularly when they were used to carry provisions to celebrations (see next section).

Left: Cheese moulds,
rootwork,
Hälsingland, Sweden
Photo: Jonas Hasselrot

Right: Decorated bowl in
fine spruce or pine roots,
Lillehammer, Norway 1996

Coiled rootwork

Outside Denmark and the Swedish lowland provinces, roots were used for coiling wherever straw was not plentiful. Birch roots were preferred especially for small baskets. Even the finest ones were taken, as small as one millimetre diameter, since these facilitate delicate work and a variety of surface patterns. But working with such fine material is time consuming and the articles are often treated as precious objects. Spruce and other conifer roots (pine and juniper) were used for larger baskets. These roots can be very long, sometimes five metres or more, with a rather uniform thickness.

The bogs in the far north are good sources of birch roots and using these for coiled work was an important part of Lapp culture. (The Lapps or Sami are the original population now mainly confined to the arctic regions of Norway, Sweden, Finland, and Russia). Coiling is suitable for robust household items needed for nomadic life, like lidded boxes and salt bottles. Traditional Lapp items have a special appearance as a result of using a central core of several roots. But they also employed the more usual technique (where the core is a single root), especially when making baskets for external sales.

Arm basket in coiled rootwork,
Maihaugen museum, Norway

Cylindrical coiled baskets were often used as cheese moulds since the technique is suitable to stand the pressure when the whey is pressed out of the curd. Medium sized birch roots were used, both for their strength and because they impart no taint to the cheese. Drainage holes can be arranged in several ways. In some base rings the core may be zigzagged to create triangular holes in both sides. An alternative way is to make the whole wall more open by using stitches with knots between successive coils. In southwest Sweden similar moulds were once made from narrow conifer-wood splints, and sold far outside the production area.

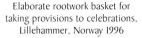

Elaborate rootwork basket for
taking provisions to celebrations,
Lillehammer, Norway 1996

Another special use for coiled baskets was to carry provisions to celebrations[3]. These, especially weddings and funerals, could last for days and the guests were expected to bring some food. That often led to competition as everyone wanted to bring the best food, displayed in the most attractive way. Usually a large, low and wide basket was employed with a tall central handle. The potential of the coiling technique was used in full to decorate the basket's body and handle. There are many beautiful examples in Swedish and Norwegian museums, and a few are still made there today, and also in Finland. I tracked down a most elaborate example for sale in Lillehammer in 1996. I was allowed to photograph it, but alas my budget restricted me to buying a smaller simpler bowl – still a work of art.

Spruce and pine roots were appreciated for their extreme softness and flexibility when soaked, and were often also used in woven work, not least in frame baskets (see chapter on Poland and the Baltics).

Birch bark

This material was in widespread use from pre-historic times, though the ways in which it has been exploited have evolved. Birch bark forests were sufficiently valued that they were listed separately in farm descriptions[4].

Folded birch bark container,
Turku museum, Finland.
Photo: Felicity Wood

If some wild strawberries or bilberries were unexpectedly found in the wood, a cornet or a simple basket could easily be made by any country person from a single sheet taken from a nearby tree and made fast with small sticks. Baskets for longer term use could also be constructed from sheets. Watertight cooking vessels were made by folding the bark into a square or oblong container (like a parcel without a top). The corners were held together with wooden pins or stitches of birch roots.

Another way was to bend the bark sheet into a cylinder so that the inside layer was then outside. The two ends could be sewn together with birch roots but a more decorative way was to cut 'hooks and eyes' into the overlapping ends. A round or oval base and lid were fitted, made of bark or wood. Such boxes were often used for butter as they were tight and did not transmit any taste. Their ability to contain aroma and moisture also made them popular for coffee, tobacco and snuff.

The length of a birch bark sheet is limited by the thickness of the tree, so two or more sheets have to be combined for larger boxes. Sometimes rowan bark was used for a special reason. The bark's grain is oriented horizontally on birches, but vertically on the rowan, and on a box the grain must go around with the curve. So if a rowan trunk is selected which is a little longer than the planned circumference of the box, then this single vertical bark sheet can be utilised. Such articles are strengthened with pieces of birch bark and birch root stitches. The base is made of two crossed sheets of birch bark since, like wood, bark has a tendency to split in one direction.

Another technique long employed in Finland and Russia, but only introduced to Sweden in the 17th and 18th centuries, was to cut the bark into soft and pliable strips and use these for plaiting. The orientation of the plaiting is normally parallel or

Milk bottle from 18th century,
birch bark, Hälsingland, Sweden.
Photo: Jonas Hasselrot

Rucksack (Finnish kont), birch
bark 1774, Hälsingland, Sweden.
Photo: Jonas Hasselrot

diagonal to the base. A typical example is a basket with a square or oblong base, where the shape changes gradually to a round or oval rim. The weave can be double: inside to the top rim, then over and down outside. Rucksacks were popular in northern parts and are made in all sizes. Children looking after cattle in the forest, or going to school could carry their lunch in one. Paniers, purses, shopping bags, and flat bread baskets were also common items as were sheaths for knives and scythes, salt bottles, and shoes. Even milk bottles were made of birch bark: in the inside an intact cylinder was taken off a log felled in the spring when the sap was rising. Circles of wood were inserted in both ends, the top one with an aperture. The cylinder was then wrapped in an outer plaited casing for protection. Similar bottles could be used to contain spirits.

Assembled wooden baskets

If some type of weaving is essential in a basket, then many Norwegian objects would have to be excluded, but the continuous range from totally woven to the totally sawn and nailed makes such a rigid definition unhelpful. Here is yet another example of the ways in which weaving and woodworking skills become joined in many articles made in forest regions. Like several other countries, Sweden and Norway have many splint-sided baskets where the stakes are fixed into holes pierced around the edge of a plank base. But the 'baskets' described here go much further towards traditional joinery work.

Some of these use the cooper's techniques we normally associate with barrels, churns, and pails. Flat wooden staves are shaped, fitted edge-on, and held in place by horizontal wooden bands or hoops. A round wooden bottom is inserted and a single bow handle fitted.

Below: Staved wood 1832,
Vefsn Bygdemuseum, Norway.
Photo: JH Munksgaard

Left: Two-handled plank base basket, Maihaugen museum, Norway

Right: Assembled basket with woven side panels, Turku Openair Museum, Finland.
Photo: Felicity Wood

Two painted wooden celebratory baskets, a willow arm basket and a plaited and painted pine splint model, all from Hordaland, Norway.
Photo: Anne-Marie Olsen

Many more are square or rectangular, built with four corner posts, four panel sides, a bottom, and often a bow handle. Sometimes the sides are solid panels but frequently they are more complex with spaced vertical and horizontal components. What is more, they often include sections of woven splint, inserted purely for decoration, and the entire surface will be painted and patterned. Such elaborate baskets were clearly designed to be taken to celebrations[5].

Specific items

Netting bags from bast

Bast is the inner fibrous bark of certain trees especially the lime or linden and is a very old material for cordage and netting. Hay and fish could be contained in bast nets for transport and the outer walls of fish traps might be similarly netted. A substitute can be made from thin hand-riven shavings of spruce or pine. Shopping bags made from

Left: Herring bag, twisted spruce shavings, Västergötland, Sweden.
Photo: Jonas Hasselrot

Separating lime bast.
Photo: K. Södring

twisted coils of bast fibres using a netting weave are a modern application of these herring bags.

Straw shoes

Coiled straw or lipwork (for example in beehives) was common in Denmark and Sweden's southern parts where cereals were more easily grown. But straw over-shoes were found in many other areas deep into the forests, as well as in other parts of northern and eastern Europe, because of the insulation they could provide from the intense winter cold. They were appreciated by market stallholders and by farmers sitting on their carts for long journeys, who could not exercise to keep warm. Naturally they were too fragile to be used when walking.

Over-shoes in coiled straw, Scania, Sweden.
Photo: Jonas Hasselrot

Notes and references

1.   Anyone who has looked through Jonas Hasselrot's wonderful book on Swedish basketry, 'Korgar: Tradition och Teknik' (1997) LTs förlad, Stockholm, will at once recognise the debt I owe to his thorough research and beautiful images. If only we had such a book on each of our European countries! Jonas willingly agreed to collaborate with me. He outlined his ideas for this chapter which I have attempted to realise, read my draft, and let me reproduce a number of his photographs - some already used in his book, and some new ones. While I have had some opportunities to travel through the other countries, and had additional contacts, it is inevitable that my treatment has a strong Swedish flavour.
2.   Johansson, Per-Olaf (1997) 'A Personal History of Splint Baskets', and 'How to Make a Splint Basket'. BA NL **80** 8 and on the author's home page http://home3.inet.tele.dk/johansso/splint.htm.
3.   Munksgaard, J.H. (1980) 'Kurver'. C. Huitfeldt Forlag A.S. Oslo. This little volume covers the whole range of Norwegian basketry with particular emphasis on the coiled root and wooden celebratory items, including many illustrations.
4.   Väätäinen, Anna-Maria (1999) 'Basketmaking in Finland: Tradition and Change'. Lecture at Cambridge University Botanic Garden, 13.07.99.
5.   See 3.

Germany

Peasants of
Vierlande, by Georg
Emanuel Opiz,
c1820,
Museum of German
Ethnology, Berlin

Sign outside basketmaker's shop, Grimma, Saxony

Resources

The top third of this large land mass in central northern Europe is mainly low lying, the centre hilly, and the southern parts are within the Alpine ranges; hence the climate varies from northern maritime down through north central European (cool summers and cold winters) to Alpine. The original forests were deciduous, merging into coniferous at higher elevations, and one quarter of the land is still under trees. The predominant type of farming has been mixed pasture and arable with the balance tilted towards arable cropping in the drier north east, and towards cattle in the wetter west and south though with pigs everywhere. Basketmakers have therefore had access to the usual range of plant resources found in most northwestern European countries. Hazel, oak, pine, spruce, larch, poplar, aspen, and ash all contributed wood splint, with root splint from spruce or larch. Small rods came from wild willow, alder buckthorn, privet, hazel, and chestnut. Rye and wheat straw were generally available. In time there were large willow plantations in the lowlands surrounding the river Oder in the northeast, though these were ceded to Poland after World War II, and many other river valleys had smaller areas.

History

"With no obvious geographical boundaries such as mountains or seas to define the limits of Germany to the east or west, 'the country in the middle' has never stopped changing shape or ethnic mix. What have remained constant are the smaller territorial regions, which for centuries had to fend for themselves while mightier powers fought military or political battles to control them. This meant there was no centralisation, no national institutions of government"[1].

Language has been the basis for unity. Briefly, the regions start from the west with the Rhinelands originally representing a bigger state between the Roman controlled Celtic region (Gaul) and the Germanic tribes to the east. From the 6th century these integrated with the Franconians east of the Rhine, but subsequently the region moved backwards and forwards between French and German control. The Saxons had come down from Scandinavia, but then expanded into Gaul (and Britain) after the Roman decline. The Bavarians similarly moved into the older Roman cities in the southern highland region and later took over Swabia and most of Franconia. Finally the Prussians originated on the Baltic coast. Their homeland has now been lost to Poland and Russia, but their inheritance (discipline, reliability, and thoroughness) is what many of us now think of as typical German characteristics.

As a consequence, we cannot simply describe the evolution of the German nation, nor of the craft of basketry within it. For centuries the regions were separate dukedoms with different resources of agriculture, energy, and minerals which naturally developed and urbanised at quite different speeds. Furthermore, the available accounts of this history are quite variable with much more recorded on those regions which developed important basketmaking industries in the last 200 years.

Parts of Germany have long been relatively densely populated with a belt of industrial areas across the middle exploiting the extensive fuel and mineral resources, and fed from farms on the easily-worked loess soils with favourable climate. Urban communities of artisans were established early in these regions as in the Low Countries, France, and Britain. But basketry seems to have lagged behind other trades with the majority of articles continuing to be supplied from the countryside. It was the last of the crafts to achieve guild status in Germany. The recorded dates: Cologne 1589, Braunschweig 1593, Bremen 1618, Leipzig 1709, and Dresden 1834 appear to span a very long period. Perhaps, as in other countries, the formal foundation of the guild was confirming an organisation which had already existed for some time[2].

Of course, after the guilds had formed, rural makers could undercut the urban masters who tried to have their legal monopolies enforced. The laws were finally changed in the 1820s, but other forms of restrictive practice remained within unions and closed shops until after World War II.

Early work was mainly in brown willow. There is no mention in some areas of white (stripped) willow, although its use was known since Roman times and the Dutch were already exploiting it. Before around 1750 the normal way of producing white willow would have been to leave the one year old rods uncut until bud break when there is a small period before the side shoots grow out and spoil their suitability. After this time growers learned the technique of cutting the crop during the winter months and pitting (standing the bundled rods in shallow water) which trebles the window of opportunity for stripping but this is not suitable where winter cold is severe.

In the late 18th century, driven by poverty, many farmers in the less fertile regions developed basketmaking as a secondary occupation and sold their work themselves in markets. Some became full-time makers and skills were passed on within families. A further degree of specialisation occurred as villages took different routes with both techniques and materials.

The initiative may have come from a single leader motivated by philanthropy, or by his desire to build up a merchanting activity. The product may have reflected the availability of a local resource, or have been based upon a new imported material. Hence the village specialities might be dough baskets from straw, carpet beaters from imported cane, chip baskets for fruit from pine or fir logs, spruce or pine root baskets, skeined willow work, pulled work (Madeira), palm-leaf bowls and baskets, or raffia work. Around the beginning of the 20th century, cane and willow furniture-making emerged.

In other areas specialisation was driven by strong demand from local industries and their transport needs. Laundry and transport baskets in white willow were made in North Rhine – Westphalia (Dalhausen); brown willow work for agriculture and metal industries and for industrial glass containers, and white willow delivery baskets for the retail trades came from towns like Hilfarth near the Dutch-Belgian border. The northern coastal areas around Hamburg, Cuxhaven, and Bremen specialised in baskets for catching and transporting fish and crustaceans, and large containers for exporting corn, coal, and other bulk products. When large-scale trading developed on the railways and through the northern ports, there were huge quantities of carboys needed for exporting acids, schnapps, and other liquids. Literally millions of containers were covered annually in the early years of the 20th century, and this work was often done by women in urban workshops.

Demi-john in peeled willow, Freilichtmuseum Domäne Dahlem, Berlin

One region whose history has been particularly well researched is Franconia, the upland region around Bamberg, Bayreuth, and Coburg at the northern edge of Bavaria. This is because the National Basketry Trade School is located there (Lichtenfels) and also the large museum (Michelau). Prof Christoph Will, one of the museum's directors, recorded some of the history in his 1978 book (translated into English in 1985)[3], and then a fuller account was published in 1994 by a later director, Dr Gunter Dippold[4]. There are some records of full-time basketmakers from as early as 1622, though in general it was only a winter occupation for small-scale farmers, fishermen, and raftsmen (who used to

Brown willow baskets used by the fishing industry.
Photo: Deutsches Korbmuseum Michelau

Left : Eel trap in brown willow - eels are a popular food in northern parts, Volkskunde Museum, Schleswig

Student from the National Basketry Trade School, Lichtenfels preparing fine willow skein, 1995

accompany rafts of floating logs down the river system as far as The Netherlands) working in brown willow. By 1760, 'fine' basketmaking had become established using white willow, whole, or skeined. A guild was formed in the village of Michelau. The Bamberg Government gave it its charter which was confirmed in 1770 by the Archbishop of Bamberg. This set down regulations to protect the local makers against competition (particularly from non-members) and to settle disputes among members – most of whom were still part-time. The techniques seem to have originated in northeast France (La Thiérache) and become established across the border in the Belgian town of Halle. One Johannes Puppert is credited with first splitting willow rods and designing planes to produce skein in Franconia in 1773, and thus beginning a new branch of the German industry which reached its peak around 1880.

When making willow skeins, the exposed surface could be planed flat, rounded (convex), or grooved (concave), and the skeins woven flat or on edge relative to the vertical stakes. Weaving was then often carried out over a wooden mould. The effects were created not only by the fineness of the weaving rods, but also the shapes and the decoration from different weaves, the use of coloured rods, and various attachments. The range of articles included handbags, needlework holders, letter trays, flower holders, wastepaper baskets, fruit and bread bowls, cradles, and baby perambulators. Such fine work catered to the desires of a large urban population for delicate and sophisticated objects. It is said that servant girls in the north German ports were judged, hired, and paid according to the quality and sturdiness of the hand baskets they carried!

Weaving fine willow skein on a mould attached to a stand, Deutsches Korb Museum, Michelau, Franconia

This industrialisation of basketmaking did not always go smoothly. With the decline in the influence of the guilds quality control became a problem, and the Bavarian government intervened to raise the region's reputation. By 1815 the guild in the village of Michelau had over one hundred Master basketmakers with a greatly improved quality and range of work. With such concentrated production, the sales clearly depended upon exports from the region. From the early part of the 19th century, the people of this region showed enormous enterprise in building markets overseas for their products. These traders initially made long journeys pushing handcarts laden with baskets all over Germany and then to Austria, Italy, Poland, Denmark, and Spain. Large firms developed particularly making fine work, employing outworkers as well as having their own premises. Gagel printed its first catalogue in 1850, containing 1390 items. Murmann began in 1865 and only ceased in 1984. In 1908 there were over 70 firms in and around Lichtenfels,

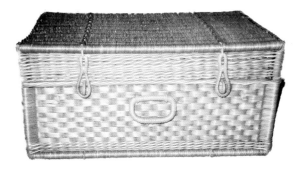

Above: Linen baskets and trunk, in white willow, Deutsches Korb Museum, Michelau, Franconia

which, because it was a railway centre, had developed into the major focus. Literally thousands of basketmakers came by train or on foot to the town each Saturday. They sold their output to the merchants and collected new materials for their next week's work. Like many other labour forces at the start of the industrial revolution, the makers worked long hours in cramped houses, often involving their whole families in some aspects of the production process, and consuming a meagre and monotonous diet. The successful merchants, in contrast, became wealthy and built fine houses which are still evident today. In 1900, some 15,000 makers were involved, but this fine basketry has declined almost to nothing because of the high labour requirement and changes in fashion for such articles. A small needlework basket may involve up to four days' work by a skilled weaver.

In Germany as a whole, since the old guild system had ceased when the profession was legally opened in the 1820s, there had been little regulation of apprenticeship even though there had been enormous developments into new types of work, and new methods of employment. These revealed a need for special training schools and several emerged between 1876 and 1904. In Franconia the local merchants had been seeking such a school as early as 1860, but it only came into being around 1880 as a travelling drawing school, and finally, in 1904 as a genuine institute in Lichtenfels modelled on the Vienna school. It was to build up generations of journeymen and masters skilled in

Basketmakers bringing their work to the merchants outside the railway station Lichtenfels, early 20th century.
Photo: Stadtarchiv Lichtenfels

the workshop, willow cultivation and business, through teaching and research into new modes. In recent years the school offered a three-year apprenticeship (year one, fine willow work; year two, other willow work; year three, furniture; with a general education throughout). Graduates could eventually apply to be recognised as Master and even today there is prestige in being called a Master basketmaker in Germany. When I visited the school in 1995, some 132 candidates had been approved between 1956 and 1994, and in the period since 1974 just over one third were female. At least seven other schools were founded in other regions of Germany between 1876 and 1881, but none of them existed for long.

It is clear that the Lichtenfels school both continued to teach the design and practical skills which had been developed over the previous 100 years, and to push forward and create more modern designs especially using willow skein. The output of two teachers, Adam Zasche and Alfred Schnieder (themselves both trained at the school) who led the fine work courses from 1922 for almost 80 years, moved away from the complex designs of handbags, dishes, trays and bowls which had once been so popular. By the 1950s, they were producing much simpler forms but without lowering the quality of materials or weaving. In one sense they have made the work look so technically perfect that they might have been made by machine. Such 'objects of desire' continue the traditions of the very finest workmanship which must, of course, have a strictly limited market on account of its cost.

The German industry went through successive crises during the late 19th and 20th centuries owing to changes in fashion, competition from other countries, and alternative packaging materials and these inevitably brought hardship. Still in the 1907 census, over 40,000 people were classified as basketmakers. Various co-operatives, trade associations, and unions formed between 1870-1930, but many individual makers failed to become members. In spite of these attempts to gain better returns by reducing competition between workers, their efforts could not stop the inevitable decline. Many left for better paid work in other industries after the end of World War II.

Clockwise from top left: Making dough baskets in coiled rye straw wrapped in cane, Lichtenfels fair 1991

Statue of basketmaker outside the Deutsches Korb Museum in Michelau, Franconia

Dough basket in coiled rye straw and wrapping cane, Lichtenfels

Nevertheless, some basketmaking (and furniture making) survives in Germany including Franconia, and anyone attending the annual Korbmarkt (basketry fair and market) in Lichtenfels could imagine being back in a mediaeval town celebrating its annual fair. The town gates are closed to traffic, and the streets almost blocked with over 60 stalls. The first fair was organised in 1979 to celebrate the former importance of the industry to the town, and involved the school and only three firms. After 25 years, it has grown into an event attracting over 100,000 people. Makers come from throughout Germany. Some stalls offer baskets from countries in Central Europe, and others from the Far East. But there are local craftsmen too. In 1995 there were still 23 workshops in the area producing baskets or furniture. And if you look very carefully, you may still see a very few new examples of fine willow skein work!

One merchant's house in Michelau is now the home of the Deutsches Korb Museum, which extends to 26 public rooms plus stores. The museum was started in 1929, occupied its first modest premises in 1934, but now serves as a wonderful record of Franconia's industry through the ages with some examples from other regions and countries.

Types of work

Professional willow

The history of fine willow skein work in Franconia was reviewed in the previous section, but many other branches of willow work have been prominent in Germany. The discipline of long apprenticeship has survived until today, and the results can be seen in widely different articles. Square work in white willow is not only made to last,

Left: Fitched log basket in brown willow by Elmar Oppel, Weismain, Franconia. A very different way of making a base from that described in the techniques chapter

but is beautiful with elegant design and surface patterns from different weaves, even in such everyday items as baskets for soiled and clean linen. Trunks, either for travel or to store household items, were obviously possessions to be proud of and are still made today.

Two current makers exhibiting at the Lichtenfels fair during my last visit had adopted quite different strategies for surviving in modern times. Elmar Oppel from Weismain, a nearby village, continued to work in brown willow creating traditional farm baskets based upon a solid wooden cross piece in the base with both base and sides in open work fitched in a spiral line. These baskets are quick to make because of the absence of side weaving, modestly priced, and could be used on the farm, in the garden, or for holding kindling and logs in the house. In addition, he made a range of traditional back baskets in both white and brown willow.

Elmar Oppel making his brown willow fitched baskets at the Lichtenfels fair, 1995

By contrast, the family firm of Witzgall had decided that it should largely leave behind the everyday traditional products, as made by the grandfather's generation, and differentiate itself from the imported products which were based on much cheaper labour and willow. Carl Witzgall designed a series of models in white or dyed willow. Their shapes are not traditional, though they have clearly evolved from classic models, no doubt influenced by the work of the school. In addition, all the rods are selected very carefully and woven in several weaves with great skill, often with a characteristic knot finish to the rods wrapping the single handles. In 1995 between three and six weavers (including father Carl and son Bernd) produced high quality work which was mainly sold by smaller shops within Germany and naturally commanded good prices

Two strong baskets in white willow from Bernd Witzgall, Lichtenfels

Above: Simulation of using a fan to winnow grain, Deutsches Korb Museum, Michelau, Franconia

Above right: Winnowing fan in white willow on wood splint: type common in the Netherlands and northwest Germany, Deutsches Korb Museum, Michelau, Franconia

from customers who admired quality crafts. Some willow laundry and picnic baskets, plus cane furniture and baskets, were also produced, but it was the style and quality of its new range which distinguished the Witzgall workshop from its competitors.

Winnowing fans

It seems likely that Roman settlers brought to these more northern parts the technique of separating grain from chaff by winnowing in a large shallow basket during the first century AD. The sheaves of corn were first threshed by beating with a flail stick, and the long straw removed. The remaining mixture of grains, husks and broken straw was then loaded into the winnowing fan and thrown into the air. Rapid vertical movements created a draught which carried away the lighter material and left a clean sample of heavier grains. The baskets were also used for carrying corn and even for holding meal. In shape, the fan is like a mollusc shell, quite flat along the front edge and gradually deepening to the rear with two small handles attached to the low sides. (The fan and shell are almost interchangeable in heraldry.)

The Latin name for the Roman basket was *vannus*. In German, *die Wanne* is a tub or bath, and the basket shape reflects this and hence the name *Kornwanne (*or corn basket). In French this basket is called *le van* and *la vannerie* has become a general term for basketmaking. In Old English the word *fann* was no doubt influenced by both Latin and French. V replaced F in several English words and a *van* or *fan* was a winnowing basket, while *to van* was to winnow with a fan.

From their initial introduction, these fans were made by specialist craftsmen in Germany for at least the next 1700 years, and comparisons with stone images from the Roman period show little change or development other than local variations in size, depth and number of ribs. There were centres of production along the river Rhine in Hesse, Westphalia and in Friesland, in Oberwill (Switzerland), and other places from which they were widely distributed by merchants, and at fairs, and exported to other countries.

The village of Emsdetten, near the Dutch border, was one such centre and the history of the trade has been recorded there in a small museum housed in an original fan-makers' workshop[5]. It is likely that the local guild existed in the 16th century and survived until 1810, but the first written proof is in a charter dating from 1645. This charter, to be administered by a group of elders, limited the number of apprentices, and sought to maintain quality standards by regulating the training period and the examination. The elders also regulated quarrels over the cutting of local willows and

Left: Winnowing fan in white willow on wood splint in the open air museum, Ballenberg, Switzerland

An elegant arm basket from the National Basketry Trade School, Lichtenfels made in willow and wood splint using the fan makers' technique of beaten work

sales of baskets. The Bishop of Münster granted the village privileges from 1721 which forbade the local makers from instructing outsiders in the specialised technique. One additional method by which the craft was kept exclusive to a limited number of families was inter-marriage amongst their sons and daughters. Records from 1750 show that half of the 450 families in the district earned money from the industry. Wives and daughters supported the men in many ways, but the actual weaving of the fans was a male occupation. The materials were white willow rods, very tightly woven around a framework of flat wooden slats, and in Emsdetten these were also of willow. Sections were cut from logs, split into four by axe, and stored until March. These blocks were then boiled, cut by knife, and split by hand into thinner slats. Finally, they were planed and cut to the required thickness and width. Three-year old stems were used for handles and rims, and were boiled before bending around forms, perhaps by the weavers' wives and children.

The one-year-old willow rods, often imported from other regions or countries, were stood in shallow water over winter, and peeled when sprouting in the spring. Peeling and drying occupied eight weeks with a further six for making the flat slats, so almost one third of the year was taken up in preparing materials.

The basket was begun in the centre with a cross of four short slats (six in other areas) bound with fine rods. More slats were added in strict order, each with a precise name, as the diameter was expanded until some 42-48 were in place. The craftsman actually sat inside the large models on the floor, turning constantly to follow the weaving in a cramped position. Each rod needed to be beaten close down onto the preceding row, using a rapping iron, with thicker rods towards the rim. A skilled worker could weave two fans in a day. The handles and rims were put on at the end, and the protruding slats reduced in width and thickness before they were brought over the rim and tucked under the final rows of weaving. The completed fans were soaked and exposed to burning sulphur fumes to bleach them.

The special fan used by millers. Wannenmacher Museum, Emsdetten. Photo: José Schilder

The fan makers of Emsdetten worked only with this technique and made seven different versions. Four or five were different sizes of the basic winnowing fan, another was much smaller and used for carrying feed to animals. Up to the end of the 19th century, a much deeper version was used by millers and bakers for holding flour, and this had three additional reversed 'handles' which projected below the base and supported it level on the ground.

This ancient method of winnowing corn was eventually displaced by mechanisation. Hand-powered rotary fans were introduced in 1870 and threshing machines from 1900. Nevertheless, some Emsdetten workshops continued to produce fans with around

Representation of a butter dealer going to Kassel market in 1770. Drawing: R Wittich

30 weavers active in 1925, and a few continuing until the 1950s. The widespread use of the combine harvester finally killed off this historic industry in 1968. It is interesting to record that the fan makers were seldom involved in repairing damaged baskets. Instead, they supplied slats to specialist workers who travelled between farms during the summer using locally cut willow rods.

This technique, known in English as scuttle work but perhaps more graphically described as beaten work, has sometimes been refined in the Lichtenfels school to create baskets of great finesse. Related techniques, where the wide slats are anchored into a solid base, may use whole white willow rods as weavers as in the grape harvesting baskets in wine regions. In other cases the weavers are narrow splint or skein, often found in back baskets[6].

Thin wood splint

Three types of chip baskets of thin pine splint from Lauter, near the Czech border, at Lichtenfels fair

In the mountainous region south of Chemnitz, near the northern border of the Czech Republic, men had long been accustomed to working in the pine forests. From the 1820s, an industry developed making a variety of 'chip' baskets (or punnets) from thin sheets of wood split at the annual rings, and this survived until the start of World War II. The various shapes and sizes were used for transporting fruit, flowers and vegetables, but also hats and caps. They were exported for use in many countries in Europe, and then much further afield, including USA. Enterprising men formed companies in several villages during the 1860s employing whole families who worked in their homes. The men split the pine logs and prepared the material, while the children performed the very simple weaving operations. At its peak around 1885, some 800 people were employed in one village alone (Lauter) so great was the demand from the USA, and the craft spread to other regions of Germany which needed rural employment. The decline started soon after and sales became confined to Europe. This is perhaps the only type of basketry which has survived by being mechanised, though in greatly reduced scale. From 1940, the log splitting was done by machine, and in the 1960s, machines even took over the weaving within a 'Kombinat', or co-operative, in the former Eastern Germany. Similar industries have existed in Scandinavia and Poland, and the technique may have had its origins in the forests of Finland.

Specific items of interest

Back baskets

At the beginning of the 21st century, it has become popular for people of all ages in western Europe to carry personal items in lightweight backpacks with two straps resting on the shoulders. Students on their world tours carry all they need for long trips in much larger versions and they are consequently known as 'backpackers'. A little earlier it was only mountaineers and hill walkers who carried 'rucksacks' (literally a bag carried behind), but the tradition is very ancient. Men, women, and children down the ages have found this method of carrying heavy loads to be one of the most suitable, even for light loads where it is advantageous to keep both hands free. Of course, if it is possible to place the load on a framework with one or more wheels (wheelbarrow, cart), or runners (sledge), or on a pack animal, then even heavier loads can be transported with less human effort. Historically, poor people did not have the capital for such resources, or the road or track surfaces were not adequate for wheeled traffic, so the human frame was assisted by some version of a back basket. Germany, Austria, and Switzerland had a particularly rich tradition of these articles and examples range from the crude to the highly sophisticated.

The materials utilised naturally varied both according to local availability and the load to be carried. In forest and mountain areas like the Alps, the framework would often be of split wood such as beech, oak, ash, maple, pine, fir, or larch; while the weavers might be thin splint made from hazel, oak, maple or lime, willow or wild vine stems, and spruce or larch roots. In the lowlands, or foothills, the whole structure might be in willow. The simplest of these would be made of unpeeled brown willow. More sophisticated baskets were in white willow, perhaps even with panels in skeinwork for lightness and decoration.

Robust back basket in oak splint -
on wooden cradle by
Karl Sporer, Lauffen,
Baden-Württemberg

General purpose carriers would be tightly woven so as to hold small objects. At the opposite extreme, baskets to carry hay, grass, or other leaves could be large, but very simple structures with the minimum of cross-weaving necessary to hold the frame together. Sometimes a pole protruded from the base on which the basket could be balanced at a convenient height for rest or loading. In some stout German baskets there is a three-legged framework or two base rails so that they can be set level on the ground. A robust model was provided by Karl Sporer from near Rottweil by the Swabian Alps in the far south west of Germany. It is built on a sturdy three-legged cradle. Both the stakes and weavers are in oak.

159

Above: Market scene in Weimar, Thüringen, around 1890. Photo: National Basketry Trade School, Lichtenfels

Above right: Back basket in willow skein, Thüringen pattern by Rudolf Rippstein, Sand am Main, Franconia

Carrying a load of back baskets to market.
Drawing: R. Wittich

The rim is neatly finished with a half-round rod inside and out, and these are lashed with cane. It was brought back from the Lichtenfels Korbmarkt in 1991 when this craftsman was still exhibiting a wide range of baskets made from wood splint.

We are fortunate to have an account of the large variety of back baskets which used to be made in the State of Hessen[7]. This is a hilly region in central Germany between Frankfurt and Kassel. At the beginning of the 20th century, some 14,000 back baskets in 10-15 shapes were sold annually from Hessen, but by 1959 this had fallen to only 350 from seven makers. Most sales in the countryside were direct from maker to customer, though merchants were established in the towns. A half-way system also existed whereby six to eight men and women (travelling in groups for safety) would make a seven- to eight-hour round trip on foot, each carrying or pushing a cartload of up to a dozen baskets. The total consignment of 70-90 articles would be left in the care of a 'basket-shepherd' to sell. This trip would be undertaken four to five times in winter, the final one just before Easter.

Thüringen, immediately to the east, was another area of rather infertile soils with many wild willows, and so basketmaking developed to supplement incomes on small farms. The guild in Kranichfeld, south of Erfurt, was founded in 1714. The test pieces to be submitted by external applicants for acceptance as a Master included a basket with six compartments, a pigeon carrier, and a decorated, lidded basket. Local applicants could get away with a single decorated piece. The patterns were twill-woven in skeined willow and might include initials, the date, a tree of life, the sun, or a heart. This region was noted for its elegant back baskets carried by farm women when taking produce to the markets. I bought a fine example in 1995 from Rudolf Rippstein, a young craftsman from Sand am Main, Franconia who trained at the German National School in Lichtenfels. He was obviously very proud of this, his premier piece, and was loath to part with it. The skeining on the three exposed sides is woven to produce a fir tree or tree of life decoration: the side against the wearer's back has simple diamond motifs. No doubt the patterns would once have been specific to an area, perhaps even the village. A photograph in Dippold's book of a market in Weimar in 1890 shows at least 10 women carrying such baskets, and several different patterns can be clearly seen. The corner posts project above the top border and allow an extra (often oval, lidded) basket to be strapped on top.

Unfortunately it is no longer possible to travel around the many different regions and see their characteristic back baskets being made. Luckily there is a particularly good collection, many on permanent display, in the Deutsches Korbmuseum, Michelau.

1. A fine willow skein creation by the National Basketry Trade School, Lichtenfels

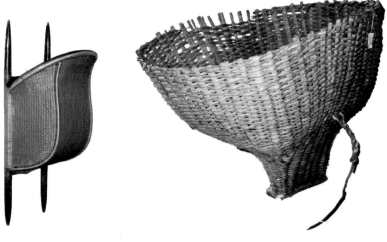

2. Lady's model in willow skein (c1500) after a Nurnberg painting, Deutsches Korb Museum, Michelau

3. Large leaf or hay carrier in wood splint, Deutsches Korb Museum, Michelau

4. Coburg type in fine white willow by Rudolf Rippstein, Sand am Main, Franconia

5. 'Stirrup' carrier in fine white willow from Saxony, Dorfmuseum, Schönbach, Saxony

6. Brown and white openwork carrier, from Hessen, Deutsches Korb Museum, Michelau

7. Small three-legged carrier in white willow from Hessen, Dorfmuseum Schönbach, Saxony

8. Plank base carrier in willow skein from Bamberg, Deutsches Korb Museum, Michelau

9. Nurnberg 'egg' basket in wood splint with leather decoration, Deutsches Korb Museum, Michelau

There is a large variety of

- sizes: for men, women and children, from huge hay baskets, to quite small town shoppers
- shape: round, oval and square sections, tall and thin, bell shaped, short and squat
- material: brown willow, wood splint, white willow rods, and skein
- construction
- and weave.

But the emphasis in the museum collection is on fine workmanship, and sophistication achieved through both form and decoration. Although there is almost no added colour or material, the craftsmen have created different effects including 'block weaving', the use of holes, openwork with fitching, surface decoration with looped rods, and patterns

Bride basket in fine willow skein,
Dorfmuseum Schönbach, Saxony

from skeined willow. A particularly rich effect is provided in some 'egg' baskets from Nuremberg, shaped like an inverted onion, woven in fine wood splint on a very large number of wooden slats. They were sometimes covered from the top rim half-way down the outside in leather which was elaborately patterned. Since they might be specially made for a young girl's dowry, this could include the bride's initials and date. Clearly a prominently displayed back basket could be as much a status symbol as other articles of clothes.

Bride baskets

Young women often received sets of finely woven baskets before marriage – hence 'bride baskets'. This was a tradition in the Schwalm villages of Hessen, but also in Marburg and Hanau. In 1912, a maker in Zella wove 34 pieces for a bride – many decorated with colours, with bells, and other ornaments. Some were for carrying on the head, others for laundry, and for garden

Left: Handbag in fine willow skein, Deutches Korb Museum, Michelau

Dolls pram in willow c1900, Deutches Korb Museum, Michelau

and field use – and the tradition persisted until the 1950s. Different dye colours were used in different areas. Some of the baskets would be filled with cutlery, crockery and textiles for the new household while the baskets themselves remained objects of prestige. But no doubt in many other regions brides would have received gifts of basketry which would be the finest example of the local traditions.

Handbags

In the 19th and early 20th centuries, large numbers of ladies' handbags were made in Franconia. Since these were fashion items, the exact design and decoration had to change quite frequently and there was a wide variety of fastenings, handles, and trim on the basic oval or rectangular shape. The main material was usually white willow, whole rods or skeined, but these were sometimes painted black to give contrasting bands and patterns. As many were sold to farmers' wives, they no doubt often carried poultry and rabbits to market. There are good selections of these preserved in the museums at Michelau and Grimma. Many individual examples can also be found illustrating earlier life-styles in old houses that have been collected into the 'open-air' museums throughout the German-speaking countries. Franconia was in competition with La Thiérache in northern France (see chapter on the Low Countries) and it would probably take an expert to reveal the true origins of individual items found today[8].

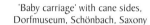

'Baby carriage' with cane sides, Dorfmuseum, Schönbach, Saxony

Perambulators

These same museums are good places to see examples of the evolution of the 'baby carriage' (including those for children's dolls). They progressed from a cradle fitted onto the sort of hand-drawn cart widely used on small farms in the early 19th century, through to elegant 'coach-built' models on large spoked wheels 100 years later. Streamlined forms woven in centre cane appeared in the 1950s, but woven bodies were finally replaced by solid panels as new materials became available and fashions changed.

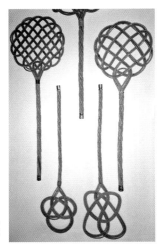

Selection of carpet beaters in cane,
Deutsches Korb Museum, Michelau

Carpet beaters

Such household implements were much valued before the days of mechanical sweepers or suction cleaners. Carpets and rugs were lifted, draped over a strong cord outside the house, and thoroughly beaten to allow accumulated dust to drift away in the wind. Furniture covered in material was also beaten. An industry developed in the 19th century to produce them based upon strong 4-7mm diameter cane imported from the Far East, in the towns of Neuensee and Lichtenfels. More than 100 different designs were made and the industry survived until well after World War II. Indeed, they are still available for purchase at the annual Korbmarkt.

Notes and references

1. Fernández-Armesto, F. (Ed.) (1994) 'The Peoples of Europe'. Times Books.
2. I have been travelling in Germany for academic visits, or on business, for almost 40 years. My contacts with basketry have, however, been strongest in Franconia, the site of the major basket museum, the national trade school and the largest annual fair and market. My understanding has been greatly helped by several visits to these centres and the kindness of Dr Bernd Wollner, Museumsleiter and Herr Alfred Schneider, Schulleiter. Fr. Natalie Gutgesell has cheerfully interpreted and translated for me for more than a decade. While all these organisations and the major books from them try to represent the history or current state of the craft throughout the Federal Republic, it is inevitable that my knowledge is biased towards the central-southern regions.
3. Will, C. (1978) 'Die Korbflechterie'. Callwey Verlag München. English translation (1985) by Edward Force, 'International Basketry for Weavers and Collectors'. Schiffer Publishing Ltd.
4. Dippold, G. (1994) 'Deutsches Korbmuseum Michelau (Begleitbuch zur Dauerausstellung)'. Schriften des Deutschen Korbmuseums Michelau Nr. 2.
5. Tapper, U. (1986) 'Das Wannenmacher - Museum zu Emsdetten'. Stadt Emsdetten.
6. Thierschmann, M. (1991) 'Die Schennkötzen aus Kammerbach und Lutter Kassel.' See review by G.M. Pot-van Regteren Altena, (1991) Wilg & Mand 3: 52-54.
7. Gandert, A. (1963) 'Tragkörbe in Hessen'. IM Eric-Roth-Verlag, Kassel.
8. Goymer, S. (1997) BA NL 80:18.

Alpine Regions

Coiled straw work on the
balcony of a farmhouse in the
Open-air Museum, Bad
Tatzmannsdorf, Burgenland,
Austria

Coppiced hazel near Appenzel,
East Switzerland

Resources

Switzerland, Austria and Slovenia all share part of Europe's highest mountain range which covers up to 70% of their land areas. (France and Italy also have Alpine regions but to a smaller extent.) Although comparatively young in geological terms, the range has been deeply dissected by rivers and also heavily glaciated so that there are many through routes between north and south. While the typical Alpine climate gives cold, snowy winters and cool summers in all three countries, this changes towards a more continental regime in the east including Lower Austria (around Vienna) while the coastal parts of Slovenia have a Mediterranean climate. Thus much of the natural vegetation has been coniferous forest, but on the plateaus and lower slopes, deciduous trees including oak and hazel grow well with willow in the valleys.

The proportion of land under arable cultivation has never been high. The lower slopes and valley fields have produced cereals (wheat and rye), vegetables and fruit, and hay as winter feed for cattle which grazed the higher pastures in summer. Straw was therefore available on the Swiss central plateau and in eastern Austria.

History

Switzerland was always sparsely populated without many towns since it had few natural resources for either industry or farming. The country grew up around its forest regions with a tradition of independence and thriftiness leading to small industries which exported sound workmanship. Austria, by contrast, except for the towns controlling north-south trade routes across the Alps, grew up not around its extensive mountain areas, but by exploiting the Danubian lowlands east of Vienna, and developing the vast Austro-Hungarian Empire which was finally lost only after World War I.

In 1815 both these countries had only some 6% of their populations in towns, rising to between 20 and 30% by 1925 (when England and Wales had 70%).

Slovenia, though settled by Slavs from the Carpathians in the 6th century, was administered by German Franks from the mid-8th century and the Habsburg dynasty from the early 14th century. Although it fell inside the communist bloc after World War II, it was always the most westward-looking part of the former Yugoslavia, and the first to break away in 1992.

The comparatively late growth of urbanisation throughout these Alpine regions would have kept basketry crafts longer in the farms and villages than in northwest Europe.

Switzerland has produced high-quality work in white willow: old baskets in the Open-air Museum, Ballenberg (below), and (left) the resident basketmaker working in brown willow, 1998

Nevertheless, Imperial Austria was the first to develop trade schools in the late 19th century. There were eventually some 30 such schools and teaching workshops deriving from the initial school in Vienna. These even served as examples for the Lichtenfels school, described earlier in the German chapter. Switzerland too was influenced by developments in Germany and Austria at this time and urban workshops were busy until the end of World War II producing high-quality work in willow. After that time, as further north, many skilled basketmakers moved into better-paid jobs, and competition from imports and new packaging caused the total industry to shrink with no apprenticeships and no school. Today, as in other regions, the surviving willow workers are serving different markets while those using other materials are mainly older rural craftsmen and women.

Traditional dough basket in coiled willow finding a new life displaying cured meats in Vienna

Types of work

Straw work

As discussed in the chapter on materials, straw is employed in basketry not as single stems, but as bundles or plaits. It is this aggregation process and the fact that the stems are hollow which gives rise to the three major qualities which differentiate straw articles from those made of individual solid rods.

Above : Coiled straw bee skeps (with willow at rear) in the Apicultural Museum, Radovljica, Slovenia

Above right: Coiled straw bee skep with two types of stitching, Burgenland Landesmuseum, Austria

First is the heat insulation provided. Thatched houses are well known to be warm in winter but remain cool in summer. So when man developed beekeeping in cold areas like the Alpine region, he often replaced the horizontal clay tubes used in the Middle East by upright hives of coiled straw. (In the main forest areas where cereals could not be grown, board, barrel, or log hives gradually replaced the use of tree-holes). Wheat or rye straw was bound with skein made from bramble (blackberry), or less frequently willow, or hazel, and sometimes spruce root. These straw hives were vulnerable to rain in the wetter districts and needed protection in the form of a loose outer cover of combed straw, or they would be kept under a roof while retaining access for the bees to the outside. Bee 'houses' where all the hives are kept close together under a verandah are still a feature of Slovenian beekeeping today, though the individual hives are now wooden boxes with moveable frames.

Left: Beehives on a sunny ledge, Austrian Open-air Museum, Stübing near Graz, Styria

Right: Traditional bee house with straw skeps under cover and accessed from inside, Open-air Museum, Bad Tatzmannsdorf, Austria

Range of coiled straw dough baskets (mostly), on sale in Piringsdorf, Burgenland, Austria

Dough baskets were widely used. These were shallow coiled bowls that were round, oval, or long in which the fermenting dough is placed for its final rise before being inverted onto the oven floor for baking. Since the yeast's activity is increased with temperature it is desirable to keep the rising dough warm, and this was achieved inside these straw bowls. In extreme cold conditions, people might wear over-boots of straw, though they were probably too bulky and fragile to use for much walking. Coiled straw mats were sometimes used on house floors.

The second valuable property of straw is its relative impermeability when tightly coiled. Most houses would have a variety of coil-work containers to hold dry goods: grain, other seeds, meal, nuts, or dried fruits. They were

Coiled straw containers for dry goods in house and barn.

Above left: Landesmuseum Joanneum, Schloss Stainz, Styria, Austria

Centre: Ptuj Regional Museum, Slovenia

Above: Open-air Museum, Bad Tatzmannsdorf, Burgenland,

Far left: Meal basket used under a hand mill, Landesmuseum Joanneum, Schloss Stainz, Styria, Austria

Left: Underside of meal basket, Landesmuseum, Joanneum, Schloss Stainz, Styria, Austria

made in all shapes and sizes with or without handles of straw or wood, and sometimes with close fitting lids. Where they were moved frequently, they might have wooden runners underneath to take the wear from the straw. In the barns or store-rooms quite large ones were used for keeping grain for later consumption, or for use as seed in the spring. The museum at Stainz in eastern Austria even has an example of a fire bucket of coiled straw. Presumably after first soaking it would hold water well enough for the purpose!

A round, oval, or kidney-shaped seedlip was used when broadcasting seed (scattering it by hand over the ploughed ground). It might have a single round wooden handle across the shorter width (like a conventional arm basket) or two attachment points for a neckband on one long side, and perhaps an upright stick or third handle on the opposite side to be grasped by the sower.

Below left and right: Coiled straw seedlips, Landesmuseum Joanneum, Schloss Stainz, Styria, Austria and centre: Ljubljana, Slovenia

Left: Egg container in coiled straw,
Landesmuseum, Joanneum,
Schloss Stainz, Styria, Austria

Right: Glass bottles protected by coiled straw plait,
Open-air Museum, Ballenberg, Switzerland

Modern coiled straw work stitched with plastic tape, Ljubljana market, Slovenia, 1996

A third characteristic of coiled straw is its soft resilience which made it suitable for holding or carrying fragile objects. The Austrians used it to make containers where eggs could be collected and held. Many types of bottles and jars were protected by being enclosed in a spiral of thick straw plait or twisted rope.

Most of these articles could of course be made of willow rods or other wood. It is noticeable that many more coiled straw containers are to be found in eastern Austria, with its drier climate and widespread cereal cultivation, than in wetter Switzerland where cattle raising predominated and willow could often be grown. Straw work was widespread in Slovenia and also in parts of neighbouring Croatia - here included in the Balkan chapter.

Root work

In the higher alpine regions where coniferous trees largely replaced broadleaves, the local population naturally utilised what was easily available – the long, even-diameter, surface roots of pine, larch, and spruce. They often used the material with a coiling technique where the root centre forms a single core and is stitched to the adjacent rows by the spiral binding made from a section of the root skin. Skeined root was also used as the weavers in stake and strand or frame construction. The Tyrolean Regional Heritage Museum in Innsbruck has examples of larch root work which illustrate these different techniques.

Root work baskets in Tyrolean Regional Heritage Museum, Innsbruck, Austria.

From left to right:
Coiled arm basket on three legs

Coiled apple basket with two handles to attach to the picker's belt

Rib basket

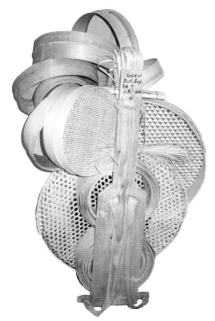

Far left: 'Dry goods' sellers in Bled, Slovenia (2004 re-enactment)

Left: A back frame loaded with sieves, Slovenia

Wood foundation

In forested regions it was natural for many people to have well-developed woodworking skills. In addition to building houses and furniture, they also made many additional articles out of wood including barrels, buckets, bowls, spoons, and dairy utensils for butter and cheese making. Slovenians in particular were well known for these 'dry goods', and the makers used to travel long distances carrying their wares on their backs and selling in fairs and markets or from door to door. Some of these articles brought together the normally separate crafts of carving, joinery, and basketry.

It is this type of work which deserves a mention here (as also in the Nordic lands chapter). Perhaps sieves with varying mesh sizes are at one extreme end of basketry (the inner surface was woven wood splint inserted within a flat wooden rim). But oval or rectangular baskets to be carried on the arm or the back, or used for gathering produce, are frequently started with a solid wooden plank base. The side stakes may be wood splint or round willow rods, and are firmly anchored in holes drilled around the periphery of the base. The weaving, again using wood splint (often spruce in Slovenia), or willow rods continues up to the usual types of border. Handles made from chestnut or hazel rods may be single bows placed centrally across the short axis, or along the length of one side, or two smaller ones facing each other.

Plank base basket, Open-air Museum, Ballenberg, Switzerland

Below left and centre: Two baskets in spruce splint on plank base, Ljubljana market, Slovenia, 1995

Below : Wood splint arm basket on plank base, Slovene Ethnographic Museum, Ljubljana

2

3

1. Back carrier for liquids (whey?) in staved timber, Austrian Open-air Museum, Stübing near Graz, Styria

2. Slatted bread carrier, Open-air Museum, Ballenberg, Switzerland

3. Slatted bread carrier with bands woven in white willow, Open-air Museum, Ballenberg, Switzerland

4. Crude hay carrier in wood slats with weaving in hazel splint, Open-air Museum, Ballenberg, Switzerland

5. General purpose carrier with weaving in hazel splint and brown willow, Open-air Museum, Ballenberg, Switzerland

6. Back basket in white and brown willow. (Note the construction of the base similar to Polish D-baskets.) Ljubljana market, Slovenia

7. Leaf or grass basket (kos) in brown and white willow skein made by Franc Kozelj from Reva, Dolenjska region, Slovenia

4

5

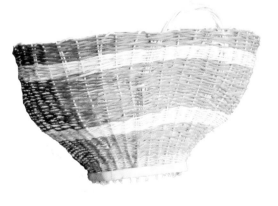

6

7

Specific items

Back baskets

These Alpine regions are the obvious places to expect loads to be carried on the back rather than on wheeled transport. The range and combination of different woodworking skills noted in the previous section is also a feature of their back baskets which show a fascinating progression.

The solid staved carrier for liquid, perhaps whey, milk, or buttermilk, would not normally be classified as a basket but more as a wooden bucket or barrel made by a cooper. Nevertheless, it stands at one end of a series. At the other end, the simple bread carrier consisting of round or flat wooden rods inserted into curved rims at the base and top, with only a single central cross support, also uses joinery skills rather than weaving.

But then exactly the same principles are found in what are clearly baskets where the coarse flat stakes are held in place at the centre and rim by a few rows of rough weaving. Such large containers would have been used to carry mown grass or hay down the mountainside for animal feed, and the absence of close weaving would keep down the weight.

Where smaller articles needed to be carried either within the farm or to and from markets, then such open work would not be suitable, and tight weaving with split hazel, round or split willow is found. Sometimes bands of unpeeled weavers are used to provide decoration. These Alpine back baskets are quite tall and thin, without handles. The load would be carried high on the back by means of leather, fabric, or willow straps. At the small base (often plank) they may be square, oblong, or semi-circular while they flow out to become oval, circular, or flattened at the rim, or even shaped against the wearer's back.

In Slovenia they made a back basket (*kos*) whose sides flowed out further to give greater volume, and provided a stout bow handle against the back and sometimes a second one on the opposite face. The load of leaves or grass could be supported by a stick threaded through, or a hand grasping it over the shoulder. They were made in split hazel or split willow, though the willow does not keep its shape so well in a large basket.

In south east Austria near Graz, a quite different construction method is found in large wood-splint back baskets[1]. These are meant to stand on the ground and usually have three feet attached to a stout base cradle, but sometimes this is extended so that the whole rests on two thick runners (as on a sledge). No doubt the largest sizes were used mainly for storage within the barns. The wide wood splint (beech, chestnut or hazel) which forms the base is narrowed as it bends up to make the side stakes. The characteristic stirrup-shaped hazel rod which pierces the base cradle to provide the feet gives stability and it is sometimes woven in to form corner posts. The final shape at the rim may be circular, strongly oval, or almost square. In the German chapter I describe a similar design but which was made even more solidly in oak splint. It was made in the Swabian Alps: a long way away, but still part of this same culture.

Detailed drawing by Fr. Simon of the construction of a Buckelkorb, a wood splint back basket from east Austria built around a three-legged cradle[1]

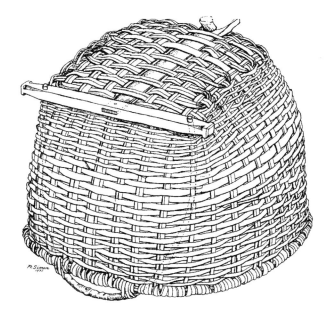

173

Finally, a rare survivor from the 19th century is on display at the Stadtmuseum in Friesach, west of Graz, Austria. This is an original ore-carrying basket, beautifully made in this same three-legged style, part joiner's art, part basketry, though quite small, presumably because the metal ore weighed heavily.

The variety of back baskets to be seen in the many museums of Switzerland, Austria, and Slovenia is remarkable. Peasant farming survived long in these regions so their use persisted well into the 20th century and they were available for collection when open-air museums were being stocked. In 2000 my wife and I attended a tiny market in an Alpine village in northern Italy (Gurro) where the local hazel splint basket was still being carried by shoppers. In other countries where farming and rural life changed much earlier, we can only retrieve craft items which are much more durable than baskets.

Cart bodies

Farm transport in the lowland parts of these regions would often have involved two-wheeled carts or four-wheeled wagons drawn by horse or oxen. In the winter sledges were used. While some loads like timber, or hay and straw would be easily carried on a flat deck with only a simple wooden framework for support, others would need to be contained. Woven bodies were in widespread use made in wood-splint, or round hazel or willow rods, or even straw plait. I came across a Slovenian farmer using such a cart to carry manure to his fields near Ljubljana in 1995.

Farm cart
Left and facing page below: Two examples of woven bodies using hazel rods on farm vehicles in Austrian Open-air Museum, Stübing near Graz, Styria

Plaited straw bags

While many uses of straw were detailed in the earlier section, there are yet more types which flourished in the past. In Switzerland, there is a whole museum dedicated to the history of fine straw work (in Wohlen)[2] and there was an industry making hats out of straw braid in the 18th century. In Slovenia too this developed, and while straw hats may not usually be considered as basketry (since they were made by sewing straw braid) another related craft clearly is. Narrow two-handled bags are made by check-weaving narrow strips of straw plait of various colours into characteristic patterns frequently incorporating the owner's initials. These bags became a regular part of the Slovene national costume in the early 20th century. There are also examples where straw braid has been used as a weaver on fine baskets producing bands of colour and texture quite different from those made by the usual willow rods.

Slovenian women carrying bags made from straw plait as part of their national costumes, parade in Bled.

Left : detail of bag

Lidded basket in willow with panels in straw plait, Open-air Museum, Ballenberg, Switzerland

Frame log baskets

During one visit to Ljubljana in April 2003, I acquired an English language copy of a most beautiful book covering the whole range of Slovenian handicrafts[3]. This listed over 20 basketmakers working at the time of publication (1999) with excellent studio photographs of their work. A particular type of oval frame basket caught my eye by the way the rib ends were anchored into two short lengths of timber fitted into the ends of the rim hoop. The following year my wife and I had the opportunity to try to track down one of the makers. Over the years we have learned how to attempt this in spite of severely limited linguistic skills. The hamlet where Franc Kozelj lived was not even shown on our excellent map, but a series of fortunate encounters eventually brought us

Frame log basket (poltr) in brown willow skein made by Franc Kozelj from Reva, Dolenjska region, Slovenia

Right: Franc Kozelj from Reva, Dolenjska region, Slovenia who makes several types of frame baskets in willow skein

to his door where sure enough he could show us his *poltr*, as well as the huge leaf or grass carrier (*kos*) which was illustrated earlier.

At the time I assumed the *poltr* was exclusive to this south-eastern part of Slovenia. Since then I have come across a photograph of a very similar design in the possession of a farm museum at Frensdorf near Bamberg across the Alps in southern Germany[4], and there is one in the museum in Villaines-les-Rochers, France.

Notes and references

1. Simon, F. (1981) 'Bäuerliche Bauten und Geräte'. Sudburgenland und Grenzgebiete-oberschützen. This book has beautiful architectural drawings of regional baskets and other craft objects.
2. Freiämter Strohmuseum, Wohlen, Switzerland.
3. Bogataj, J. (1999) 'Handicrafts of Slovenia – encounters with contemporary Slovene craftsmen'. Rokus.
4. Smyth, P. (1991) 'Osier Culture and Basket-making'. The author has written an account of past basketmaking in Northern Ireland, but on p67 included an image of a frame basket in the Frensdorf Bauernmuseum, near Bamberg which is strikingly similar to a type still made across the Alps in Slovenia.

Today some Swiss village houses display old winnowing fans as decoration

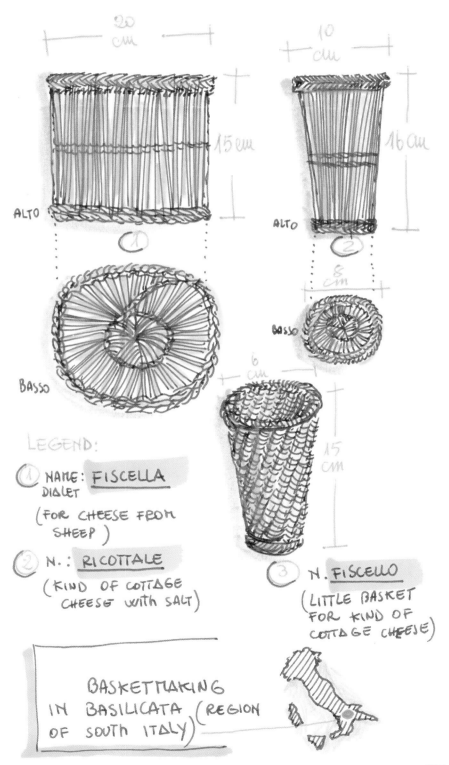

20 cm

15 cm

ALTO

①

Basso

10 cm

16 cm

ALTO

②

8 cm

Basso

6 cm

15 cm

③

LEGEND:

① NAME: FISCELLA
DIALET
(FOR CHEESE FROM
SHEEP)

② N.: RICOTTALE
(KIND OF COTTAGE
CHEESE WITH SALT)

③ N. FISCELLO
(LITTLE BASKET
FOR KIND OF
COTTAGE CHEESE)

BASKETMAKING
IN BASILICATA (REGION
OF SOUTH ITALY)

Cheese moulds as used in Basilicata
sketched by M Cecere

The Italian climate changes a lot from one region to another. Sheep and lentils are produced below the desolate slopes of the Monti Sibillini

Resources

This long thin land stretches 1300km from its border with Switzerland to its southern sea coast on a level with North Africa. With the Alps in the north and the limestone Appennine hills stretching from Genoa in the northwest corner right down into Sicily, only one quarter of the country is easily cultivable: the coastal regions and northern plain. Nevertheless, this plain is larger than the whole of the Netherlands. These features produce an extraordinary variety of climate and topography, which in turn dictate the vegetation, and hence the materials available for basket making.

From the Alps down to Florence the summers are hot and the winters freezing with rainfall concentrated in summer and autumn. Below Rome the typical Mediterranean climate has hot, dry summers with rain in autumn and winter leading to semi-arid conditions. Cereals are autumn sown and harvested in spring. Other crops have to be drought resistant or rely on irrigation. The vegetation is reduced to wiry grasses and shrubs where the soils are too poor.

The alpine coniferous forest gives way in the centre to deciduous woodland. Plants utilised in basketry have included chestnut, ash, elm, beech, lime, pine, cork oak, clematis, blackberry, dog rose, Spanish broom, and no doubt many other shrubs. Cultivated trees include olive, hazel, mulberry, and willow. Pastures provide grasses (and the asphodel in Sardinia) while arable fields give wheat and rye straw. The extensive marshes used to contain rushes, sedges, reeds, and hemp. Many roadside and waste areas in coastal regions have been colonised by the bamboo-like grass or tall reed, the Mediterranean cane. The palm *Chamaerops humilis* grows in some mainland areas and in Sardinia.

History

The Greeks brought their city states to areas of fertile soils near Naples and into Sicily in the 8th century BC, cultivating vines and olives. They already had sophisticated basketry skills which they utilised to make a range of items for everyday city life and for religious ceremonies including the deposition of grave goods. The Etruscans, who were skilled craftsmen, developed parts of the west coast and created cities, including Rome,

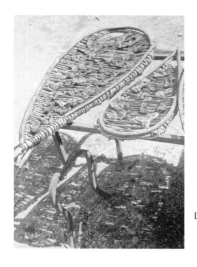

Drying figs in the sun on a graticcio,
Sesto, Lucca 1982.
Photo: Gastone Venturelli

Citrus fruit in Alghero market,
Sardinia

between 800 and 500BC. This Roman civilisation remained until the 5th and 6th centuries AD.

Under Roman rule, the lowland areas were gradually taken over by estates with villas and large arable farms worked by hired or slave labour. But very large parts of the peninsula are uplands which continued to be occupied by Italian subsistence farmers whose way of life had evolved over millennia. Their descendants remained to farm the land for centuries after Imperial Rome had gone. We are fortunate that the classical Greek and Roman civilisations left a great deal of written evidence of man's activities from these times. While the authors naturally concentrated on urban matters, and on the estates which supplied their cities, the diligent researcher can glean much from their writings on the way of life of the native Italian peasants.

Joan Frayn has compiled a list of the minimum equipment which would have been possessed by such an Italian smallholder in the Roman period from 500BC to 200AD[1]. It is of interest to reproduce it here since it tells us something authoritative about the families' activities and hence their likely requirements for basketry. The articles are grouped in three categories: the more durable items, those containing a considerable proportion of wood or other perishable substance leaving little trace for the archaeologist, and those not present on every holding – depending on specialist activities.

Perishable	Baskets, broom, dibble, flat trays, hurdles, ladders, plough, rope, shovel, sieve, winnowing fan
More durable	Axe, bucket, candlestick, handmill, hoe, jars and basins, knives, ladles, lamps and lanterns, milk boiler, milking pail, pestle and mortar, poker, pruning knife, rake, saw, scythe, spade, wine vat
Not on every holding	Beehives, loom, oil press, troughs, yoke and harness

General purpose baskets would have been used for carrying or holding everyday goods, both on the smallholding and for taking things to and from neighbours and markets. In addition, more specialised baskets were needed. These would be to sieve and winnow grain; contain bees and catch swarms; hold olives for pressing; strain oil, wine and honey; gather grapes; dry fruit; collect grass and hay; make cheese; provide shoes and muzzles for oxen and horses; and fans for the fire, besides forming components of furniture and cart bodies.

Carrying hay in a gabbia da foraggio,
Gallicano, 1979.
Photo: Gastone Venturelli

These same written records include references to the wide range of plant materials which was employed. They also confirm that suitable willow varieties were being selected and cultivated for basket making, though no doubt many smallholders continued to rely on those wild types which were available locally. In addition there have even been a few basketry items preserved in very wet or very dry conditions and discovered by archaeologists, as well as others shown in sculptures and mosaics illustrating their use[2].

Much has been written about the 'colleges' of ancient Rome (voluntary associations of traders or employers devoted to a specific line of commerce or production), but there is little mention of basket making[3]. After the chaos following the decline of the Roman Empire, Italy was divided into Duchies. Normans settled in the south in the 11th century. After this, northern Italy began to flourish again and was one of the most urbanised regions of Europe by medieval times. Records surviving from the 12th and 13th centuries show that cities like Genoa, Bologna, and Siena had well-structured groups of artisans working at, and controlling, their various trades, and these must surely have included basketry. On the other hand, no craft or professional guilds existed in the countryside. Spain ruled in the 16th century and Austria in 18th century, so that a great deal of cultural interchange must have occurred. The city states were only united into a single country in 1870, and at that time Italy was still largely agricultural with widespread poverty driving massive emigration until 1900. As in other countries, new demands for baskets to take goods in and out of the growing urban centres then led to the opening of more than a dozen trade schools at the beginning of the 20th century. Today it is the fifth most densely populated country in Europe after the Low Countries, Britain, and Germany.

Types of work

With this history of early development of northern cities and industrialisation, but also of rural poverty in the south and in the mountains, we would expect a wide range of basketry to have survived until recent times, from professional willow work to ancient peasant designs in many other materials. I have therefore been surprised how little willow work is represented in the numerous Italian ethnographic museums which we have managed to visit. This may be because they usually have a rural bias. Or it could be that my sample has been unlucky: it would take a lifetime to visit (and find open) all the 476 ethnographic museums listed in the extensive guide published in 1997[4]!

In this, as in other chapters, there is only space to feature a few of many types of work produced in such a highly varied country.

Rush work

The region south of the Po delta and northwest of Ravenna is now devoted to pastures and fruit production, but the land was once poorly drained and covered in a variety of wetland species. Naturally the local population made the best of this difficult environment. They harvested the reeds, sedges, rushes and small trees, and produced a wide range of articles including mats, strings, ropes, brooms, chairs, poultry cages, hats, bags, shoes, baskets, and roof-thatch.

These activities finally finished by the 1970s, but a group of enterprising people formed the Centre for Marshland Ethnography in the village of Villanova di Bagna Cavallo which had earlier been an important manufacturing centre for wetland products. Examples of these articles are preserved and displayed, and the voluntary staff aim to keep the old crafts alive through documentation, courses, and festivals. The Centre emphasises five different plants: reed, reedmace, sedge, freshwater rush, and the pointed rush which grows in brackish water. In addition it utilises willow and the Mediterranean cane.

We called in during the spring of 2000 and the Centre's energetic curator Maria Rosa Bagnari introduced us to all these products. This has led to a valuable relationship with the Basketmakers' Association of Britain. Several members have been to the annual festival in September, and some have taken classes in rush work which is the Centre's primary focus.

Many different shapes and sizes of rush bags were made from the inner leaves of the reedmace which was harvested in August and dried for several months. The long leaves were then damped and split lengthwise. Stakes were cut to length, sufficient to go across the base and up both sides. The base was woven first and this was then nailed to a wooden mould before continuing the weaving around both sides.

Broad, soft rushes from the bulrush or reedmace are familiar in chair seats. The rushes are twisted together into a continuous coil which is then wrapped around the rails and across the seat frame. In Tuscany the same technique is used to create baskets by threading the coil around a wooden frame and ribs.

Above left: Weaving a rush bag over a mould, Centre for Marshland Ethnography, Villanova di Bagnacavallo, Ravenna. Photo: E Sailler Airone

Above: Shoes made from rush, Centre for Marshland Ethnography, Villanova di Bagnacavallo, Ravenna

Twisted rush on a simple wooden frame from Tuscany. Pigeon nest by Donati Giulio, Asciano and miniature arm basket (below)

Weaving the fiscella from narrow-
stemmed rush.
Photos: M. Cecere

The narrow-stemmed rushes grow widely in wet places in Italy and throughout the Mediterranean. One use to which they have been put since Roman times has been the dainty cheese moulds into which fresh curd was pressed to drain and begin maturation.

Pressing the sheep's milk curd
into the rush moulds.
Photo: M. Cecere

Below: Lidded grain storage bin
in coiled straw, Civico Museo
Etnografico Romagnola, Forlì,
Emilia-Romagna

Right : Sieve (or cheese strainer)
in coiled straw, Bosa, Sardinia

Most cheese was traditionally made from sheep's milk, and flocks were frequently on the move in a system of transhumance. They followed the pasture growth from low to higher ground, or from inland to the coasts, on an annual cycle. The shepherds would gather these rushes and weave the *fiscelle* themselves during mid- to late summer. In the Basilicata region of the far south, they used *Juncus conglomeratus*, and their pattern involved a large number of bottom stakes held in place by one ring of fitching and continued through one or two rows of upset to form the side stakes[5]. The side had one central row of fitching and a simple plaited border. A related type also with open-work fitched sides was used in the Salento (Apulia) region in the extreme southeast as both a filter and container for ricotta cheese (a soft cheese made from whey) which needs to be drained after heating[6]. When the fresh ricotta cheese was turned out upside down, it carried the impression of the basket on its surface. Today, when plastic has replaced rush, the new moulds are made to give a similar pattern on factory-made ricotta. Further north, in the Aurunci region, both base and sides were much more closely woven using *J. acutus*[7].

Coiled work

Willow is not naturally suited to the drier areas of Italy and its islands Sicily and Sardinia, and so alternative vegetation has had to be utilised which in turn demands different weaving techniques. Coiling can utilise many types of grass, sedge, and straw for the inner core. The plainer versions occur throughout the peninsula, primarily where tight weaving is

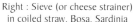

Coiled platters in dyed raffia. Left: from ISOLA, Sassari, Sardinia, and right: from Castelsardo, Sardinia

required to contain grain, seeds, or flour often in large quantities. The stitching material used in the south was sometimes palm leaf, and this tradition continues today using the imported leaves of another palm growing in Madagascar, usually called raffia. This is often dyed to produce brightly coloured patterns.

In Sardinia, another wrapping material was created from the dried and split stems of the asphodel, a plant of the lily family. This species is widely distributed on the island growing in dry stony soils but also in wet pastures where it may reach a height of 150cm. The stiff flower stalks are harvested in late spring and dried. Later they are split lengthwise and dried further. Sedge stems or asphodel leaves are coiled and sewn together with split asphodel stems. The products are platters, bowls, and even large, flat storage containers for grain, flour, and other farm and household goods. The larger ones were left plain while use was made of the natural colour variation (pale buff to dark brown) to weave traditional patterns in the smaller items. In the finest examples, the central flat disk was covered with a patterned woven fabric. The tradition is being continued by women in Castelsardo and other villages who often work in the doorways of their houses. ISOLA, the Sardinian craft organisation, markets some delightful modern interpretations.

Shallow grain container in coiled asphodel, Casa di Grazia Deledda, Nuoro, Sardinia

Left: Grain basket in coiled asphodel, Museo Nazionale delle Arti e Tradizioni Popolari, Rome

Left: Coiled work for sale in Castelsardo, Sardinia

Right: Coiled platter in asphodel with fabric centre, Museo Sardo di Antropologia ed Etnografia, Cittadella Universitaria, Cagliari, Sardinia

Bottle covers

From left above:

Willow,
Museo della Cultura Popolare
Padana, San Benedetto,
Po, Lombardia

Fine willow,
Wine museum, Torgiano, Umbria

Coiled straw (or grass) plait,
Wine museum, Torgiano, Umbria

'Cane' and willow,
Museo civico,
San Ferdinando di Puglia

Bottle covers

Fragile glass bottles have always needed protection, particularly when round bottomed, and examples of woven willow or coiled or plaited straw covers are common for flasks, demi-johns, and carboys. The flasks of Chianti wine, so popular in Britain after World War II, were half covered in straw and given a coiled flat base so that they would stand on a table. The Aurunci mountains, northwest of Naples, have their higher slopes covered in rope grass which has been utilised in ways similar to the esparto of southern Spain. The dried material yielded fibres which were processed into ropes. These, and simple lengths of grass plait were used for coiling around demi-johns, as well as being sewn together to make bags and baskets[8]. But the very finest work is seen on smaller bottles used to hold spirits or liqueurs, and Sardinia has a continuing tradition using narrow rush. Maria Raimonda Pinna covers slender wine bottles to produce some of the

Livia Forte and her work in coiled
plaits of rope grass
(Ampelodesmos), Maranola, near
the Aurunci mountains.,
Latina province,
Photo: D. Novellino

184

Coiled straw (or grass) plait,
Museo del Lavoro Contadino,
Brisighella, Emilia-Romagna

most exquisite articles imaginable in her home in San Vero Milis and markets them through ISOLA. I first noticed these in a shop selling local produce in Alghero and was permitted to photograph them. I needed to return to the island briefly the next year when the Castelsardo museum had reopened, and determined to visit the maker. Not having her address, I was helped successively by the local bartender, one of her customers, and then several immediate neighbours who encouraged me to persist even when normal polite knocking had convinced me the house was empty. I was eventually asked to return after lunch, and then welcomed to an amazing display of fine craftwork spanning three quite different techniques. I had inferred from the entry in her sales brochure (translated as 'a basket factory') that Maria had a team of outworkers, but it soon became clear that she was the sole creator of these beautiful stake and strand fine-rush bowls, coiled bowls, and covered bottles. In spite of my lack of Italian or Sardinian, we spent a delightful afternoon. She demonstrated the technique of using fine rush (as used in traditional cheese moulds) to create delicate shallow bowls, and I came away with samples of the different rushes and the finished items, including a prized slender covered bottle.

Fine rush-covered bottle
by Maria Raimonda Pinna,
San Vero Milis, Sardinia

The base begins with a two-across-two slath, but extra stakes are gradually inserted until there are no fewer than 120 at the rim. These continue up the sides while gradually reducing in number by about two-thirds at the narrow neck. The weavers produce an astonishingly rich surface decoration in several ways: by varying the number of stakes passed in front or behind, by changing the weave, and by using dyed weavers (dark brown instead of natural). Even the cork stopper has its own separate cover. The result is perhaps the finest piece of basketry I have ever seen (although some split-bamboo work in China used material of even smaller diameter). Maria has been featured over many years in articles and books on Sardinian craftwork and we must hope that she has passed on her skills to a subsequent generation.

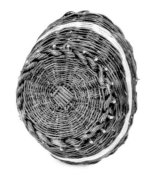

From left to right: Brown and white willow, Torgiano, Umbria

Underside showing base

White willow, Torgiano, Umbria

Specific items

In addition to the major types of work already featured, there are several specific baskets and materials which, while perhaps not unique to Italy, are certainly characteristic and well worth noting.

Arm baskets

Some of the commonest baskets in any country are simple round or oval articles with a single arch handle, designed to be held on the crooked arm or in the hand with the arm fully extended. They are used domestically for gathering, transporting or storage. In many countries they would today almost always be made in willow, but in Italy one can still find them in other materials or styles.

'Rope' borders are characteristic of central regions, from the Po Valley and Umbria down to Lazio and Tuscany (and are also found in Spain). In some brown willow examples from near Perugia, five or more rods (the ends of the vertical side stakes) are twisted around each other while at the same time being twisted around one or two similar strands, as in a rope, to form an attractive border. The central handle may be formed from two or three such ropes, and the foot may be worked in a similar way. Where the technique is used, the basket sits on this basal rope and the base stakes are trimmed slightly proud of the side weaving to ensure the ropes stay in place.

From left to right: Hazel rods, Canepina, Lazio

Hazel splint on plank base, Museo Civico dei Costumi e delle Tradizioni Locali, Gurro, Piemonte

Thin chestnut splint, Museo delle Tradizioni Popolari Canepina, Lazio

Trees grown for their fruit or nuts have provided by-product stems as alternatives to willow. Hazel and sweet chestnut groves produce thin shoots which emerge from the ground around the main stem. These can attain considerable lengths during their first year while remaining slender and unbranched. I found it hard to believe that hazel was used in this way until I was driven up into the hills above Canepina to be shown the

rods growing in abundance and given a basket made from them. Unwanted stems from olive trees and grape vines grow out in the same way. These, as well as fine elm rods, dogwood and myrtle, may be used for the base and side stakes where the weavers are willow, 'cane', or clematis.

On the Amalfi coast south of Naples, chestnut splint was still being used in 2001 to make arm baskets. The base and side stakes are some 3mm thick and 20-35mm wide. The weavers are narrower, around 5-7mm, and beaten down tight. Bye stakes are added as the shape flows out to the rim. All the stakes are then reduced in width and thickness, bent over, and tucked under the penultimate row of weaving. For fruit picking the baskets are sometime lined with canvas. Since I would judge that none of the arm baskets illustrated here was made in a professional willow workshop, it is perhaps surprising that half of them are built up from the separate round or oval base which is the characteristic technique of such workshops. We often observe that part-time basketmakers use the frame technique. While some Italian frame baskets can be found, they seem far less common than, for example, in France.

Drying tray – *graticcio*

The *graticcio* is the simplest type of frame basket. It is an almost flat tray usually created by bending an ash, willow, or chestnut rod back onto itself so that it has one round and one pointed end. A second rod may be similarly positioned below, and slightly inside, the first to form the first pair of ribs. Three or four additional single ribs are inserted along the long axis. Alternatively, the second rod may be placed on top of the first after the weaving is completed to create an edge to the tray. The weavers of clematis, grapevine, twisted rush, split bramble, chestnut, willow or wild rose go across the short axis. There are no handles. In other forms, two rim rods may be fastened to produce a spindle shape with points at both ends. Or the shape may be defined within two rods forking from a main stem and finishing with a flat end. It is a simple peasant basket for use at home to dry fruit or tomatoes in the sun or a cool oven.

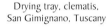
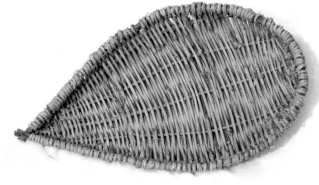

Above: Donati Giulio who worked in rush, clematis and willow, Asciano, Tuscany, 2000

Drying trays (graticcio) woven in a variety of materials
From left to right above:
Fine willow and clematis, Montalcino, Tuscany

Spanish broom and wild rose weavers; and (far right above) frame made from a forked ash branch
San Paulo Albanese, Basilicata

Right: Valletto in brown willow, collected in Annecy (France)

Far right: Carrying the valletto in the Tuscan countryside 1979.
Photo: G. Venturelli, Centro Tradizioni Popolari di Lucca

Below: Three varieties of valletto collected in the Lucca area of Tuscany for the Centro Tradizioni Popolari di Lucca.
Photos: Cortopassi di Luciano Ceccotti

Mountain carrying basket – *valletto*

I first found this basket on a stall in Annecy (France) in 1990 and only gradually tracked down its origins[9]. The *valletto* is another frame basket bearing some resemblance to the drying try, although deeper. It is also based upon a chestnut, ash, or willow rod bent through almost 180 degrees so as to create one round end. The

other end may take various forms: a point, a square where the two rod ends are not quite brought together, or a curve where one end is brought inside the other. In most cases the shape is sub-oval or trapezoidal – the round end is wider than the flat or blunt end, and is also deeper. Two side handles are created by not bringing the cross weaving (brown willow or cleft chestnut) right to the rims. These distinctive baskets were for carrying items in the garden or farm (on the shoulders or against the waist) or for drying corn cobs or wool, and were found in the hilly areas of Tuscany and right up into the French Alps and Switzerland. A very similar basket was made in Ireland and the West coast of Scotland where it was used for holding a long baited fishing line in small boats[10] (see p72). Did it perhaps have Celtic origins?

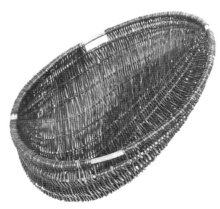

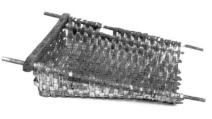

Forage carrier - *gabbia da foraggio*

The *gabbia da forragio* is another crude basket used on small farms especially in upland areas like Tuscany. It may be constructed from two large rods, each bent into a circle with diameter 50-70cm, even up to 150cm. These are placed one above the other, 30-40cm apart, and often joined by vertical or angled stakes scallomed onto the base circle or attached by a simple twist. Inside the base circle is a much smaller one. These two are joined by radiating spokes in the form of a twisted willow rod doubled on itself. The smaller circle has to fit comfortably onto the carrier's head and may be a rope of several twisted willow rods. The overall construction (chestnut, mulberry, or willow circles and usually willow stakes) may be very open, with as few as nine widely spaced vertical stakes. In other examples the more numerous stakes will be held in place by a central row of fitching. The basket is filled with grass, hay, or leaves and carried on the head using one or two hands on the base circle or spokes to steady the load. Crude it may be, but it is a very practical solution to the challenge of keeping the weight down while enclosing a large quantity of loose material for transport back to the farm.

Cage for hen and chickens - *cesta da choiccia i pulcini*

This is another large round structure with openwork sides and a central hole in the base. Half filled with hay, the open basket served as an open-topped nest for the broody hen to incubate her eggs. On hatching, the basket is inverted, the hole covered, and it becomes a cage to contain the hen. The chicks can get out between the stakes but are called back by the hen. In

some cases this cage may be the same as the forage carrier described above, but then there have to be many more vertical stakes (and spokes) placed closer together. In other cases it is made using the 'Perigord' weave, a continuous spiral of plaiting. Variations on this basic design are found throughout Italy from Tuscany across to the Veneto and in France it is call *la mue*[11].

Left: Diagonal stake work in split 'cane' and rush

Right: Diagonal stake bowl in split 'cane' and rush in Alghero market, Sardinia

Diagonal stake work

The traps for fish and crustaceans which are found all along the northern Mediterranean coasts are featured later in the chapter on Cyprus, Greece, Malta, and Turkey, but other baskets are made by the same technique in Sardinia. The side stakes are fine rush set at some 20° to the vertical and secured with twine (originally made from twisted rush) where they cross. The structure is given rigidity by a spiral of split 'cane'. Bowls, two-handled maunds, and arm baskets were all seen in Alghero in 2002[12].

Notes and references

1. Frayn, J. M. (1979) 'Subsistence Farming in Roman Italy'. Centaur Press.
2. Gaitzch, W. (1986) 'Antike Korb und Seilerwaren', Schriften des Limesmuseums Aalen Nr 38, Wurttembergischen Landesmuseums, Stuttgart; Barbier, G., Blanc, N., Coulon, G., Gury, F. and Pichonnet, M. (1999) 'La Vannerie à l'Époque Gallo-Romaine'. Musée d'Argentomagus, Saint-Marcel, Indre; and Bobart, H. H. (1997) 'Basketwork Through the Ages' reprinted by the Basketmakers' Association. All these books have illustrations of basketry items from Roman times.
3. Epstein, S.A. (1991) 'Wage Labor and Guilds in Medieval Europe'. University of North Carolina Press.
4. Togni, R., Forni, G. and Pisani, F. (1997) 'Guida ai Musei Etnografici Italiani'. Leo S. Olschki, Firenze.
5   Cecere, M. (1998) 'Massari e Masserie - forme del lavoro e cultura materiale in Lucania'. Oros & Ganos. This beautiful book celebrates the passing of the large rural estates in the hills of Basilicata, southeast of Naples, and documents the everyday lives of those who worked there.
6   Minonne, F., Mele, C., Albano, A. and Marchiori, S. (2006) 'Salento (Apulia) Southern Italy'. ICEB2005: 668.
7   Novellino, D. (2006) 'Central Italy (Maranola)', ICEB2005: 664-667, and 'Basketry in the Aurunci Mountains (Central Italy)' BA NL 119:25-32, and (2007) BA NL **120**: 45-50.
8. See 7 p667, p29 and p45.
9. Beconcini, P., Giusti, M.E. and Venturelli, G. (1985), 'L'Intrecciatura Tradizionale in Area Lucchese'. Edizioni Quasar. This (out of print) report is a well-illustrated catalogue, with supporting essays, of an exhibition mounted by the Centro Tradizioni Popolari di Lucca in the far northwest of Tuscany.
10. Hogan, J. (2002) 'Basketmaking in Ireland'. Wordwell.
11. Pichonnet, M. (2006) 'Ces Papés - mémoire et tradition de la vannerie en France', Les Brins d'Osier.
12. See also Kuoni, B. (1981) 'Cestería Tradicional Ibérica', Ediciones del Serbal, p261.

Poland and the Baltic States

Coiled straw figure of St Barbara,
Warsaw

Primitive measuring vessels for corn
made from hollowed logs,
State Ethnographic Museum, Warsaw

Resources

Levelled by successive ice ages, the four countries Poland, Lithuania, Latvia, and Estonia occupy part of the north European plain, and are bordered on the south by the slopes of the Carpathian mountains. The soils, which include a fertile strip of clay along the coast, become generally poorer sands further south. Central Poland has a typically continental climate with very cold winters and warm summers, but the Baltic regions are milder under the influence of the sea. The natural mixed forest has been partly cleared for arable cropping though trees still cover one third of Poland. Pine, spruce, juniper, birch, and lime have produced stems, roots, bark, and bast for use in basketry. There are extensive wetland areas around the numerous lakes, river valleys, and coastal bays which provide good conditions for wild and cultivated willow, and also reeds and rushes. Cereals have been widely grown: wheat on the heavier soils and rye on the poorer sands.

History

Today's four independent countries have only recently emerged from successive occupations by the previous empires of Germany, Austria, Sweden, and Russia. While it is convenient to treat them as a group, their origins and some of their histories are diverse. Western Slavs settled in Poland (as well as the Czech Republic and Slovakia) while Lithuania and Latvia were founded by Baltic tribes from west central Russia around 2000BC. The Estonians' ancestors arrived in around 3000BC and were related to the Finns.

Christianity took a long time to replace pagan beliefs, especially in Lithuania, but by the 13th century their societies had evolved as in other parts of Europe. Craft traditions could be classified into three parallel streams. First were the utilitarian crafts of the commoners in towns and peasants in the country which satisfied everyday needs. Next were the journeymen, non-guild members who worked at the manorial complexes of the landed gentry and the larger monasteries. Third were the guild members and independent artisans working in towns like Warsaw, Riga, and Tallinn. There was a tailor's guild in Estonia from 1363, and a goldsmiths' guild from 1393. As in other countries, these governed their crafts, maintaining exclusivity through secrecy. Masters had to have the correct social background, serve long apprenticeships, and submit test pieces for approval. They were often foreigners brought in by the ruling powers. For example, in Tallinn there were more than 50 areas of craftsmanship in the 14th century, mostly in metal and leather, and these grew to 73 in the 15th century. The masters were

all German in the more prestigious guilds[1]. We can be sure that basketry was not among these. Throughout the centuries

"wherever raw material for (weaving) was abundant, (basketmaking) often became the specialist profession of the poorer village inhabitants".[2]

The monopoly of the German masters began to decline after 1785 in Estonia, and all guild privileges were abolished in 1866.

For a long period between the 15th and 19th centuries, Poland and Lithuania were allied in a commonwealth which formed one of the largest empires in Europe and extended down to the Ukraine. It was during this period that there was a shift of power from the monarch to the nobility. The wealth of the landowning class grew with the export of grain to other parts of Europe through the Baltic. The peasants were increasingly tied to the land (to prevent them moving east to pioneer new farms for themselves), and were forced to spend much of their time working on their lords' estates. This was the time when western Europe was developing a society which included independent farmers who rented, or even owned their land. The commonwealth was eventually divided amongst Austria, Prussia, and Russia so that Poland ceased to have a separate existence from the late 18th century. Hence social reform and economic modernisation came late to this region (emancipation of the serfs was not completed before the 1860s), and industrialisation developed unevenly in spite of there being coal resources in Silesia (western Poland).

As long as the peasants did not own their own homes they did little to decorate or embellish them, but devoted their handicrafts to items displayed outside: travel wraps, sleigh blankets, gifts from the bride to wedding guests, and of course traditional costumes. Then during the 1800s, many future owners of manors were educated abroad and were influenced by new ideas then current in Germany and elsewhere. On their return they arranged handicraft instructions for their house servants. These in turn spread new patterns, techniques, and fashions to the general population.

When the peasants started to buy their land and houses after 1860, there were two contradictory trends. On the one hand a transition towards urban ideals – which were in many senses international. But in opposition to this, a national awakening and ethnic self-consciousness so that traditional handicrafts became valued, and ethnographic museums were founded to preserve their heritages.

After World War I there was a brief period of independence for these countries, but this ended in 1940. The three small states were absorbed within the Soviet Union after

Display of fine Latvian basketry from their communist era craft guilds, collected by Mary Butcher

World War II while Poland became a Russian satellite. Forced collectivisation and deportation ensued, and industrialisation was brought rapidly into the three republics often based upon workers from other Soviet regions. The existing craft organisations were banned so that national handicrafts became a form of protest against communist ideology, and new associations were quietly formed. From the perspective of basketmaking these two trends are fascinating. Such predominantly agricultural economies without large urban populations had not needed to build up large craft workshops until the Soviet Union encouraged them to export throughout Europe, both in order to supply the needs of the new industrial workers in the eastern bloc and to bring hard currency back from the west. This development took place primarily in Poland, but occurred to a lesser extent in Lithuania.

In Latvia there was a determined effort to preserve and even revive traditional skills. In the 1970s several craft guilds were recreated in Riga and other parts[3]. The members collected wild willow, pine roots, and birch bark and instructed newcomers in their preparation and use. Very high standards of workmanship were required at competitions after long training before the title of Master of Applied Arts could be granted. This was possible when everyone worked for the State and had time and energy left over but little money to spend or freedom to travel. A common joke in communist-controlled countries was "We pretended to work, and they pretended to pay us".

After the collapse of the Soviet regime in 1991, the large Polish state-controlled cooperatives have struggled to survive in the realities of the free market, and the professional industry has contracted. At the same time, the incentive for previously underemployed urban workers to indulge in traditional handicrafts has also decreased[4].

Types of work

Coiled straw

In spite of the availability of willow, the use of straw was widespread in Polish and Lithuanian basketry traditions. Of course the two materials are used for different purposes, with straw employed where the basket needs to be impermeable to fine particles like small seeds or meal, or to provide insulation. Many large circular storage baskets were used in a variety of shapes: some straight-sided cylinders, others flowing out to wide mouths, still others like amphorae with close-fitting lids and side handles. The colder climate compelled farmers to continue growing wheat and rye as their main cereals

when their counterparts in Balkan countries began exploiting maize after its introduction from the Americas in the late 15th century. Maize can be stored outside in the ear in ventilated corn cribs (often basketwork – see chapter on the Carpathians), whereas wheat and rye would have been put into straw stacks then threshed and the grain stored indoors in large coiled straw containers. Smaller articles include seedlips (to hold seed when broadcasting by hand), two-handled shopping bags, and a range of open and lidded containers for the house.

A feature of Polish straw containers is the range of materials and methods used to wrap the coiled straw cores and to stitch them to the previous one. In almost all cases the wrapping is sparse so that the straw core is largely exposed. While the outer bark of blackberry canes is commonly used throughout Europe, many Polish baskets use willow skein or split pine root in its place. Others use cord made from twisted hemp. But different techniques dispense even with such wrapping elements and instead use strands of the same straw (perhaps in the same way as three-way plaiting in Ireland)[5]. These produce new surface patterns, some quite decorative.

It is noteworthy that straw hives were not prominent in most of Poland even though hive beekeeping was known from at least 900AD. Across the whole of northern Europe east of the Elbe, man traditionally practiced tree beekeeping by identifying hollow trees where wild bees nested. He 'managed' these by fitting doors for easier removal of wax and honey, and marked the trees to declare ownership. Gradually this method was supplemented by the use of log hives kept within gardens, and these were

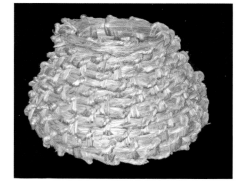

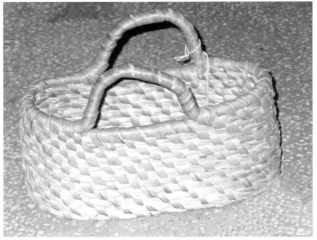

often sawn sections out of living trees. Further west and south, where forests were not so extensive, beekeepers used straw, wicker or cork hives (or mud and pottery hives in the Mediterranean)[6].

I came across a wonderful example of Polish straw coiling skill in 1996 displayed in the window of the Museum of German Ethnology in Berlin. This was a nativity scene made around 1960 by Marcin Lorkiewicz comprising no fewer than 13 human figures including the holy family, three kings, angels, and shepherds with some of their flock. Judging by the size of figures, this must have been a major undertaking.

Finally, as noted in other regions where woodworking skills co-exist alongside basketry techniques, the two may be combined. A wooden base may have holes pierced around its edge, and the straw coil is stitched to this using the normal wrapping material.

Coiled root work

Where grain fields give way to coniferous forests, as they do in parts of Poland and the northern republics, pine and spruce roots were used in similar ways to the coiled straw just described. These roots have the advantage of long lengths of uniform thickness, but their diameter is much less than a normal coil of multiple cereal straws so the baskets are finer and usually smaller. Roots can also be split into two skeins to make the stitching element. In addition to oval and round storage containers of all sizes, some with side handles or tightly fitting lids, several other articles were made. Scoops, or measures for grain and meal had a cranked wooden handle attached. Slightly dished platters and bowls, and elegant water-carrying jugs with spouts and handles were used in farm households. Vases were decorated with rings of dyed wrapping skein. Modern Latvian workers vary the stitches to produce richly decorated surface patterns on lids of their shallow containers[7].

Coiled root work in the State Ethnographic Museum, Warsaw

Clockwise from far left: Large storage vessel, Jugs, vase, Grain scoop or measure, platters

197

Collection of Polish professional work in white, buff and brown willow

Professional willow work

The good growing conditions for willow in Poland mean that basketry based on wild and cultivated willow must have been carried on for centuries, no doubt with specialists in some of the larger towns. But large-scale professional production for domestic sales and export was probably started in the late 19th century. As in some areas of Germany, there were deliberate efforts by local landowners to bring in Austrian instructors to help exploit local willow supplies and provide employment in disadvantaged areas where farms were small and soils poor. A local willow, *S. konopianka* was used for coarse agricultural baskets while *S. americana*, imported from USA, provided good material for finer domestic ware, and much was boiled to produce buff rods.

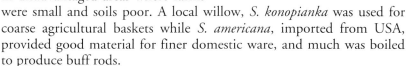

Right: Fancy work in fine buff willow by Marian Gwiazda, Willow Master at the Basket School, Kwidzyn, Poland. Collected by Ann Brooks

Below: White willow work from Lithuania for sale at the Korbmarkt, Lichtenfels, Germany 1995

After World War II, the communist regime encouraged these centres to form cooperatives and supplemented their own small training departments with a specialist secondary school at Kwidzyn on the Wisla river between Warsaw and Gdansk. The school took in pupils from the age of 15 for a three-year training, with the opportunity to specialise in basketmaking during the final year. In 1991, Mary Butcher made a study of this industry and noted that 18-20 students were taking this option annually and then working professionally all over the country. Some of this account is based upon her subsequent reports[8].

Prior to the political changes in 1989, several companies (cooperatives) were each employing hundreds of workers growing and processing

Sewing basket with lid in fine white willow by Andris Lapins, Riga, Lativa

willow, making baskets and furniture, and organising home and export sales. Basketmaking was the seventh largest industry in Poland as recently as the 1980s.

In the villages within 100km of Rudnik there were 400-500 makers, a high proportion of them women mainly working at home. The system was quite similar to that found in Franconia in southern Germany in the early years of the 20th century.

Some makers grew their own willow, but much was produced by the exporting firms, who also boiled and stripped the rods to produce buff willow – the favoured material. Some white willow went into finer work and also brown (unpeeled) rods for farm and fishing baskets. The month's production was taken to the central depot, sorted, and loaded into containers which were then sent by rail to Gdansk for shipment to Germany, Denmark, and the USA. Trains left Rudnik every week loaded with these baskets.

Typical products of these professional businesses were arm baskets in several shapes and styles, cradles, linen baskets, and baskets for logs and dogs. Chairs, stools and tables were also made, and more delicate articles like screens, wall decorations, and amphorae.

Frame baskets

Stake and strand baskets made within a family for its own use are frequently based upon some type of framework. The simplest involves a single round or oval 'hoop' which forms the top rim. Carefully shaped ribs are inserted, attached to this rim at each end to

Below left: Very finely worked frame basket in hazel,
State Ethnographic Museum, Warsaw

Below right: Crude lidded frame basket with horizontal ribs in wood splint,
State Ethnographic Museum, Warsaw

Left: Frame basket with lids in root work, State Ethnographic Museum, Warsaw

Right: Juniper frame with split pine root weaving by Stanislaw Kumanrowicz Sulejow, central Poland, collected by Mary Butcher

Above: Frame basket in thin wood splint in pine or maple

Below: Frame basket in hazel splint, State Ethnographic Museum, Warsaw

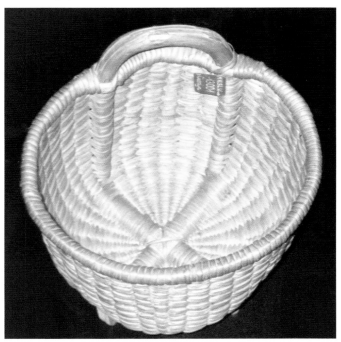

form the skeleton or framework of passive elements. The sides and bottom are then filled in with the active weaving elements. Where the article is to be an arm basket, then there will be an additional hoop which crosses the rim hoop at right angles to form the handle and the central spine of the base. The lengths of each pair of ribs, and their positions within the 90⁰ space from rim to base, determine the shape of the basket.

While some Polish frame baskets are quite crude, others reveal extremely high standards of craftsmanship and would have involved many hours of careful work. The weaving materials included willow, split pine root, and hazel splint. Mary Butcher described the making of a medium sized juniper frame with split pine root weaving in 1991 which took the maker 10 hours even when the weavers were pre-prepared[9]. The first ribs were placed parallel to the handle hoop, while the later ones were horizontal, parallel to the top rim. This is an unusual arrangement which is found in several different examples in the Ethnographic Museum in Warsaw. In Law and Taylor's encyclopaedic study of Appalachian white oak basketry, the authors give a classification according to rib positions and include this variant[10]. No doubt Polish farmers continued their methods with new materials when once they had become established in the eastern states of the USA.

A beautiful variant is featured in two almost round baskets in Warsaw's Ethnographic Museum. Finely made in hazel splint, the frame is formed by two flat base sticks which cross in the centre and rest on four short legs at their ends. Six to nine flat ribs are inserted in each of the four junctions in addition to the arched carrying handle in one of them. A pair of rim hoops is fitted around the rib ends and lashed with finer splint which pierces each of them to secure the border. (This same design also occurs across the Baltic in Sweden).

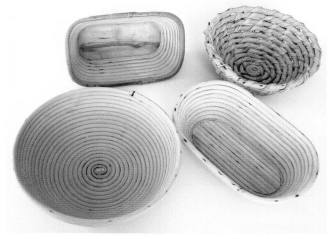

Specific items

Coiled willow

In Latvia, members of the communist-era craft guilds excelled in all the types of work featured in this chapter but in addition adapted the techniques normally used in coiled pine root work to the fine willow varieties which they could grow on their allotments. A problem with willow rods is, of course, that they taper from butt to tip. Some craftworkers make a hoop of white willow, shave it to an equal thickness along its length, and join end to end by overlapping. The next 'coil' is in fact a similar, slightly larger hoop made in the same way but placed with the join in a different position. Instead of being the usual spiral, the result is a set of tightly fitting separate concentric circles bound together with fine skein. The complex patterns in such plates and bowls are created by the type and density of stitching.

A much cruder tradition of coiled work is found in the round or oval dough baskets used in Poland (and also in Germany) which leave their spiral imprint on the rye loaves favoured in both countries. The modern versions have replaced the white willow rods by centre cane, and successive coils are nailed or stapled to each other.

Chip baskets or punnets

Pine and birch woods are widespread on the poorer sandy soils and have long supported the production of simple cheap punnets for soft fruit - major crops in these lands. The baskets were made in many sizes and shapes, but the basic design is the same. Was the technique learned from

Above left: Dough baskets in coiled willow,
State Ethnographic Museum, Warsaw

Above right: Modern dough baskets in coiled centre cane, from Germany

Left: Shallow bowl in concentric rings of white willow stitched with willow skein, by TINE guild member, Riga, Latvia

Left : Loaves showing marks of the coiled baskets used during rising

Below: Peasant women selling wild strawberries from punnets, Zakopane, Poland, 1993

the Finns, or was it evolved separately? The trees are cut, the bark removed and the trunks planed to produce 4-6cm wide splints, some 1mm thick. No doubt these were originally split by hand along the grain. The base is simple check-weaving and the sides are brought up around a wooden mould. The top rim is strengthened by internal strips 5mm thick with perhaps a thin band outside and a low double strip handle. In the past these would have been sewn together at the rim with fine splint or cane, but today are nailed or stapled. Families would have made large numbers of them in their homes as a means of supplementing the income from their small farms. A factory collected their output and made up orders, many going to Scandinavia where they competed on price with the local products[11].

Cart bodies

A world away from fine decorative work: anyone who travelled in rural Poland until quite recently will have noticed that a farming family's normal form of transport was a horse pulling a narrow four-wheeled wagon. It would be in daily use between farmhouse and their scattered strips of land, but would also convey them to and from markets. When needed, a willow lining could be lifted onto the cart body, either to contain loose material or perhaps to give some protection to the family.

Two cart bodies in brown and white willow, State Ethnographic Museum, Warsaw

These very large baskets were sold in markets at least until the 1950s, made in plain brown willow or with patterns made by occasional rows of white.

Oval market baskets

Peasant women in southern Poland still bring their produce to market in large oval baskets. Their arch handles don't project much above the sides which often flow out at each end. The base may be constructed in several ways. Some are woven around a set of long rods crossed by several shorter sets as illustrated in the techniques chapter. Often

Group of market baskets from southern Poland in brown, buff and white willow

the long set is replaced by a squared length of timber drilled at intervals to take the shorter cross sticks. The ends of the handle bow may be bent under and pass through this timber ensuring that the handle is well anchored and can carry a heavy load.

An interesting third variant was collected from a market in Krakow close to the Tatra mountains. It has a round base woven around a short timber stick crossed by the handle ends. Brown willow rods are inserted in the four angles of this cross, in just the same way that ribs are placed in the angles between the rim and handle hoops of a true frame basket. The base weaving circles all around the cross in round rod, or splint, with more 'ribs' being added as necessary. When completed, the 'ribs' are pricked up vertically along the sides but allowed to flow out strongly at each end. This creates a pronounced oval form at the rim from the initial round base.

Bases of baskets showing the methods of construction

D-shaped mountain baskets

These baskets are found along the whole length of the Carpathian chain from Slovenia to Romania but also occur in south-east Sweden[12]. Their characteristic features are the semi-circular base and the bow handle on the flat side, often of unpeeled hazel. Those collected in Krakow and the rural market at Nowy Targ have their bases woven in quite a different way from the wood splint plaiting often found in Croatia. The vertical handle rod has its two ends joined by a cross piece (see over), but closely related to the method just described for the oval market basket from the Tatra and the round hazel splint models in the frame section. A second stick butts onto this, to make a T-frame in the horizontal plane. The first base sticks are inserted into the two angles and the weavers taken back and forth to produce a fan-shaped base through adding more 'ribs' as required. These 'ribs' are then pricked up to form the side stakes and, eventually, the top border. In the example shown on p204, the 'ribs' are brown willow rods while the base and side weavers are hazel splint with a final band of brown willow. In cruder versions the rough wood splint may be juniper, and in previous times some baskets of this shape were in coiled root work.

D-basket in coiled root work, Zakopane, Poland

203

D-shaped mountain basket from near the Tatra mountains in hazel splint and brown willow

Notes and references

1.   Reeman, V. and Õunapuu, P. (2004) 'Crafts and Arts in Estonia - past and present'. Estonian Institute, Tallinn.
2.   Szacki, P. (1995) 'Folk Crafts - guide to the permanent exhibition'. State Ethnographic Museum, Warsaw.
3.   Goymer, S. (1991) 'Latvia'. BA NL **59**: 5-7, and Butcher, M. (1995) 'The Great Latvian Basket Exhibition', BA NL **75**: 18-19. Also 'Vāceles un Cibas' (1989). Catalogue of the Latvian Ethnographic Museum; and in the 1998 book by Astra Pope (Mājturíba – pinumi), Zvaigzne ABC, the author mentions six different guilds in four Latvian towns. She introduces the basic techniques of willow basketry and also birch bark work, rush plaiting, and straw coiling.
4.   Goymer, S. (2002) 'Latvia 2001' . BA NL **100**: 10-14.
5.   Hogan, J. (2001) 'Basketmaking in Ireland'. Wordwell.
6.   Crane, E. (1999) 'The World History of Beekeeping and Honey Hunting'. Duckworth.
7.   Butcher, M. (1999) 'Contemporary International Basketmaking'. Merrell Holberton.
8.   Butcher, M. (1991) 'Basketmaking in Poland'. BA NL **59**: 11-33.
9.   See 7 p22-23 and 8 p31.
10. Law, R.N. and Taylor, C.W. (1991) 'Appalachian White Oak Basketmaking - handing down the basket'. University of Tennessee Press.
11. See 8 p27-28.
12. Hasselrot, J. (2002) 'Bowstring Baskets'. BA NL **100**: 32-33. In this short article he discusses the construction of the bow handle, but there is also an excellent six-page clearly illustrated account of the method of making the Swedish version on p142-147 in Hasselrot, J. (1997) 'Korgar - tradition och teknik'. LTs förlag, Stockholm.

The Carpathians

Carved and painted headboard,
cemetery at Sapînta,
Maramures, Romania

Two contrasting sides of Romanian basketmaking in 1995

Right: Stacks of varnished arm baskets in buff willow skein for despatch from the Marginex factory, Gherla, Translyvania

Far right: Smallholder selling garden produce from a hazel splint back basket in Baia Mare market, Maramures

Resources

This grouping of four central European countries, the Czech Republic, Slovakia, Hungary, and Romania, is joined or enclosed by the great sweep of the Carpathian mountains and their western extensions in the Tatra and beyond. These uplands form the northern edges to the Czech provinces of Bohemia and Moravia, then to Slovakia, and finally curl around to fill most of Romania. They circle much of today's Hungary which has a flat area to the east, the Great Plain, and then gradually rises to reach the higher ground of eastern Austria.

The climate throughout is continental – hot summers and cold winters – while the rainfall decreases towards the east. The vegetation was mainly deciduous forest except where the altitude dictated coniferous trees, though the dry Hungarian plain was grassland. Cereal production is important throughout with wheat and barley in the north while maize has long been cultivated in the warmer southern lands. Fruit and vegetable production includes vines as far north as southwest Moravia though the southern countries also drink spirits based on large crops of plums. Peppers, tomatoes, and squash are all characteristic of hot summers. Willow grows well in many areas as well as hazel. Straw and rush provided other basketry material.

History

While these countries are geographically well defined, lying between the Danube and the Dnestr (flowing into the Black Sea) they are ethnically diverse – from the edge of the Germanic world into that of the Slavs. The region has major east-west routes, particularly the Danube valley, and it formed a buffer between Western Europe and the eastern borders. It has been organised in large part by empires centred successively on Rome, Budapest, Istanbul, and Vienna.

The Czech Republic, ethnically Slav but culturally part of central Europe, was strongly influenced by Germany. For 400 years it was part of the Habsburg (and eventually Austro-Hungarian) Empire. Urbanisation started early, particularly the growth of Prague, and Bohemia's coal and mineral resources were the major focus of the Empire's industry in the 19th century. Slovakia was less well endowed and more mountainous.

From the 9th century the Magyars ruled Hungary until the Turks took over the east in 1526. At this point, the western portion was absorbed by the Habsburgs who regained the whole only 160 years later. Romania was part of the Ottoman Empire for much

longer, until the 1820s. In 1890 almost the whole of this region was in fact within greater Hungary, though around half of its people were of ethnic minorities.

But, as in the Baltic and Balkan lands, the big difference between development in this region and that in northwest Europe began in the period between the 14th and 15th centuries. At the beginning of this period, all of Europe was affected by economic and social problems which produced a crisis in the feudal system. General disorder was caused by pestilence, population decline, falling grain prices, civil wars, feuds, and invasions. East European seigneurs reacted by demanding higher payments from their peasants, restricting rural mobility and enlarging their own estates at the expense of the lower orders. By contrast the English nobility reduced the feudal obligations of their manorial servants.

This divergence occurred because western kings managed to establish their predominance over the nobility in the 16th century, whereas in the east the weakened kings and princes needed the support of their noblemen, and they made concessions to them in respect of their relations with the rural population.

As a result the east, poor in cities, populations, fuel sources, and manufactures, developed an agrarian system based on landed estates dependent upon a huge class of serfs who both paid taxes and owed day labour as well as tithes to the Church. This reached its highest development in the 18th century and lasted much longer: emancipation of the bonded peasants only began in the mid-19th century. When the Empress Maria Theresa made new laws which started to limit the power of the landowners in 1848, three quarters of the Hungarian population were still in the peasant class. Farming practice had hardly changed since medieval times so that grain yields were only one third of those current in the west.

With its dense network of towns, broadly based craft activities, and lively markets, Western Europe had forged ahead into quite new societies with vastly different needs for goods and services. Only when the eastern agrarian system had begun to break down did these trends gather momentum in the Carpathian lands. In the middle of the 19th century some 2500 fairs were held annually in 600 locations in greater Hungary. Village and town artisans had to meet a growing demand for their wares as specialist agriculture (tobacco, onion, and pepper growing) became widespread[1]. But the fairs lost their role as the primary hubs of interaction when road and rail systems were created in this region. Even then, the evolution into more mobile societies was halted at the start of World War I, and was only to make fitful progress through much of the 20th century.

White willow in Madeira weave or pulled work. Two dough baskets presented by Dr Nedopil, Prague, Czech Republic, and large farm or market basket from Orosháza, Great Plain, Hungary

The relevance of this to our study is that the consolidation of serfdom from the 14ᵗʰ century actually conserved cultural conditions, and the early ethnographers were able to identify many phenomena of medieval origins still present in the 19ᵗʰ and 20ᵗʰ century folk traditions. Hence the characteristic basketry styles and products featured here are mainly peasant traditions (except for the 'factory' production of willow work). There may well have been high quality basket work produced for the privileged families of the eastern capital cities, many of whom were German, since city guilds had existed in other trades from medieval times. But there seems to have been nothing like the development of the profession in the west which catered for their urban customers and the large-scale transport of foods and other commodities.

Types of work

Coiled straw work was traditional in many parts of this region but there are close similarities to that found in nearby Austria. The emphasis here is on some other forms which seem to me to be characteristic at different times in the region's history.

Madeira

This type of weave, usually in willow, is frequently found making part or the whole side of a basket and creating its own border. Groups of two to six rods are worked together alongside each other to produce a curving open effect. It is sometimes called 'pulled work'. While it can be seen in many other parts of Europe, it is particularly evident in the Carpathian and Balkan regions. Is this because it is commonly employed by the Roma, or gypsies who are so often the basketmakers in these countries?

Three bow-handled baskets in fine willow from Transylvania, Romania

One of the simplest articles is the shallow round or oval bowl without handles worked in fine white or buff willow rods and with a foot created by a plaited border at the edge of the base. It would have been used to hold fruit or bread on the table or, lined with a cloth, to hold rising dough.

But the technique is not confined to these delicate bowls. Sometimes the baskets are made in much stouter rods, and are then strong enough to be used in the garden or farm to harvest produce, or feed animals. A bow handle

Rush and maize items for sale from roadside stalls in Izvoru Crisului, Translyvania, Romania (except back basket):

Clockwise from left:

Coiled bread or cake storage basket

Maize bags

Coiled back basket, in rush, Hungary

Patterned bag

Slippers

Decorative bowl

may be fitted thus converting it to an arm basket which might take produce to or from market.

In the Museum of Ethnography in Budapest there is an exhibit depicting a bride's trousseau of the 19th century. Many of the smaller items are contained in four substantial baskets in Madeira weave. Apparently it was customary to display the presents in the farm's yard during the church ceremony.

Rush work

The region still produces objects from leaves of the reed mace, *Typha angustifolia*. Mary Butcher has described the work of Janos Hanis of Orosháza on the Hungarian Plain using the coiling technique[2]. His output includes traditional round and oval baskets with tight-fitting lids for storing bread and cakes, flowerpot shapes for raising dough, and a bulbous form for storing dried plums. The same rush material was also used for chair seating[3]. Transylvania is the region of the Carpathian mountains which was transferred to Romania from Hungary in 1920, and many of the population are ethnic Hungarians. Rush basketry using the coiling technique is still made there, but the material is also employed in plaited and stake and strand work to produce decorative bowls, two-handled bags, and even slippers. These are often sold to tourists returning to Oradea from Cluj at roadside stalls, especially in the village of Izvoru Crisului.

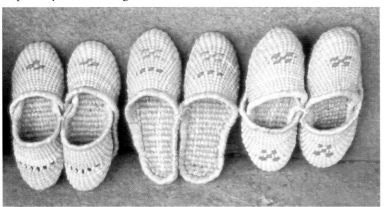

Professional willow worker in Morkovice, Moravia, Czech Republic

Willow work in white and buff (and plastic wrapping on bow handle) from Morkovice, Moravia, Czech Republic

Willow laundry baskets on casters in use as rubbish carriers, University of Brno, Moravia, Czech Republic

Below: Fruit carrier in buff willow, Budapest, Hungary

Below right : Professional willow work from Cluj, Romania and Orosháza, Hungary

Professional willow work

Where urbanisation did occur, as in parts of the Czech Republic, it was natural that professional willow workers would achieve the same high levels of workmanship as their German neighbours. Museums in Bohemia and Moravia have plenty of examples of such work alongside more rustic baskets.

In early 1992, shortly after the political changes in these countries, I visited Morkovice which had long been a centre of willow work using largely Moravian-grown rods. Under communist rule a substantial cooperative had existed employing some 320 workers, mainly women, some working in their homes. A training school had been established only three years previously, and the Director was still quite confident that his business could continue to compete with Far Eastern work based upon quality. Their output was almost entirely in skeined buff willow and cane, and was all articles used in and around the home: shoppers, baskets for pets, waste paper, linen, and flowers; as well as lampshades, plant pot holders, magazine racks, fancy trim around trays and mirrors, and small chairs and tables. A third of their work was exported, mainly to countries in northwest Europe. As the Czech Republic was reabsorbed into Western Europe it seemed very unlikely that the cooperative would in fact survive. Denied access to the wider world, its population had previously been satisfied by these products, but they now appeared dated.

The male basketmakers in Morkovice were working privately making articles in whole rods, both white and buff. These included maunds and arm baskets, but I also caught sight of some more modern adaptations such as oval laundry baskets mounted on casters, and a square carrier fitted up as a handcart on pneumatic wheels.

Strong general purpose maunds and market display baskets in attractive brown willow were also a feature of much Hungarian work. One of my favourite items is a fruit carrier in buff willow. It is a very large rectangular basket apparently lifted by a handle on each of the shorter sides. Inside there are no fewer than 18 smaller versions stacked in two layers with the upper nine resting on a wooden framework. The whole structure was clearly designed to transport a large quantity of ripe fruit without crushing.

A few years later when exposure to the realities of free markets was beginning to hurt, we toured a branch of the Marginex business in Gherla, Romania. In 1995 the factory was still employing 100 or more workers. Bundles of dried brown willow rods were stacked in the yard. Most were then boiled in large tanks and unloaded by means of overhead gantreys and machine-stripped to produce buff. The larger rods were then split and shaved to produce skein for weaving. The basketmakers were seated on chairs, working on sloping lap-boards. This factory was turning out large numbers of arm baskets or shoppers in at least 20 styles: round or oval, open or closed weaving, and achieving a variety of patterns from different weaves and bands of brown willow. Some styles were woven around light metal frame 'moulds'. Most were then clear-varnished, dried, and stacked ready for dispatch to markets throughout Europe. The enterprise had been started in 1971 by the Government and had employed up to 210 workers. Until 1989, when this and similar factories were all within the Soviet orbit, their baskets were both bartered with other communist nations and sold cheaply into Western Europe in order to gain hard currency.

Above left : A fancy arm basket made by a Roma worker in buff willow rods and skein, Tirgu Mures, Romania

Scenes from the Marginex factory, Gherla, Transylvania, Romania

Above: A trio of different designs

Below : Weaving with buff willow skein

Below left: Boiling tanks for producing buff willow

Below right: Varnish drying on a batch of arm baskets

Fine back basket in hazel splint by Iona Peteas, Ocna Sugatag, Maramures, Romania

Above right: Three hazel splint baskets from stalls in Izvoru, Crisului, Transylvania, Romania

Round farm basket in hazel splint, some dyed, and its Roma maker, Maramures, Romania

Above: arm basket, right: cradle. Two hazel splint frame baskets in Sibiu, Transylvania, Romania

Wood splint

Travelling through markets in northwestern Romania in 1995, it became obvious that both stallholders and customers were using a particular pattern of back basket. It was made of quite narrow (6-7mm) peeled hazel splint closely woven onto wider splint stakes with one or two small handles on the top rim. Some had decorative patterns formed from bands of unpeeled splint. We failed to locate one for sale, but subsequently acquired a beautiful example through the good offices of one of my students who grew up in the region. It was made by Iona Peteas in the village of Ocna Sugatag in Maramures county within sight of the Ukrainian Carpathians. This could well be of very ancient origin since Hungarian and Romanian culture often survived best in these distant parts of Transylvania far from the influence of urban developments.

We found several other baskets in the same (or similar) splint. The 'gondola' or hen basket shape may not be traditional, since it became wildly popular throughout Europe during the 1950s. Another frame basket may also be an imported design since Dorothy Wright illustrates two related models, one from the Scottish islands[4]. One might view it as a conventional frame basket with two oval hoops forming the rim and the spine/bow handle. The two sets of ribs have been fitted as usual along the long axis and anchored into the wrapping diamond where the hoops cross at right angles. An extra set of ribs is then fitted to fill the space on one side between the rim and handle hoops. The weaving then proceeds, crossing from one side of the rim hoop, past the spine, the second side of the rim hoop, and to the handle hoop before returning. This leaves an opening on only one side of the 'handle' which has now become one side of the new rim. In this Romanian example, two small handles have been attached to this, and to the other original rim to create a bag.

A third barrel-shaped container has both base and lid constructed in the way previously described for one of the oval market baskets in Poland. They begin with two crossed sticks which are joined by the 'eye of God' wrapping. The 'ribs' are inserted into the four angles between them with the weaving spiralling around. These 'ribs' continue up the sides to a simple lashed rim on the main body and on the lid's overlapping edge.

Four hazel splint shapes from near Kezmarok, northern Slovakia, collected by Owen Jones

Some of these techniques may have been moved around Europe by the migration of farming families. For example, ethnic Germans moving into Hungary in the 1750s seemed to have taken with them a method of weaving a basket base which Mary Butcher had only previously noted from the Hessen region[5].

In 1993, this same author studied the making of round frame baskets from an *Acer* species by a Roma family, the Karoly brothers, a short distance away in northeast Hungary near the Slovak border[6]. A 10-15cm diameter tree was felled, roasted on a low fire overnight, cleaved into segments, and split into growth rings while hot. Further hand-splitting produced fine splint which was woven onto the rim hoop of wild briar to form a deep bowl shape in two sizes, 30 and 60 cm diameter. These were used for a multitude of tasks in the household and smallholding.

Just a little further along the Carpathian chain, Tim Wade described a range of splint baskets still being made near Kezmarok in northern Slovakia[7]. These included oval arm baskets, the typical Carpathian D-shape carried on the back, and others similar to the swills used in Cumberland (see the British Isles chapter). Owen Jones accompanied him in 1996 and brought back several examples which we have been able to photograph.

Oak splint basket from Czech Republic, collected by Owen Jones

Below: Gate from hazel or willow rods in the Village Museum, Bucharest, Romania

Specific items

Gates and fences

These structures may not be typical baskets but they certainly use normal materials and weaves to provide fixed or movable barriers. Simple openwork gates or closely woven hurdles, both on wooden frames, are made from hazel rods. More unusual are the continuous hazel or willow fences using several different weaves, and often topped by a thatch or shingle roof to shed the rain. There is an excellent display of these in the Bucharest Village Museum, though one would not expect smallholders to be creating new ones for real use in the 21st century.

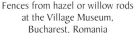
Fences from hazel or willow rods at the Village Museum, Bucharest, Romania

Grain stores

With their high summer temperatures, Hungary and Romania have grown maize for over 300 years. In autumn the maize cobs were picked and often stored whole at a relatively high moisture content. They were placed in narrow containers so that the air could circulate easily and moulds were discouraged from forming. These were

Outdoor grain stores for maize cobs, the Village Museum, Bucharest, Romania

usually based on a stout wooden framework raised clear of the ground to avoid rats, and permit easy emptying by gravity flow. They had an aperture near the top for filling, and another at the base from which to remove the cobs. The walls would normally be woven in willow rods over hazel or similar stakes. The whole structure was finished with a pitched roof of thatch or wood shingles. Similar stores with wire-netting sides could still be found quite recently in the mid-west of USA.

On the other hand, the wheat and other small-grain crops would be threshed from the ears and stored dry. Large willow baskets were woven into a variety of shapes, usually around stakes inserted into a plank base. They were often then coated internally, and sometimes externally too, with a clay, lime, and perhaps cow dung mixture to seal the gaps between the weavers. These grain stores were kept dry inside the house or adjoining barn.

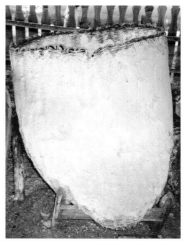

Beehives

While many of the poorest people would have continued to rely on extracting honey and wax from wild bee nests in trees, hive beekeeping was known in Hungary from the 13th century. Sections of hollow logs were used by forest dwellers and coiled straw skeps by those who grew wheat or rye. But a third type was in common use in this region until very recently. This was woven from willow or split hazel. The framework of stakes

Beehives in Translyvania, Romania.
Left: Log hives and coiled skeps, Open-air Museum, Cluj

Above: Hive woven from hazel splint, Bran

was often based on several stems emerging as a whorl from a branch or perhaps split out from it. The short section of branch formed a crown piece which served as a handle. The outside would be coated with clay and cow dung to make it weatherproof. When visiting the small farm belonging to the grandmother of another of my students near Tirgu Mures in Romania, I was shown a collection of such hives made by her late husband, and I brought one back to England in 1995. There are still many to be seen in museums throughout the country. In her comprehensive world history of beekeeping and honey hunting, Eva Crane had an illustration of the upper part of a crude, but similar, woven willow hive preserved in a peat bog in Lower Saxony, Germany, dated some time before 200AD[8].

Miniature splint basket, with decorated eggs from northern Romania

Easter stick in centre cane from Morkovice, Czech Republic

Easter sticks

These are hardly baskets, but fertility symbols from the Czech Republic and Hungary. "At Easter time and around May Day, young men give the girl who takes their fancy a 'tap' with these sticks and sprinkle her with scent. If the 'intended' is sufficiently taken with her admirer, she responds by giving him a painted egg. Easter sticks are made from fresh willow in bright 'fertile' colours, usually with a green bow tied at one end"[9]. The tradition was very much alive in the Czech Republic in 1998[10]. I was presented with a stick in Morkovice, Moravia (though this one is made in centre cane) and saw eggs being painted at the Open-air Museum at Prerov Nad Labem outside Prague. The most exquisite decorated eggs I have seen are produced around Brodina in the far north of Romania, the region of the painted monasteries[11]. The decoration on duck and goose eggs is with beeswax, dyes and inks.

Notes and references

1. Kovács, A.S. and Szacsvay, É. (1997) 'Folk Culture of the Hungarians'. Museum of Ethnography, Budapest.
2. Butcher, M. (2006) 'Eastern and Central Europe - an introduction to basketry in Eastern and Central Europe'. ICEB 2005: 684-687.
3. Butcher, M. (2004) 'Reed Mace Seating in Hungary'. BA NL **68**: 20-22.
4. Wright, D. (1997) 'The Complete Book of Baskets and Basketry'. Charles Scribner's Sons pp123-125.
5. Butcher, M. (1999) 'Contemporary International Basketmaking'. Merrell Holberton, p22.
6. Butcher, M. (1994) 'Maple Baskets from the Gypsies of Hungary' BA NL **69**: 25-27 and see 2 p685-686.
7. Wade, T. (1996) 'Timber, Trade and Tourism'. BA NL 77: 14-15.
8. Crane, E. (1999) 'The World History of Beekeeping and Honeyhunting'. Duckworth p241.
9. Gilmour, J. (1996) 'Easter Sticks', BA NL **76**: 12-13.
10. Fuller, S. (1998) 'Feedback on Easter Sticks', BA NL **85**: 21.
11. The Transrural Trust, a charity based in Oxfordshire, helps women in this remote area of Romania to earn some income through their amazing skill of egg decorating for which this region is renowned. The eggs are imported into England as well as being sold to visitors to the painted monasteries (www.transrural.org).

The Balkans

Painting by Zdenka Serdic (who worked for nearly 40 years in the museum) depicting Croatian villagers in folk costumes at a rural festivity.
Exhibition catalogue, Ethnographic Museum, Zagreb

Old Croatian arm basket with plank base, wood splint stakes, and willow weavers in Zagreb's Ethnographic Museum

Resources

The Balkan region occupies a broad peninsula from Croatia down through Bosnia, Serbia, Montenegro, Macedonia, and Albania, to Bulgaria. (Western Turkey, Greece, and Cyprus are treated in the next chapter.) The northern band is continental in climate and out of touch with the sea other than along Bulgaria's Black Sea coast, because of the lie of the mountains. By contrast, the coastal regions are fully Mediterranean. Many parts are mountainous and little suited to commercial agriculture though they have provided the native populations with subsistence for millennia. The broad, flat Danube valley from Croatia through Serbia and north Bulgaria is more favoured.

The main plant species utilised in basketry have been willow (wild and cultivated), hazel, chestnut, olive, vine, the Mediterranean cane, and clematis, as well as reeds, rushes, maize bracts, and cereal straw. I have been informed that pine roots were used in the Rhodope Mountains of Bulgaria, but have so far failed to confirm this. The Ethnographic museum in Zagreb (Croatia) also has old baskets formed from sheets of birch bark.

History

The origins of agriculture in Europe were in the Fertile Crescent in the Near and Middle East at least 13,000 years ago. It seems likely that one route by which these activities spread into Western Europe (perhaps 7000-8000BP) was via Turkey, and one would expect the Balkans to have had a very long history of settlements though the mountain ranges would not have provided suitable sites for cereal cropping. We know that Greek culture developed urban living 3000 years ago and influenced the Dalmatian coast. This area subsequently had many centuries of Venetian rule when fishing and trading would have been important. But during the times the West was developing less feudal societies, most of this region became occupied by the Turks. There followed a rule more primitive than the societies which were occupied which remained in some parts for nearly 500 years. Bulgaria virtually lost contact with the outside world until the end of the 19th century. Furthermore, once their national identities re-emerged in the 18th and 19th centuries, many of these countries continued to suffer from conflicts between the Catholic, Orthodox, and Muslim faiths based upon events of long ago (e.g. the battle of Kosovo Polje in 1389 when the Serbs were defeated by the Turks). Their agrarian societies persisted long after Western Europe was developing industries, trade, and transport, in part because the Balkan states were pre-occupied with achieving independence. Under Turkish rule they had left trade and finance to foreigners, so

Old Croatian baskets in Zagreb's Ethnographic Museum.

Far left: Lidded arm basket in brown willow

Left: Brown willow frame basket for drying nuts

when they drove out the very people who were most active in their economies, they hampered the pace of change. Communism again isolated them for a further 40 years.

The result is that the predominant basketry styles from the region reflect the same types of simple rural activities already noted from the Carpathians, apart from some industrial production of willow goods which was encouraged during the Communist era and exported throughout western Europe. Smallholders made their own requirements during slack times. The main professional makers were from the Roma populations, still active today, who combined this work with other trades.

Western Croatia was part of the Habsburg Empire from the early 16th century and benefited from a long period of Austrian influence. Nestling in the old town, the fascinating daily market in Zagreb still has large numbers of women from the surrounding villages bringing their produce or taking away their purchases in baskets, often locally made. Several stalls up near the Cathedral offer articles in willow, coiled straw, and rush, as well as the wooden goods so famous across the border in Slovenia. Peasant farming methods have changed less in rural eastern districts because Soviet dictated 'collectivisation' did not take hold. Here, traditional basketry was still prominent in local markets at the end of the 20th century.

Above and left: Baskets in use in Zagreb market in 1997

Below: Old lady bringing flowers to sell in Zagreb market, May 1994

In my searches for traditional work in Bulgaria, I had the opportunity to study today's industry (late 2003) and gain an insight into how it had emerged after state control during more than 40 years of Communist rule until 1989. During the 20th century, willow had been cultivated commercially in the three main river valleys (Danube, Marica, and Camcia) with a research station at Svistov trialling new cultivars. Today the industry is concentrated in villages near Shumen in the northeast corner and on Belene island in the Danube. With high summer temperatures and the main demand being for thick rods which are split for skein, it is essential to irrigate the willow beds weekly from May onwards. The village of Khan Krum used to have

Covering a glass bottle in buff willow skein, Prolet workshop, Shumen, Bulgaria

upwards of 20 growers, but only two or three were active by the time of my visit. One had a quarter hectare of 50-year old stools behind the house irrigated from a shallow well. The rods grow up to 4m in height and 10-20mm in diameter in the season. Another grower had 7ha on waste ground along the river edges where flood irrigation was possible. On Belene island (once an infamous prison, and still reserved for offenders) the land is more or less at river level, and 10ha of rods are grown on the prison farm for its own workshops and others around the country.

Biser Ivanov at his family stall near Sofia's main market, Bulgaria, 2003

Most rods are harvested mechanically in October, and boiled before stripping to produce buff rods. Individual craft workers buy these rods and split the thicker ones into three or four with a hand-held cleave made of iron, aluminum, or bone (see materials chapter). Finally they may plane the triangular lengths into flat skeins using a simple hand-powered machine. The better work is woven with the outer skein, but some low-grade work is made with the inner pieces.

The quality of the output from Belene and other prisons varies with the maker's skills. Once trained in the workshops, prisoners may not remain long before release. They can be given a certificate of competence, and some find basketmaking a useful trade since unemployment rates are high. Demand for prison output ebbs and flows, and there seemed to be little effective marketing. They made many small decorative items but also tables, chairs, and cradles. While these Bulgarian workshops manage to gain some

Buff willow skein work from Belene prison workshop, Bulgaria including a photo frame, wall decoration and case around a cigarette lighter

Chair in willow rods and
skein by Dimitar
Atanasov, Stara Zagora,
Bulgaria

Dimitar Atanasov outside his
workshop in Stara Zagora,
Bulgaria, 2003

orders from Western Europe, their type of skein work finds it difficult to compete with even lower-priced articles from Belarus, Romania, and the Far East.

A careful search on two days in 2003 through the large and busy produce market in Sofia, the capital city of Bulgaria, failed to reveal a single trader bringing goods in baskets, nor a single shopper carrying one to take away his or her purchases. There were two stalls where Roma traders were offering baskets, and a few one-man urban workshops nearby. No doubt each large town in Bulgaria still has a handful of makers working on a small scale. In addition there are a very few workshops producing quantities of buff willow goods for local and export sales.

One exception to the general rule that the only 'professional' basketmakers were gypsies was Dimitar Atanasov operating from a modest workshop in Stara Zagora. His grandfather (born 1910) had been taught the trade during a two-year course in an applied agricultural school in Pleven, and had lived from his profession for most of his life (though more or less illegally during Communist rule since the work was meant to

Roma women hand-stripping
buffed willow rods, Shumen,
Bulgaria

be reserved for handicapped people). Dimitar was trained as an electronic engineer and employed in the local large chemical manufacturing complex. Like many state industries, this could not survive after the political change of 1989, and he set up his own small basketry shop using his inherited tools and the skills he had learned from watching his grandfather, He makes a complete range of baskets and small furniture including customers' commissions, but struggles to make even a modest living. Most items are rather flimsy in skeined buff willow rather than whole rods to keep his prices down. Dimitar prefers working in white willow and in whole rods, but finds it difficult to get small enough rods and such work would not sell readily. Nevertheless, a well-made infant's crib in his workshop would have stood comparison with work in the West, and he displayed a good range of covered glass bottles for home-distilled brandy which is still popular and legal in the Balkan countries.

Such one-man workshops producing a wide range of willow work are not very common in Bulgaria, but Prolet, the new business created by Paraskev Paraskevov, seems unique. This former engineer saw an opportunity with the demise of a state-controlled workshop on the Danube. He controls all the separate processes from a headquarters in Shumen. Willow is grown on 4ha of good flood-irrigated land, processed, woven into a variety of products, and supplied to shops throughout the country. Most of his items are woven in buff willow skein. He prefers the surface from hand-peeled rods so he does not use mechanical stripping machines. Fresh-cut rods are boiled for three hours, then hand-stripped by a team of colourfully dressed Roma women using upright metal brakes, and dried outside for several days. The rods are then split and planed by simple machines in old farm buildings to produce skein. Workers weave this mainly on moulds to make arm baskets, and others for dogs and cats, laundry, and hampers. There is limited internal demand for these and so the company's main focus is on wooden furniture (chairs, tables and sofas) covered with skeined buff willow, often varnished. This has in turn led to general shop-fitting (storage and display units, bar counters, etc) in the same style.

Collection of willow work in Madeira weave.
Clockwise from top left:

Large arm basket in white from Sofia market 1975

White oval bowl from Prolet workshop, Sumen

Posy basket in white and brown, Sofia

Round bowl in white by Ibrahim Shabanov, Plovdiv

Two small bowls in white and buff, given by Prof Aliko, Tirana, Albania

Types of work

The contrast already noted between the Mediterranean coasts and the inland areas with continental climates is reflected in some very different basketry styles. Several are also seen in other parts of Europe but have been featured in this chapter because they are particularly well developed in the Balkans.

Madeira

This type of work is widespread throughout the Balkans and often comes from the Roma or gypsy craft workers. The closeness of the side weaving varies from dense to very open. Small round or oval bowls in fine, white or buff willow would have been used to hold a variety of foods including rising dough. These are the only basketry items I have so far managed to discover from Albania. Much larger maunds, closely woven with side handles formed from two bundles of weavers, were seen in Hvar, an island off Croatia's Dalmatian coast.

Strong white willow maund in Madeira weave, marketplace Hvar, Croatia

In Bulgaria the technique was used for quite large oval arm baskets. One of these has the bundles of weavers forming the openwork sides grouped into fives and sixes alternately. The plaited finish around the base usually creates quite a deep foot which keeps the basket off the floor or table.

I visited a Roma family headed by Ibrahim Shabanov in Boliarzi village near Plovdiv. There were around 10 other basketmakers nearby. In addition to producing buff willow baskets and small furniture, he sometimes cut standing willow and stripped it to produce fine white rods for small Maderia baskets for bread or fruit. He used bunches of seven weavers for the border, and formed two side handles by pulling up a top loop of five of these on opposite sides.

In the Sofia market Biser Ivanov and his family were mainly selling brooms, but also produced dainty conical posy baskets made more attractive by using two brown rods with four white in each bundle of six for the Madeira borders.

Coiled straw bee skeps on sale in Zagreb market, Croatia

Coiked straw work collected over several years from Zagreb market, Croatia. Seedlips, dough baskets, large bowl, and bee skep for catching swarms

Coiled straw work

Croatia still displays plenty of coiled straw items both in its museums and markets. My collection includes bowls for the table, large containers for grain and seeds, both round and long dough-rising baskets, seedlips for sowing grain, and a skep which has already helped me recover many a swarm of bees back in Oxfordshire. The sewing material is usually thin narrow splint made from willow or hazel.

Two coiled straw containers in Zagreb's Ethnographic Museum

Wood splint work

All along the more wooded inland regions of the Balkans, the people naturally utilised wood splint primarily from hazel stems, but no doubt from other species too. In western Croatia which borders on Slovenia, one finds the same type of splint baskets built up from a plank base (already described in the Alpine chapter). But further east near the Serbian border, in a region confusingly called Slavonia, the D-shaped back basket is still in use on farms. The square base is woven in check weave from 3cm wide flat strips of chestnut or hazel which are then taken up to form the side stakes. A stout round rod is bent through 180° to form two corner posts with a wire or twisted rod between the two ends keeping it in shape. The weaving is in 1cm wide hazel splint, with or without the bark. It flows out a little so that the rim is almost semi-circular with one flat side carried against the back. The top ends of the side stakes are thinned then bent over and tucked under the top rows of weaving and sometimes lashed quite decoratively. In 1996 there were many well-made examples in the rural market at Nova Gradiska, in at least three sizes. The large size would hold 15kg of potatoes and was used in the fields. Smaller and shallower ones were for gathering salads and vegetables from the garden.

Right: D-basket with plank base, splint stakes and weavers, Ethnographic Museum, Zagreb

Back basket (hay carrier) in wood splint on plank base, Ethnographic Museum, Zagreb

Left: D-baskets in hazel splint for sale in market at
Nova Gradiska, eastern Croatia 1996
Below: Strong arm basket in hazel splint, Sofia, Bulgaria

Farmer's wife demonstrating how
the D-basket is carried (hazel
splint) near Nova Gradiska 1996

Much more surprising to me was to discover a single oval arm basket on a rectangular base made of similar materials but on sale in a city shop in Sofia, since a thorough search with a local professor had previously found only willow workers throughout Bulgaria. Here the rim is finished by two rods fitted inside and outside, and lashed with splint. A feature is the arch handle formed of two stout sections of splint which cross in the centre, and fit down under the side weavers. Four holes have been made on each side with a hot iron, and small wooden pegs inserted to fasten the handles to the side stakes. A peach basket from over the border in Greek Macedonia is quite similar in construction, though its handle is simpler.

Frame baskets

Part-time rural makers often used the frame technique for their work, and several countries have already been singled out for special mention. There must surely be many interesting frame baskets to be discovered in this region, but the last two decades have not been the easiest for travel in these strife-torn countries, particularly those in the central mountainous areas where basketry might have been expected to survive in the villages and farms. There are however good examples in both Bulgaria and Croatia.

One type shown in the Agricultural Museum in Sofia, but seen also in an hotel in Shumen and in the Village Museum across the Danube in Bucharest, is a round arm basket with seven almost equal pairs of ribs. The first three pairs are inserted normally into the 'eye of God' lashing which joins the rim and handle hoops. The weaving, in clematis, begins to cover their ends and proceeds for a few centimeters. An additional four pairs of ribs are then placed between the earlier three with their points barely tucked into the lashing. The weaving is completed but leaves the end sections of these four pairs exposed lying on top of the first section. This is an elegant way of avoiding congestion from too many ribs at the start, and is most attractive.

Frame basket with weavers in
clematis and exposed rib ends
(far left) and arm basket (left) in
brown willow used for collecting
rose petals, both from
Agricultural Museum, Sofia,
Bulgaria

225

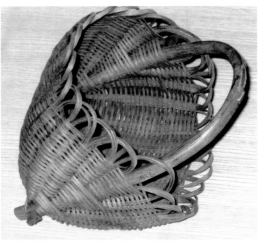

Right: Egg basket woven in willow skein with unusual rim attachments, Agricultural Museum, Sofia, Bulgaria

Far right: Fruit-picking basket in wood splint with looped border, Ethnographic Museum, Zagreb, Croatia

Below: With handles to hang on branches or feet to stand in the ground, Ethnographic Museum, Zagreb, Croatia

Below: Ox wearing muzzle. Photo: Ethnographic Museum, Zagreb

Right: Ox muzzle, Ethnographic Museum, Zagreb

A very finely made egg basket, also in the Sofia Agricultural Museum, solved this same problem of accommodating more ribs as the shape flows out and down in the more usual way. The later pairs are much shorter. But it emphasises the beautifully-shaped, flat, wood handle and rim hoops by keeping the rim largely free of weaving. This is achieved by cutting four wide mortices in the lower part of the rim hoop. Some of the weavers pass through these to anchor the upper ribs, but most of the rim remains exposed.

Bulgaria is renowned for its tradition of growing fields of roses used to distill the aromatic oil known as 'attar of roses'. In the valleys around Karlovo and Kazanlak the flowers are gathered early in the mornings in June and carried to the stills. I had hoped to find that they were picked into beautiful frame baskets to complement the sight and scent of the rose fields. The reality is that all the rose petal baskets preserved in Sofia's Agricultural Museum are quite ordinary brown-willow arm baskets which might be used for a dozen other jobs in farm, garden, or market!

Other frame baskets used for fruit picking, and displayed in the Agricultural Museum in Zagreb, have ingenious ways of using the handle 'hoops' as supports either by hanging on a branch, or sticking into the ground. One of these uses a method very similar to that noted in local berry-gathering baskets from near Kassel in Germany, and a large one from the Hautes Pyrenées in France is also similar. The ribs are inserted through holes drilled in a cross piece which is fixed to the bottom ends of the handle bow[1]. Another has close similarities to the *cageole du Comminges* mentioned in the French chapter[2], p114.

Specific items

Muzzles

Small-scale farmers would not often have had horses to help with their work, and instead relied upon cattle, donkeys, or mules. Where cattle were used to pull carts or implements there would be a need to prevent them eating crops while passing or resting, and so basketry muzzles were fitted over their mouths. A variety of models can be found in museums: close woven clematis from Sofia, and other openwork designs from Croatia. Perhaps the smaller calf-muzzles were used to control the time when the young animal was allowed to suckle its mother.

Fish traps for lakes and rivers

The freshwater traps in this region are similar to those made in Western Europe, and quite unlike the special Mediterranean traps for sea fish and crustacea (described in the next chapter). I found one stout model for sale in Sofia market, in semi-green (part-dried) willow rods, in stark contrast to the rather flimsy, buff-willow skeinwork which surrounded it. Several other shapes were seen in the Agricultural Museum in Zagreb. But this Croatian museum also has examples of a quite different trap used in another way. It is a simple cylinder or tube with both ends open. The side stakes are thin wooden slats. In some, these are held together by close-woven, brown willow rods, in others by just two or three separate rows of fitching with their top ends held by a hoop. The fisherman stands in the water with the trap held up, away from the bottom, and drops it smartly over any fish which come within its circumference! Similar traps are found in Hungary.

Stencil decorations

Above left: Maize bract bag collected at Sofia market, Bulgaria

Right: Rush bag collected at Zagreb market, Croatia

Rush bag, Sofia market, Bulgaria

Most woven baskets are left plain and unadorned. It is therefore all the more striking to see a proportion of those used by stallholders and customers in Croatia's markets with simple flower motifs painted on their sides in blue, red, white, and green. They seem most frequent on the display baskets of florists though some customers' baskets have them too. In Nova Gradiska they were seen on rectangular arm baskets, plaited probably from white and buff willow skein, brought by smallholders selling their produce.

Rush and maize bags

Tall rushes can be found in wet places in most of these countries and are used in a variety of ways. In Bulgaria (as also across the Danube in Romania) they find their way into inexpensive shopping bags which are lightweight and flat, so that when empty, they take up much less room than a rigid structure. Several quite different methods of construction are employed.

One technique is to use the folded rush leaves like rods in willow basketry. In a flat bag collected in Sofia, a rectangular base has been made in check-weave, the stakes pricked up, and the sides woven probably over a mould. A plaited border holds the two handles also in plait, and the top is closed by a simple fastening. A somewhat similar bag also from Sofia is made from maize where the 'stakes' are a twisted string and the weavers are flatter lengths both made from the cob bracts, some of them coloured to produce a geometric pattern.

In a much larger flat bag from Zagreb, the relatively fine rush (weft) has been tightly woven over twine (warp) to produce a sheet some 70cm square. It incorporates four rows of thicker three-ply rope which will eventually provide the handles and carry the load. This square sheet is folded onto itself, and the ends sewn together with twine. Finally, a separate border is attached to enclose the tops of the vertical side weavers.

Yet another style of bag from Sofia is based upon two flat coils forming the sides and handles, and simulating the multiple petals of a flower by leaving long lengths of each rush unwoven.

Notes and references

1.   Thierschmann, M. (2001) 'Bilberry Basket'. BA NL **99**: 17-22.
2.   Bertrand, B. (2006) 'La Vannerie Sauvage – initiation'. Editions de Teran (with DVD).

Cyprus, Greece, Malta, and Turkey

Red-figured Greek coffer
showing women at home,
470BC.
Photo: British Museum

Resources

This group of countries is the southern extremity of the Balkan region. Malta, Greece and Cyprus have typical Mediterranean climates with hot, dry summers and mild winters with winter rain, though the mountainous Greek mainland is naturally colder. Much of Greece is broken into hundreds of islands, so communications are not easy. There are a few flat areas more suited to intensive crop production, but in general farming has remained small-scale with cereals, fruit, and vegetables. The main livestock have been sheep and goats. On the other hand, Turkey is a large landmass, much of it mountainous, and its easterly position means that the summers are hot and dry while winters are bitterly cold. Milder conditions prevail along the long Mediterranean coastlines on the south and west, and the Black Sea to the north. There are also some lowland areas, particularly in Thrace, which is the continuation of northern Greece or southern Bulgaria.

The tree resources consist once again of willow, chestnut, hazel, olive and vine plus the chaste tree and myrtle. Straw is usually available besides reeds and rushes wherever there is adequate moisture. A very important basketry plant is the Mediterranean cane.

History

This region is the closest part of Europe to the Fertile Crescent so that we would expect the crafts of plaiting and weaving to have had a long history here. Archaeological evidence from Çatalhöyük in central Turkey (Anatolia), shows that coiling, plaiting, and twining were indeed practised at least from 7500BC[1]. Classical Greek civilization began to develop from around 2000BC, and progressed through a Mycenaean phase originating from the island of Crete around 1600BC. It suffered a sharp decline after 1300BC before more settled conditions from 1000BC led to urbanisation – the emergence of hundreds of separate city states. Improving technology, including metallurgy, was associated with population growth and emigration to found new cities around the Mediterranean.

We know quite a lot about the basketry items used in classical Greece from both written records and from sculptural work which has survived. These include such farming aids as baskets to gather grapes, fruit, and nuts; hold cheeses; and winnow grain. In addition there were travellers' baskets and long-necked provision baskets carried by soldiers. As societies became more sophisticated then rites and ceremonies would have become more formalised and elaborate. For example, various baskets were used to hold sacrificial knives and chaplets of flowers to be worn by the priests, images

Typical products of the Argos workshops in 'cane' and brown willow

Far left : Transport basket, Historical and Folklore Museum of Corinth, Greece

Left : Beehive, Peloponnesian Folklore Foundation, Nafplion, Greece

of gods, and sacred barley in services honouring their deities. The baskets themselves were gradually regarded as sacred instruments, and were adorned with flowers and either carried in procession on the heads of basket bearers or priestesses, or borne in horse-drawn chariots. They became associated with the goddess of tillage symbolising abundance, and hence were used at marriage rites. Gifts to a newly-married couple were conveyed to their house by women in procession led by one carrying a basket. Infants were placed in the winnowing fan as an omen of future health and prosperity.

In the city states which supported the flowering of beautiful stone buildings, sculpture, metalwork, jewelry, and pottery, it seems inconceivable that there would not also have been a simultaneous development of fine craftsmanship in the previously humble weaving of baskets – at least those utilised in public ceremonies. One can imagine that such willow articles would have achieved a peak of quality in this civilization.

The classical period ended with internal fighting and the region became the eastern part of the Roman Empire with its capital established in Byzantium (later re-named Constantinople, and then Istanbul). The western part (based on Rome) was eventually broken up, but the Byzantine Empire survived for a further 1000 years as a Greek-speaking Christian territory until the Ottoman Turks finally occupied it in the mid-15th century. At first the Ottoman Empire was widely admired in the West, and Istanbul grew into one of Europe's few large cities in the 16th century with organised guilds of basketmakers and mat makers. But this prosperity declined, and the region failed to match the social and industrial transformations taking place in western Europe. The Empire disintegrated piecemeal with Greece becoming independent in 1821 while the final shape of Turkey was settled only in 1923.

Since we have little detailed knowledge from post-classical times, the basketry styles and products featured below inevitably reflect the work current today and in the last century. Some will be relatively unchanged from those developed over millennia by small-scale farmers and fishermen using the materials which grow readily in these climates. In a few cases we are lucky to have written accounts to draw upon. One such concerns the industry which grew up in Argos, southwest of Athens in the Peloponnese region of Greece. Factories were built to process the crops which flourished on the surrounding plains into that essential Mediterranean food ingredient – tomato paste. During the 1930s these factories purchased 10,000-15,000 baskets annually from each of the many workshops in Argos. Supplies of willow and 'cane' from the surrounding villages proved inadequate for this new demand, and they had to be brought in from Sparta and Preveza on the west coast. Skilled workers too were drawn from other regions, and Argos became one of Greece's most important centres of the craft.

Fisherman mending nets with fishtraps suspended above him, Castelsardo, Sardinia

The workshop owners employed foremen who were paid piecework for the weekly output of their teams of wage-earning basketmakers. Working hours were from sunrise to sunset. They were housed in simple sheds with raised platforms for working on and with covered soaking pits in the ground. The disruption of World War II and the move to wooden containers for bulk transport caused the decline of the industry, though it continued in a reduced form during the 1970s.

A recent review of the surviving basketry crafts in Turkish Thrace and Anatolia concluded that only a few craft workers are still active in those areas[2].

Types of work

Once again, some basketry styles which are featured here are also quite widespread in other parts of the Mediterranean.

Traps for fish and crustacea

A stronger trap in Castelsardo, Sardinia

Above: Fish trap from Italy, Museo Nazionale delle Arti e Tradizioni Popolari

Right: A Cretan trap. Photo: R. Stathaki-Koumari and HOMMEH

Along many of the Mediterranean coasts and islands, the local fishermen have constructed conical or cylindrical traps (sometimes called bow-nets) which are of very different appearance from those used on the Atlantic coasts. Within their style, the size and shape varied with the species being pursued. While those most often illustrated look quite fragile because of their lightweight rods, there is a good selection in the museum in Castelsardo (Sardinia) which are much more robust and were used for crabs and lobsters. The lightweight models are made using side stakes, often pointed rush or common bulrush, set at 20^0 to the vertical in both directions. The horizontal member is a continuous spiral which may be 'cane' splint, or myrtle. Where these cross they are secured with twine, once made from the tips of rush leaves split and twisted into a two-ply string. This splint gives the whole structure a degree of rigidity and can be finer or coarser according to the target species. An inversion at one end provides a non-return device to funnel the fish towards the bait and hold them until the trap is next inspected. A removable round cover allows access from the opposite end.

Other authors have illustrated them from Bodrum (Turkey[3]), Crete[4], Malta[5], Corsica[6], Elba, and Ischia[7], and Spain[8]. Besides examining museum examples in Nafplion (Greece), I was delighted to see them still in use in Sardinia stacked up on a slipway in Bosa, and stored in a fisherman's hut in Castelsardo.

The same construction method is sometimes also employed to make maunds, arm baskets, and bowls and these are illustrated in the Italian chapter.

Split 'cane' work

One can find the giant reed (*Arundo donax*) growing throughout European countries bordering the Mediterranean from Spain to Turkey. It is often referred to as cane, *canna* (or similar words), but it is utilised especially in Greece and Turkey where it largely takes over the normal role of willow. The unbranched hollow stems are split lengthways into up to six rods which may be smoothed and reduced to a constant width but are often employed in a rough form. 'Cane' is normally used in conjunction with other rods (including brown, buff or white willow, hazel, chaste tree, and wild olive). These then form the base, side stakes, border, and handles while the skeined 'cane' appears only in the side weaving. However, examples can be found where some or even all of the other component parts are in 'cane'.

Arm baskets and maunds can still be seen in many parts of Greece. Argos has already been mentioned as a once-famous centre of the craft. Maunds of different size and shape were specific to each use and made by the thousands by professionals in many workshops during the early part of the 20th century[9]. The side weaving was 'cane' with the exception of bands of brown willow. These varied in number (one to five) and width according to the use for each basket.

The horticultural models were made in ascending height from 35 up to 75cm. These were for: dessert grapes; transport of courgettes, tangerines and grapes; tomato gathering and transport; citrus fruits and olives; artichokes; melons; tobacco leaves; water melons; and back baskets for harvesting wine grapes.

The largest maund made in Argos (five bands) was for carrying lamb carcasses. Other customers were bakers (display), fishermen (keeps for bait, traps, baited lines, and display), beekeepers (hives, swarm catchers), quarries (stones and lime), and housewives (bread containers, crockery drainers, laundry). The museum in Nafplion has examples of these and others for catching wild birds and transporting carrier pigeons. In addition, large numbers of glass containers for wine, oil, and other liquids were covered in 'cane'

Small table basket for bread, olive stakes, clematis base, and split 'cane' sides from Bodrum-Mugla, Turkey. Photo: Z. Füsun Ertug

in the same workshops. Although these were all working baskets, it is easy to see in their forms echoes of some classic Greek ceramic vessels.

I first collected an arm basket in a street market in 1985. It was in a small Greek town, wonderfully named Megalopolis! A different model without handle was the result of a chance discovery in 2001 and, although it was on the Adriatic coast of Italy, illustrates well what sometimes happens in basketry research. We had driven to the Gargano peninsula which juts out in to the Adriatic sea three-quarters of the way down the eastern coast of Italy. We were to visit a museum which turned out to be almost devoid of baskets. This was in Monte Sant'Angelo, perched some 800m above the coast and approached up a steep winding pilgrim road. We followed signs to a bakery, and soon found ourselves touring a very modern building which produced large traditional loaves with a natural leaven, and delivered them all over Italy. Stacked up alongside the mechanical mixers were piles of baskets made in nearby Bari. The dough is placed on a floured cotton liner inside each one and rises for several hours until ready for baking. It is then inverted and positioned with a long-handled peel on the hot oven floor. The owners allowed us to take photographs and presented me with a basket. I frequently use willow *bannetons* made in France when baking our own bread, but this large 'cane' version from the Italian bakery would make a loaf of several kilos, and I have yet to find the right occasion to use its generous capacity.

Arm baskets for sale in Megalopolis, Greece 1985

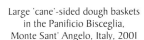

Large 'cane'-sided dough baskets in the Panificio Bisceglia, Monte Sant' Angelo, Italy, 2001

In southwest Turkey, small arm baskets for carrying eggs or herbs, and bowls for serving bread are based on olive stems as stakes, clematis weavers in the base, and 'cane' sides[10]. This same method of curving the top halves of the side stakes (olive or willow rods) to make a border and then down as a side decoration is also widespread throughout Greece.

Arm basket with decorative hoops, (olive or willow) and 'cane' weavers, Skyros, Greece. Photo: Museum Falteitz, Skyros and HOMMEH

Rush work

This general term covers a wide range of materials growing in damp or very wet conditions, from fine stiff *Juncus* species to much larger *Typha* species with quite broad leaves. Different weaving methods are employed, even with the same material.

Coiling with *Typha angustifolia* is used in central Anatolia in Turkey to produce mats and conical containers[11]. Other coiled articles are made with one or more flat sides. This is unusual since the coils (as in straw work) are more often kept in smooth curves. In Cyprus

Range of round and square baskets.
Coiled rush work in Sultansazligi, Develi-Kayseri region of Turkey.
Photo: Z. Füsun Ertug

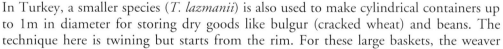

a two-ply twisted rope was coiled and sewn together with string to create a small lidded jar to hold a snack of olives. Plaiting with rushes is also found in Cyprus and this type of weave is seen in both bowls and arm baskets.

In Turkey, a smaller species (*T. lazmanii*) is also used to make cylindrical containers up to 1m in diameter for storing dry goods like bulgur (cracked wheat) and beans. The technique here is twining but starts from the rim. For these large baskets, the weaver

uses a flat metal ring (or tube section) as a moveable inner support or mould[12]. This is brought down gradually inside the basket as the weft elements (two continuous lengths of twisted rush) are woven in front and behind of the soft warp elements (side stakes, also twisted rush).

Olive snack basket made from coiled two-ply rush rope from Nicosia, Cyprus, Peloponnesian Folklore Foundation, Nafplion, Greece

Left: Method of twining the container using a tubular metal mould

Far left: Twined rush container for storing bulgur or beans from Aksaray, Turkey.
Photos: Z. Füsun Ertug

Right: Cheese mould in Styrax sp. from Crete, collected by Mia Pot

Above: Cheese mould in fine rush from Skyros, Greece. Photo: Museum Falteitz, Skyros and HOMMEH

Right: Small sewing basket in Cyperus papyrus by Byron Papadopoulos, Nisi, Lake of Ioannina, Greece. Photo: R. Stathaki-Koumari and HOMMEH

Far rght: Oil pressing bag in rush from Limasol, Cyprus, Peloponnesian Folklore Foundation, Nafplion, Greece

As in other Mediterranean regions, Greek shepherds used to make their own simple cheese moulds from rushes gathered where their flocks grazed (see earlier reference in Italian chapter). The fresh curds were pressed into these to drain and begin their maturation. Not surprisingly, both the type of rush and the type of weaving varied, and two different examples can be observed: openwork from Chios, Greece; and close woven work from Cyprus. Some of the flatter, bowl-shaped moulds are strikingly similar to those made today by Maria Raimonda Pinna in Sardinia, though hers have close-woven sloping sides (see materials chapter p36).

Small sewing baskets and hats were woven from *Cyperus papyrus* gathered from the waters of Lake Ioannina up near the Albanian border, while rectangular trays and lidded bags were made from *Typha latifolia* in Macedonia. The fine rush *Juncus inflexus* was plaited into circular bags to contain the linseed grains during oil pressing.

Coiled straw work

Sewing basket of coiled straw sewn with a straw weaver from Iraklion, Crete. Photo: Museum of Cretan Ethnology, Voiroi and HOMMEH

The women of Greece, Turkey and Cyprus have a tradition of coiling straw. They made quite thin coils, very different from the usual work we associate with beehives or meal storage vessels in other regions. The objects they created played important roles in family and religious life and were made with great care. Unbroken wheat stalks were selected, and successive coils were attached to each other either by additional flattened straws which

wrapped them completely, or by twine which left the straw core exposed. Some of the wrapping straws were dyed so as to produce coloured patterns. The simplest shape was a flat disk, but others were curved up to form shallow or deep bowls, and some had lids or side handles. The rim and foot might have additional decoration in the form of one or more coils attached as zigzag edges.

In Crete, such items had their everyday use as wall decorations, to hold spools of wool near the loom, or as sewing baskets. But in addition, a young girl would make and decorate a set of six special baskets for her future wedding[13]. They would then hold the bride's clothes, the gifts (perhaps towels) she would offer, the wedding rings on a hand-woven towel covered with rose petals, special breads for the church, a bread offering for the mass, and linen for the nuptial bed. The groom would also send his gifts to the bride in similar baskets (*paneria*). Others would hold rose petal confetti. Later they would hold fruit, nuts and rusks offered to those who came to congratulate the new mother on her baby's birth, and then new clothes for the christening. On feast days they would be used for flowers or coloured eggs and Easter bread. After a death they contained the special funeral bread. In Cyprus the coloured decorations are often elaborate.

237

Right: Fishing line basket in split 'cane' and olive rods with cork rim to hold the hooks. Mykonos, Greece.
Photo: R. Stathaki-Koumari and HOMMEH

Conical fruit picker in hazel splint from the Black Sea area of Turkey.
Photo: F. Ertug

Arm basket in frame construction from Volas, Thessaly, Greece.
Photo: K Arkoudoyiannis and HOMMEH

Specific items

Conical fruit picker

An interesting conical basket has been described from the Black Sea coast of Turkey[14]. Made from hazel splint (sometimes willow), the side stakes seem to be inserted into a small wooden cone. The splint weavers receive additional stakes as they progress up the sides and the mouth is finished with one or two hoops lashed onto the weavers. It is suspended vertically by a string attached to the rim and can be hung on a branch while being filled with grapes or other fruit.

Fishing-line basket

Men exploit the available fish species with baited lines or nets all around the Greek coasts. A simple round maund (*paneri-paragadi*), often with stakes of wild olive and weavers of split 'cane', has a rim of cork attached on top of the rope border[15]. The many fish hooks are inserted into this rim and their barbed points kept safely out of the way.

Frame baskets

It is interesting that the same technique is used in some Greek baskets as was previously noted in Bulgarian examples in the Balkan chapter. The wrapping where the rim and handle hoops cross is in the form of a bold 'eye of God'. Alternate ribs are exposed by laying them on top of the first rows of weaving before tucking their ends into the wrapping.

Bird traps

Long cylindrical structures were made – quite different from the flat traps which were featured in the French chapter. The side weaving in split cane is sometimes covered in animal skin as camouflage.

Notes and references

1.   I have not yet had the opportunity to study basketry at first hand in Turkey, but believed it important to include at least its western parts in this study. Fortunately the IVth International Congress of Ethnobotany was held at the University of Yeditepe in Istanbul in 2005 and its published proceedings (ICEB 2005) include a lot of information. Furthermore, Dr Füsun Ertug, the Congress Secretary, has been most helpful in answering my many queries relating to the work which she described in her own contributions: Ertug, F.Z. (2006a) 'An Overview of the Plaited Crafts of Turkey (Anatolia and Thrace) ICEB 2005: 297-306; (2006b) 'Turkey' ICEB 2005: 673-679.
2.   See 1a p302.
3.   See 1a p299.
4.   In 1985 the Hellenic Organisation of Small and Medium Sized Enterprises (HOMMEH) published the results of an initial study of basketry in Greece. The first part was a quite thorough study of the craft in Crete while the second was described as a 'sampling' from various other Greek districts. I must thank the Director of Crafts and Affiliated Companies for permission to lean heavily on this work. Stathaki-Koumari, R. (1985) 'Basket Weaving in Greece'. HOMMEH Edition.
5.   Gray, G. (2000) 'A Basket-free Zone?' BA NL **92**:28-30; and Jones, G. (2005) 'Short Review of Basketry on Malta and Gozo'. Geraldine Jones was awarded a bursary by the Worshipful Company of Basketmakers, London to study the construction of these fish traps.
6.   O'Bryan, G. (1989) 'Corsican Fishing Baskets'. BA NL **51**: 14.
7.   Will, C. (1984) 'International Basketry for Weavers and Collectors', Ed. Force, E., Schiffer Publishing Ltd, p74.
8.   Kuoni, B. (1981) 'Cestería Tradicional Ibérica' Ediciones del Serbal pp259-261.
9.   Efthymiou-Chatzilacou, M. (1979-80) 'Basket Weaving in Argos' Ethnology 2: 57-82, Peloponnesian Folklore Foundation, Nafplion.
10.   See 1b p679.
11.   See 1b p674-676.
12.   See 1b p677.
13.   See 4 p35.
14.   See 1a p299.
15.   See 4 p37.

239

The Eastern Borders

Nesting doll,
Moscow, Russia

Right: Decorated cylindrical lidded containers in birch bark sheets, Russia

Far right: Staved wooden basket, Russia

Exhibition in Schloss Kittsee Museum, Austria

Russia, Belarus, the Ukraine, and Moldova cover a huge land area which has a strong claim to be the eastern edge of Europe. These countries occupy the eastern plains from the Barents and White seas right down to the Black Sea, and are home to some 200 million people. While the Russian Federation extends all the way east to the Bering Sea, most of its population lives in its European region, west of the Urals.

This area has no sharp natural boundaries except the rivers whose valleys dissect the plateau and which have provided both centres of settlement and a network of communications. The continental climate has rain and snowfall decreasing to the south and east. The northern regions bordering Finland are birch scrub, or spruce and pine forest. Coming further south into the Ukraine there were woodlands and tall grassland on the Black Earth soils until these were replaced by mixed farming and small towns in the 16th and 17th centuries. Further south again, the treeless prairie was first colonised and cultivated only in the 18th and 19th centuries after the clearance of Turkish-speaking nomads.

Many of the points made in previous chapters about central and eastern countries apply equally here. In particular, the vast proportion of this huge area continued to have agrarian economies with relatively little urban development much later than the north-western countries. Most people existed in the countryside living as serfs who worked for the landowners until the late 19th century, although there were of course some centres of wealth and urban culture. These contained craftworkers employed by the court and aristocracy, who were often from other lands.

It was only in the mid-19th century that willow-based industries were started, particularly around Moscow. Schools were opened from the end of that century, and just before the Revolution of 1917 over 30,000 workers were active in the trade[1]. No doubt the peasants continued making their traditional articles from bast, roots, straw, birch bark, and wood splint.

I have travelled several times to northern Russia but have seldom seen fewer baskets anywhere than on the streets of Moscow and St Petersburg, even in the late 1980s when thousands of citizens were searching for food or consumer goods in long queues. They seemed to prefer light bags which could be folded away, but were always at the ready. My knowledge is therefore limited to the exhibits I have seen in museums in other countries, the few objects on offer in tourist shops, and more recent information from friends who have visited ethnographic museums. I still hope to explore Europe's eastern limits more thoroughly, to understand better the traditions, and see what has survived.

It is natural that basketry in the north is closely related to that already described from the Baltic States and Finland. These are the lands where birch bark has been used in folded sheets, or in plaited strips, to produce bowls, boxes, rucksacks, slippers, and small household items like salt cellars. Coiled rootwork was common, and wild willow was employed for arm baskets in the frame technique as well as for fish traps. Further south we would expect some extensions of wood splint work from the western borders of Poland and Romania. Modern factory-produced willow articles are similar to late 20th century Polish, Carpathian and Balkan work.

Plaited birch bark from Russia in exhibition, Schloss Kittsee Museum, Austria

Above: Rucksack

Centre: Boots, shoes and salt cellars

Far left : Decorative piece in willow skein by Alexander Tilly, Samara, Russia

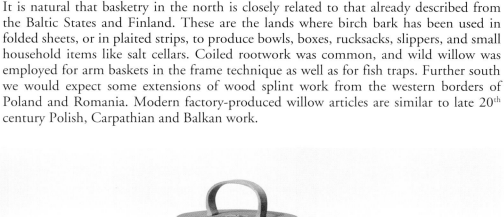

Modern tourist items from Russia in birch bark, fine wood splint, and straw

Notes and references

1.   Doobrovskiy, U.M. (1993) 'Thirty-two Lessons of Willow Weaving' quoted in letter of 1999 to Mia Pot-van Regteren Altena from Alexander Tilly who taught decorative art in a school in Samara (formerly Kuybyshev) east of Moscow.

Detail from arm basket in white willow by David Drew from his 1986 London exhibition

Modern shopping uses different baskets, Abingdon, 2008

- Early man developed basketry techniques to help him catch his prey, carry food, and provide shelter in his camps. As he adopted agriculture and more settled living, so he developed the skills to make a wider range of containers to catch, carry, display, store, and prepare food and other possessions; and to improve his shelter. Baskets performed traditional roles in many societies which gave them complex cultural significance[1].

- Populations grew and colonised extra land, selecting more efficient strains of plants and animals, and producing these more reliably and in greater number. The total amount of basketmaking increased, but the activity remained within each family group.

- With the adoption of urban living by a proportion of the population, there was a growth in specialist professions including warriors, priests and rulers, and the need for others to service them with food, clothing, housing, furniture, and household goods. So we have the emergence of people who specialised in basketmaking for a least part of their time. Some would themselves be town dwellers, and would group together in associations or guilds to protect their interests within the community, while others would remain in the countryside.

- The craft seems to have achieved near perfection in the whole range of techniques very early. It became almost static[2].

- The growth of towns in turn demanded that a proportion of the rural population change from self-sufficient farming to commercial agriculture and fishing, and others to mining and quarrying, creating new needs for basketry. Improved transport systems using road, water, and eventually railway allowed and encouraged the movement of more goods over longer distances. All this increased the need for different types of containers in much greater numbers, and hence more professional makers. The favoured material was often willow so there was an increase in its cultivation, but work in wood splint, straw, rush, cane, and grass also expanded.

- The growth of technology then began to provide alternative solutions for many of the needs which basketry had been satisfying. New materials (cardboard, plastic) were manipulated by automated processes (thus saving labour costs) to create containers which had more convenient shapes and were non-returnable. Mechanisation allowed bulk handling of many commodities, loose, or in boxes, nets or sacks, or on pallets.

Competition from the Far East: a traditional French open arm basket in white willow (left) and (right) a cheap copy from China, 1989

- These new solutions caused a huge reduction in the need for baskets by all types of users: food producers, manufacturers, wholesale and retail traders. Also, urban consumers shopped less frequently and carried their goods further from market to home in their cars, or had them delivered in vans. Cheap oil provided the basis for plastics. Retailers provided more and more plastic or paper bags emblazoned with their corporate logos for the unprepared or overladen customer. Supermarkets provided long-lasting hand baskets or trolleys made of wire.

- The number of self-sufficient rural families also declined continuously, and many of today's country-dwellers have adopted an almost urban way of life. As a result, the making of farm and garden baskets in this sector has decreased, and so too has the cultural significance of baskets in all sorts of activities.

- Finally, for those traditional basketry needs which have survived, competing sources of supply have arisen based on wage differentials within Europe, and now between Europe and the Far East and Africa.

But while this pattern of development may be evident in every part of Europe, its timing has certainly not been synchronized. Those countries which adopted urban living early, like England and The Netherlands, and quickly went on to develop commercial farming and manufacturing industries, built complex transport systems at a time when baskets were still the main type of container. They therefore lost most of their subsistence farmers and the basketry skills which were part of that ancient way of life. Instead, they grew their professional basketry industries based upon cultivated willow. These peaked around 1900 but then dwindled to almost nothing by 2000.

By contrast, some of the central and eastern countries remained primarily agrarian economies until much later. By 1970 they still had large rural populations. Even where communism had forced them to pool most of their land, they continued to farm up to one or two hectares in a traditional way and retained many of their old skills. As their industries grew, and transport systems developed, these countries were able to proceed straight to some of the newer container systems provided by more modern technology. So their willow-based basketry industries never assumed the importance seen in the industrialised nations. On the other hand, state planners were able to see the potential for supplying the remaining domestic basketry needs of countries in north-west Europe based on their own much lower wage rates. They actually grew this branch of their basketry industries while the corresponding English and Dutch businesses were fast disappearing.

Baskets in use for garden produce: potatoes (left) and damsons (right)

Today, even in the former communist states, the old rural way of life is in decline. Children fail to practise their parents' traditional skills. Mary Butcher has written about the loss of age-old knowledge of the suitability, harvesting, processing and preparation of a range of plant materials "when it is no longer transmitted between generations"[3]. In these same countries we now also see the closure of their factory-based basket enterprises when the harsh realities of capitalist economics finally intrude.

In western Europe the numbers of professional basket workers continued to fall as the last of the apprenticed members reached retirement, and most of the training schools and disabled workshops had closed[4]. There was an inevitable knock-on effect on willow cultivation with the areas and numbers employed falling further.

Nevertheless, baskets continue to be made and sold – so what is happening?

Wood splint and 'cane' baskets still being sold in quantity in 1995, Barcelos, Portugal

Traditional products for traditional purposes

In spite of the generalisation that urban-dwelling Europeans no longer need baskets to catch, carry, display, store or process food and other items, many are still used for some of these purposes. A proportion of this huge population (about 730million) still buys arm baskets and bags for shopping. Many still use woven containers for soiled and clean linen, for logs, pets, and picnics; and even have cradles, trays, and garden hurdles. In countries which have retained a relatively high number of farming families, additional baskets for harvesting garden crops, rising dough, storing produce, or keeping bread or cakes are used, at least by the older generation.

Since most of these purchasers are price sensitive, the majority of such goods today originate in countries with low wages. This often means the Far East: China, Taiwan, Philippines, and Africa. But Europe still produces considerable numbers in Spain and Portugal, Poland, Romania, Bulgaria, and the Balkans; and some of these utilise local materials other than willow. While the previous State or cooperative factories may have ceased trading (see chapters on Poland and Romania), their facilities and staff have sometimes been reorganised by individual entrepreneurs.

Left: Crib or cradle in white willow by Sally Goymer who combines English traditions with techniques from other countries in northern Europe

Right: La trinité, a complex piece in white willow (40cm diameter) created by André Rousseau in Paris around 1890. Today a few are made by Danielle Martin in the Cooperative at Villaines-les-Rochers, France. Each takes a whole day to complete

Even in northwest Europe with its higher costs of living, some craftsmen and women continue to sell traditional products. How do they do this? Many will just accept relatively low prices and thus effectively a low rate of pay – nothing new for a basketmaker! Perhaps they need to work from home, value independence, have some type of disability, or combine making these products with other activities which pay better. Selling such domestic items at markets or craft fairs can bring them into contact with the public after long days alone in a workshop[5].

But some craftworkers can command higher prices even for domestic baskets because a segment of the market recognises high-quality work, and has the resources to pay for it. Examples have already been given from Finland, Latvia, Germany, Britain and Ireland. This segment may expand in future based upon rising prosperity and the increasing interest in issues around sustainability which are already evident in food purchasing in some countries.

The two cooperatives in France may be special cases. Their members argue that by representing a high proportion of the French professionals (and hence cutting out damaging competition on price), and of course by maintaining very high standards of workmanship, they have made themselves price makers rather than price takers. They continue to sell large volumes of products even into their traditional markets: the retailers of fish, cheese, charcuterie, bread and cakes. Naturally some of their baskets have to be in new shapes and sizes to fit in with modern self-service retailing methods.

Basketry in white willow used in modern bread retailing, made by the Société Coopérative Agricole de Vannerie, Villaines-les-Rochers, France.
Photo: Coopérative Vannerie de Villaines

Traditional products for new purposes

While the vast majority of traditional craft items were always utilitarian objects, with a clear use, that did not mean that their aesthetic qualities were not appreciated. People with money chose to use items where the workmanship was of the highest quality, especially clothes, furniture, or room decorations. And our peasant ancestors also took pride in their few possessions, especially items which they wore or carried since they indicated many subtle ranks within the social hierarchy.

Left: Small arm basket well made in white and brown willow showing the maker's tag - Graham Glanville, Whithorn, Scotland

Right: Slatted tray in white and brown willow and hazel, the type of bold modern work produced by Jenny Crisp, Leominster, England

Now that many more people in the West have money to spend on things other than food and housing, it is not surprising that some take an interest in high-quality traditional baskets, even when they have no intention of using them for their original purpose. Their interest may simply be as 'ethnographic objects of a bygone culture'[6] to which the owner feels some connection. But they may be bought for some new use, or as objects like items of pottery, glass, or sculpture.

Part of the exhibition of David Drew's work at the Crafts Council Gallery, London in 1986

For me, one early event which impressed by the sheer beauty of well-made baskets from a traditional maker was the 1986 solo exhibition at the Crafts Council Gallery, London devoted to the work of David Drew. Some 250 baskets in white and brown willow produced in the previous nine months were displayed and offered at prices which clearly announced that such work should begin to be valued alongside the more usual gallery crafts. Many other talented makers must have been grateful for such a bold statement which has surely helped them have their own work appreciated and collected[7].

In spite of this, there still seems to be little evidence of a collector's market for traditional baskets in Europe by private individuals. In the United States there has long been fierce competition to acquire good examples of such work, both native and from immigrants. I have at least three collectors' guides dating from the 1970s[8].

People outside northwest Europe, who have not yet reached the same levels of disposable income, may nevertheless wish to express their national identities by displaying traditional objects. Such a move has already been noted for the Baltic States where old craft traditions were deliberately revived in the 1970s. A recent lavishly illustrated book on Slovenian crafts shows many old forms in a range of materials and promotes the individual makers[9]. But this may not always apply. Instead there can be a rejection of the old symbols associated with poverty in favour of universal 'modern' furnishings and décor.

Examples of traditional items being produced long after their original use has disappeared can be found in many countries. Some of these have already been illustrated in the appropriate chapters.

- From France we may include the eel trap, winnowing fan, *hotte* (back basket for harvesting grapes), *manne à vendange* (large receiving basket to hold 60 to 80kg grapes), sparrow trap, and *égrappoir* (large sieve used in the grape harvest)

- from England the quarter-cran herring basket and Cumbrian swill, the skib in Ireland

- from Germany, Austria, and Switzerland the large back baskets

- from Norway the coiled rootwork celebratory baskets

- from Sardinia the bottle cover in fine rush.

In addition, small or miniature versions often, but not always, made by retired craftworkers in several countries. These include models of Galician grape harvesting baskets in chestnut splint, and plaited grass objects (using Ampelodesmos) in the Aurunci mountain area of Italy.

Lluis Grau and Anna Champeney have a very practical approach to the problems of preventing the loss of traditional work in their adopted home of Galicia, Spain. They accept that by themselves they are unable to return the living basketry traditions to each region. What they can do is to seek out the old craft workers and record their methods, products, and language in words and pictures. By learning these techniques and forms they can then offer to teach courses in order to preserve them. They seek to be a link with the past and to transmit this knowledge and skill in the hope that others will eventually produce and even develop what is otherwise destined for extinction[10].

Jacket in white willow by David Drew on a 9litre cider jar by John Leach, Somerset, England 1988. Photo: R.J. Whittick

Hot-air balloon basket in willow and cane built on a strong metal frame and with leather protection 1989

Products which have been revived or introduced into new markets

Many traditional basketmakers have seen opportunities for extra products to replace or supplement those whose market has declined. The growing popularity of hot-air ballooning in Britain and elsewhere requires strong people-carriers in

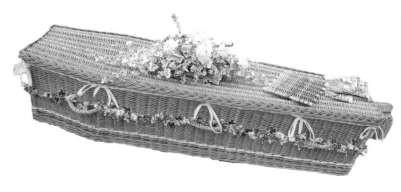

Traditional coffin in peeled willow inlaid with coloured bands. The Somerset Willow Company, Bridgewater, England

steel-reinforced willow or cane to hold from three to 50 persons! One English firm was already making two a week in the 1970s[11], and another made four or five a week in 2001[12].

The modern balloon basket may be a relatively new product, but the willow coffin is clearly a revival. By 2008 this same firm was making 35-40 coffins a week as interest has grown in 'green' burials based upon quickly renewable resources. Even here there is strong competition from Asia and Central Europe. These two products have brought much needed work and required the training of new young makers.

Right: Matthew Lewis demonstrating and selling willow baskets, garden sculpture, and plant support structures at a hedge-laying competition, Oxfordshire, 2000

Below: Living willow fence and below right: 'globe', both by Anna Patrucco, Italy

Woven drawers have also become fashionable in many modern kitchens. Several English craftworkers have made these their major product since customers are prepared to pay premium prices to upgrade this part of their houses.

Garden structures (arches, bower seats, arbours) and supports for tall-stemmed or climbing plants proved a useful new line for English makers, but they were soon copied by Far Eastern suppliers

who can sell much more cheaply through commercial garden centres[13]. Outdoor sculptures of human or animal figures and living willow fences are now parts of the basketmaker's repertoire[14].

There have always been sectors of basketmaking devoted to furniture, and again greater prosperity has led to many people investing in chairs, benches and tables for use outside or in their new glazed conservatories. The Bulgarian firm Prolet, from Shumen, has also specialised in such products for the new shops and bars which have opened in recent years after decades of drab décor. These are made in buff willow skein which is woven on to wooden frames to produce display units, partitions, and bar counters for the growing consumer culture.

In the hills northeast of Cannes in the far south of France, Edmond Ghiglione (Italian by birth) continued to make the large willow baskets utilised by florists along the wealthy coast. But he, and now his son René, extended the tradition by experimenting with new shapes for a different clientele drawn to the numerous craft boutiques in their village of Biot. They used several varieties of willows left unpeeled. In 1989 their workshop displayed a most unusual range of platters, horns of plenty, and variations on classic back baskets with many subtle colours. Ten years later René was working in the same way and to the same high standards[15].

In recent years, Lithuanian workers have been taking beautifully made white willow 'flowers' to the annual Lichtenfels Korbmarkt where they are in great demand.

Right: Terry Bensley, one of the last of the English apprenticed basketmakers, demonstrating the making of the Great Yarmouth herring swill, a frame basket in brown willow and cane, at the Basketmakers' Association 2006 summer meeting in Suffolk. Terry calculated he had made 80,000 baskets in 52 years at work

Work produced by class members at a 5-day course run by the Basketmakers' Association in Buckinghamshire, England 2001 and tutored by Anne Hermans from Belgium

When I was there in 1995 customers were snatching them before the stallholders had time to display them alongside their other baskets.

Another line of diversification has always been the making of individual pieces for shop displays, or for use in theatre, cinema, and television productions often to reproduce historic scenes, though even here there is competition from other countries.

Teaching

Below: Garden sculpture in willow by Jocelin Whitfield

In addition to surviving by producing the several categories of products reviewed in the preceding sections, many traditional basketmakers have been able to supplement their incomes by teaching or demonstrating at shows and fairs. They have transferred some of their skills, mainly to amateurs with a hobby interest – although some of these may in time turn professional In Britain, the Women's Institute movement had a long record of organising classes for its members, originally including cane basketry and then the use of hedgerow material. In 1975 a group of mature students from the first course in Contemporary Basketmaking, developed at the London College of Furniture, decided to form the Basketmakers' Association, and this was soon holding exhibitions and organising its own courses often tutored by the last of the apprenticed men[16]. Now almost every British professional spends some time teaching.

Comparable situations have developed in several other countries including France, Germany, the Netherlands, Denmark, Sweden, and Finland. In others the initiative may have been based in the surviving national training schools. One happy consequence has been a sharing and cross-fertilisation of traditions from different regions through invitations to teach or study in another country. There is now plenty of evidence that some of today's professionals have incorporated into their regular work techniques acquired from another part of Europe.

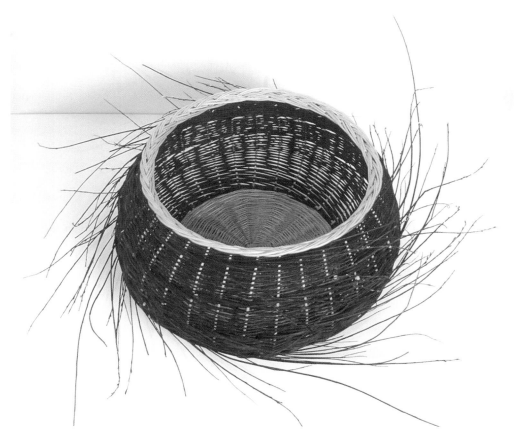

Objects derived from traditional baskets or using traditional techniques

"Originally the handcraftsman was a supplier of all man's basic needs. Everything made, whether utilitarian, ritual or merely decorative (and often one cannot separate these functions) (was) essentially a craft object. Later …. there was an intellectual separation between the idea of craft and that of fine art, which eventually (at least in Europe from the Renaissance onwards) came to be regarded as superior"[17]. Today developments in the fine arts have perhaps produced a reaction. A renewed interest in virtuosity in the handling of materials has appeared, and the long distinction between craft and art may be breaking down. A new generation of contemporary makers has emerged using both traditional and new materials, and all the classic techniques. The dividing line between their work and the containers which have constituted the subject matter of this book may be that they are not intended for use. Their artistic creations are made only for display - public or private, indoors or outside.

The background to the emergence of a new basketry has been traced by Mary Butcher in her several contributions to 'Contemporary International Basketry[18]. The book accompanied the exhibition of the same name organised by the Crafts Council in Britain in 1999, and is a useful starting point for anyone wishing to pursue this branch of the craft. A more recent volume is the catalogue which accompanies the European Baskets exhibition organised by the Crafts Council of Ireland in 2008[19]. I have illustrated this development with a very few examples, which are closely related to traditional work. These are of course only at one edge of the new movement, but they perhaps provide a bridge between it and the long European tradition which I have tried to document.

Notes and references

1.   Butcher, M. (1999) 'Contemporary International Basketmaking'. Merrell Holberton pp25-31.
2.   Lucie-Smith, E. (1981) 'The Story of Craft - the craftsman's role in society'. Phaidon Press p23.
3.   Butcher, M. (2006) 'An Introduction to Basketry in Eastern and Central Europe'. ICEB 2005: 684-687.
4.   Collins, E.J.T. (2004) 'Crafts in the English Countryside' Countryside Agency. This is a survey of the state of craftwork in England and has a section on basketry by Upton, V, Sully, J. and Collins, E.J.T. pp153-166.
5.   Brigden, R. (2008) 'Rural Crafts Today' Museum of English Rural Life. A record of a film project 2006-2008 which documents 10 different crafts and assesses their preservation and presentation in English museums and archives. Includes a DVD of 10 short films and a CD with these assessments, and graphics banners for an exhibition at the museum in 2008.
6.   See 1. p34.
7.   Crafts Council (1986) 'David Drew: Baskets'. Illustrated booklet with essays and photographs on the occasion of the touring exhibition of his work.
8.   Teleki, G.R. (1975) 'The Baskets of Rural America' and (1979) 'Collecting Traditional American Basketry' E.P. Dutton, also Thompson, F. (1977) 'Antique Baskets and Basketry'. A.S. Barnes and Co.
9.   Bogataj, J (1999) 'Handicrafts of Slovenia - encounters with contemporary Slovene craftsmen'. Rokus.
10.   Grau, L. (2008) 'Split Wood Basketry of Los Ancares'. Report to the Basketmakers' Association, 24pp.
11.   Rogers, F. (1982/83) 'Balloon Basket'. BA NL **24** 14-15.
12.   Excell, J. (1989) 'Balloon Baskets'. BA NL **48** 10-11.
13.   Basham, A. (2000) 'How to Make Hurdles from Willow (Osier) - following an East Anglian pattern'. The Basketmakers' Association; and Tabor, R. (1944) 'Wattle hurdles' in Traditional Woodland Crafts. Batsford.
14.   Warnes, J. (2000) 'Living Willow Sculptures'. Search Press.
15.   Fuller, S. (1999) 'Nice Baskets'. BA NL **90** 47-49.
16.   The Basketmakers' Association published a comprehensive booklet (25th Anniversary) in October 2000 celebrating its first 25 years of existence. This contains numerous short articles describing the founding, growth, and development of the Association which has contributed so much to the craft's survival in Britain.
17.   See 2: pp 8-11.
18.   See 1.
19.   Butcher, M. and Hogan, J. (2008) 'European Baskets'. The Crafts Council of Ireland.

Glossary of English Technical Terms*

		Illustration or further explanation on page
Arm basket	with a single arch, bow or cross-handle for carrying on the crooked arm, or hand	186
Assembled	made from components using techniques other than weaving	50
Base sticks	short lengths of rod forming the foundation of the base	45
Bast	the fibrous inner bark of a tree, especially lime	33 and 145
Beaten work	see scuttle work	45
Bolt	a bundle of rods of one size	31
Bracts	leaf-like parts of the maize plant which enclose the cob	35
Brown willow	dried willow rods with the bark still on, whatever the colour	30
Buff willow	willow rods after boiling and stripping, which leaves the skin stained brown by the bark tannins	30
Butt	the thick end of a tapering rod	-
Bye stakes	stakes added after the initial set usually as the basket's circumference expands	45
'Cane'	the stem of *Arundo donax*, naturalised in many Mediterranean countries	37
Check weave	a simple plait	42
Chip	thin wood splint, often pine, used to weave punnets	32
Cleave	to split a rod longitudinally into three or four using a tool called a cleave	31
Corner posts	the four stakes in the corners of square work, often thicker than the other stakes	46
Creel	sometimes a specific kind of pannier or back basket made in Ireland, Scotland, and other north-western parts, but sometimes a general Scottish term for a basket and particularly a pouch-shaped basket for fish	74 and 68

*The Basketmakers' Association issued a list of equivalent basketry terms in French, Spanish (Castilian and Catalan), German and Italian in July 2007

257

Cuttings	willow is normally propagated by cutting 20-35cm lengths (sets) from one-year-old rods in late winter and pressing them into the ground. This will normally be done before the buds have sprouted	64
Daub	a mortar applied to wattle walls	9
Fitching	openwork in the fabric of a basket (usually siding) with the stakes held in position by one or more rows of a two-strand weave	45 and 47
Flat	rectangular basket with hinged lid for transporting fruit or vegetables which could crush	66
Flow	the outward slant of the sides of a basket	203
Frame	the one or more rigid members to which the ribs (stakes) are attached in the frame method of construction	48
Green willow	fresh-cut rods (more often used semi-green or part-dried)	29
Lapping, lashing, or wrapping	binding with skeined material	123
Leg	a short section of coppiced tree trunk which raises the annual growth of shoots out of flood water or to make cutting easier	29
Lip work	work using coiled straw	169
Looping	basketry made with a single continuous weaver	49
Maund	a large round (or oval) more or less straight-sided basket, often with two small side handles	137
Netting	basketry where netting techniques are used with stiffer elements to give a rigid structure	50
Open work	where the weaving does not fill all the spaces between the stakes	47
Oriental cane	several species of tropical creeper imported from the Far East and used whole, skeined, or as the central core (distinguish from 'cane' from a tall reed growing in Mediterranean countries)	34
Osier	another name for willow	28
Pairing	a weave where two weavers are worked alternately over and under each other forming a twist	45
Plank base	a solid piece of wood with holes drilled around the edges to anchor the stakes	44
Picking (knife)	for cutting off the projecting ends of weavers when a basket is completed (today often done with secateurs)	7 and 48
Pitting	standing green willow rods in a shallow pond (or pit) until bud burst in April/May when they are stripped to produce white willow	29
Plait	a weave where all (two or more) elements are active	42
Pot	sometimes a small basket for soft fruit, sometimes a trap for crabs, lobsters etc.	66 and 76
Pricked up	willow stakes turned up over the point of a knife after they have been inserted in the base	45

Punnet	a small basket made of thin wood splint	140
Rand	a single rod worked in front of one stake and behind the next	45
Rapping	beating down the rounds of weaving with a blunt-edged heavy iron tool to achieve a tight finish	7 and 46
Ribs	the shaped stakes in a frame basket	48 and 113
Rim hoop	usually a single thick rod or length of splint bent into a round or oval and forming the top edge of a frame basket	48
Rive	to split wood along the grain	26 and 28
Rod	a whole shoot of one year's growth (older rods are usually branched but may be trimmed and used in specific roles)	30
Rope handles	wrapped with a spiral of finer rods	65
Scallom	a method of fixing a stake to another rod by cutting away part of the stake's thickness at one end and wrapping the reduced part around the rod	39
Screw block	a device to clamp sticks in position during the weaving of a base	46
Scuttle work	the technique of weaving willow rods very tightly around stakes made from wooden slats	45
Seedlip	seed basket used when sowing by broadcasting	169
Sets	see cuttings	64
Siding	the side of the basket and the weave used there	45
Sieve	either a cylindrical market basket for fruit or an article with a slatted base used for sieving	66 and 171
Shave	a device which planes the triangular section cleaved from a rod to remove the inner pith and produce a skein	48
Shopknife	for general purpose cutting	7 and 48
Skein	the shaved outer skin of a rod normally after the bark has been stripped off and the inner pith planed away	151
Skin	the outer part of a rod under the bark	-
Slath	the arrangement of sticks used to start a base	45
Slats	flat strips of wood used as stakes in scuttle work	46
Slewing	a quick weave using two or more rods together as though they were one	45
Slype	a long sloping cut made on the butt of a rod often to make it easier to force the end of a stake into the base	45
Spine	one or more thick rods forming the keel of a frame basket (and often continuing to form a handle hoop)	48
Splint	(also spale, spelk, split) thin strips split from saplings and pole-sized trees and used as stakes and weavers	27
Square work	baskets with corners and straight sides, whether square or rectangular	46
Stool	the base part of a coppiced tree, at or above ground level	29
Stripping	removing the bark from a rod	30

Stroke	a movement in basketmaking, repeated as part of a weave, like a stitch in sewing or knitting	-
Swill	general purpose round or oval basket usually with side hand-spaces, often in splint	73
Tip	the thin end of a rod	-
Twining	working two or more weavers together where they change positions as they pass successive stakes and hold these in position	47
Twisted rod handle	twisting a willow rod partly separates the fibres and allows it to be bent without kinking	137
Tying in the slath	the first few rows of pairing which fix the slath (base sticks) in position	45
Upright shave	a device with two upright adjustable blades used to produce skein of constant width by pulling the material between them	48
Upsett	setting up the sides of a basket (usually by several rows of waling which holds the stakes in position after pricking up)	45
Wale	a weave where three or more rods are worked in sequence in front of two, three or more stakes, and behind one (or more)	45
Warp	the static element around which the active element (weft) is woven, in basketry usually stakes, ribs or coils	43
Wattle	simple weaving of round or split rods used as a wall filling, normally covered with a mortar (daub)	9
Weaver	the flexible material (weft) which is woven around the stakes, ribs, or coils	43
Weft	the active element woven around the static warp element	43
White rods	willow which has had the bark stripped off (without boiling) to reveal the creamy-white skin (sometimes bleached to enhance its appearance)	30

Abbreviations

AD	anno domini
BC	before Christ
BP	before present
BA NL	Basketmakers' Association Newsletter (quarterly)
ENOV	École Nationale d'Osiériculture et de Vannerie de Fayl-Billot
HOMMEH	Hellenic Organisation of Small and Medium Sized Enterprises
ICEB	Proceedings of the International Congress of Ethnobotany
MERL	Museum of English Rural Life, University of Reading

Source List

Organisations and contacts

Britain

The Basketmakers' Association
Membership Secretary, 37 Mendip Road,
Cheltenham, Gloucs, GL52 5EB
www.basketassoc.org

The Worshipful Company of Basketmakers
Clerk to the Company, 29 Ingram House,
Park Road, Hampton Wick,
Kingston upon Thames, Surrey KT1 4BA
www.basketmakersco.org

The Scottish Basketmakers' Circle
www.scottishbasketmakerscircle.org

Ireland

The Irish Basketmakers' Association
Secretary, Willow Works, Knockmore,
Co. Mayo

The Netherlands

Wilg & Mand
Klipper 19, 1186 VR Amstelveen

Vereniging van Vlechters
Secretary: Corry Hansen, Enkhuizen,
Vrijdom 7 1601 HM
www.vlechters.nl

France

Syndicat Professionnel des Vanniers de France
École Nationale d'Osiériculture et de
Vannerie, Maison Darboy
24, rue Georges Darboy, Fayl-Billot,
F-52500 Haute Marne
www.ecole-nationale-de-vannerie.com

Société Cooperative Agricole de Vannerie
1, rue de la Cheneillère - BP 3,
37190 Villaines-les-Rochers
www.vannerie.com

Spain

The Catalan Basketmakers' Association
contact: Monica Guilera, Avenida 310,
Num 20, Castelidefels, Barcelona

Sweden

Jonas Hasselrot
Täppgatan 10, SE-151 33 Södertälje
jonas.hasselrot@telia.com

Denmark

Danish Basketmakers' Association: Pileforeningen
c/o Åne Lyngsgaard, Blegindvej 102,
8362 Hoerning
www.pileforeningen.dk

Germany

Association of Basketmakers, Lichtenfels Regional Craft Association
Innungsverband der Korbmacher
Kreishandwerkerschaft Lichtenfels, An
der Mainau, D-8620 Lichtenfels am Main

Switzerland

Swiss Basketmakers' Association: IGK (Interessengemeinschaft Korbflechterei)
Schweiz, Bernstrasse 9, CH 3117 Kiesen
www.korbflechten.ch

Museums

Great Britain

The main British museums with collections of traditional basketry are listed below as well as some smaller ones from which items have been illustrated here.

The Museum of English Rural Life (MERL)
The University of Reading,
Redlands Road, Reading, RG1 5EX
www.merl.org.uk

Gloucester Folk Museum
99-103 Westgate Street, Gloucester, GL1 2PG
www.glos-city.gov.uk

Abbott Hall Art Gallery and Museum
Kendal, Cumbria, LA9 5AL
www.abbothall.org.uk/molli.shtml

Scottish Fisheries Museum
St Ayles , Harbourhead, Anstruther, Fife, Scotland, KY10 3AB
www.scotfishmuseum.org

Somerset Rural Life Museum
Abbey Farm, Chilkwell Street, Glastonbury, Somerset BA6 8DB
www.somerset.gov.uk/museums

Norfolk Rural Life Museum
Beech House, Gressenhall, Dereham, Norfolk, NR20 4DR
www.museums.norfolk.gov.uk

Museum of East Anglian Life
Stowmarket, Suffolk, IP14 1DL
www.eastanglianlife.org.uk

The Elizabethan House Museum
4 South Quay, Great Yarmouth, NR30 2QH
www.nationaltrust.org.uk

Luton Museum
Wardown Park, Luton
Bedfordshire, LU2 7HA
www.luton.gov.uk/museums

Museum of Lincolnshire Life
Burton Road, Lincoln, LN1 3LY
www.lincolnshire.gov.uk/museums

Museum of Welsh Life
St Fagans, Cardiff, CF5 6XB
www.museumwales.ac.uk/en/stfagans

Maritime Museum
Queen Victoria Square, Hull, Yorkshire, HU1 3DX
www.hullcc.gov.uk/museums

Coates Willows and Wetlands Visitor Centre
Meare Green Court, Stoke St Gregory, Taunton, Somerset, TA3 6HY
www.englishwillowbaskets.co.uk

The Longshoreman's Museum
The Esplanade, Ventnor, Isle of Wight, PO 38 1JT
www.isleofwightattractions.co.uk Longshoremans.htm

Scottish Agricultural Museum
Ingliston, Edinburgh, EH28 8NB
www.scotland.com/museums/scottish-agricultural-museum/

Time and Tide Museum
Blackfriars Road, Great Yarmouth NR30 3BX
www.24hourmuseum.org.uk/ museum_gfx_en/AM19771.html

Swinford Museum
Fox House, Filkins, Nr Lechlade, Gloucester, GL7 3JQ, Gloucestershire
www.24hourmuseum.org.uk/ museum_gfx_en/SE000352.html

Northern Ireland

Ulster Folk and Transport Museum
153 Bangor Road, Cultra, Holywood, Co. Down, BT18 0EU
www.uftm.org.uk

Ireland

The National Museum of Ireland
Museum of Country Life, Turlough Park Castlebar, Co. Mayo
www.museum.ie/en/intro/country-life.aspx

In addition, The Basketmakers' Association has a museum list (available on application to the Sales Office) and the UK's rural museums are listed at www.ruralmuseumsnetwork.org.uk.

France

Musée de la Vannerie et de l'Artisanat
Grand Café du XIXe siècle, rue Carnot, 30300 - Vallabrègues
www.tourinfos.com/fr/r0011/d0030/ m0001/j0007/p001798.htm

Musée de l'Osier et de la Vannerie
22 rue des Caves Fortes,
37190 Villaines-les-Rochers
www.culture.gouv.fr/mpe/carto/ fiches/188.htm

Société Coopérative Agricole de Vannerie
1, rue de la Cheneillère - BP 3 -37190 Villaines-les-Rochers www.vannerie.com/

École Nationale d'Osiériculture et de Vannerie (ENOV),
Maison Darboy
24, rue Georges Darboy, Fayl-Billot, F-52500 Haute Marne
www.ecole-nationale-de-vannerie.com

Musée des Vallées Cevenoles
95 Grand-Rue, 30270 St Jean-du-Gard
http://pagesperso-orange.fr/
museedesvalleescevenoles

Musée de la Vannerie
La Glaneuse, 84160 Cadenet
www.vaucluse.fr

Château de Troussay
41700 Cheverny
www.chateauxtourisme.com

Musée des Arts Populaires
22 rue du Monceau, Laduz 89110
www.culture.fr/sections/regions/
bourgogne

Artisans et Paysans de Lozère
4 rue de l'Ange, 4800 Mende (shop
selling locally produced work)

La Vannerie Bussièroise Cooperative
Bussières-les-Belmont
52500 Champsevraine
www.vanneriebussieroise.fr

Musée National des Arts et Traditions
Populaires
Centre d'Ethnologie Française
6, avenue du Mahatma Gandhi
750116 Paris
www.musee-atp.fr (a large collection but
very little on display)

Musée du Compagnonnage
8 rue Nationale, 37000 Tours
www.musee-du-compagnonnage.info

Foire aux paniers et à la vannerie
Issigeac, near Bergerac, Dordogne is held
annually in July.
www.issigeac.fr

Musée de la Vie Rurale et Forestière
Site abbatial, Rue du Chamiteau
02830 Saint-Michel, France
www.abbaye-saintmichel.com
(close to the Belgian border with a
collection of fine willow skein work)

Low Countries

The Netherlands

National Vlechtmuseum Noordwolde
Mandehof 7, Noordwolde
http://noordwoldevlechtdorp.nl
(annual festival end of August)

Stadsmuseum IJsselstein
Walkade 2 IJsselstein, 3401 DS IJsselstein
www.stadsmuseum.nl

Visserijmuseum Vlaardingen
Westhavenkade 53/54, 3131 AG,
Vlaardingen
www.visserij-museum.nl
(sea-fishing museum with fishing baskets)

Nederlands Openluchtmuseum
Schelmseweg 89, Postbus 649
NL-6800 AP Arnhem, The Netherlands
www.openluchtmuseum.nl
(open air museum with baskets in many
of the buildings)

Belgium

Vlechtwerkmuseum
Maascentrum De Wissen, Maaspark,
3650 Dilsen-Stokkem
www.dewissen.be/vlechtwerkmuseum.php
(a modern Belgian museum devoted to
the former willow industry)

Museum De Zilverreiger
Scheldestraat 18 , 2880 Bornem-Weert,
Antwerp
www.museumsite.be

Spain

Museo do Pobo Galego
San Domingos de Bonaval
15703 Santiago de Compostela
www.museodopobo.es

Museo de Artes y Tradiciones Populares
Carretera Colmenar Viejo KM 15,500
28049 Madrid
http://Museo de Artes y Tradiciones
Populares/default.html

Museo Folklorico
Plaza Catedral, Ripoll, Gerona
(Spanish Basketmaking Fair, Salt,
Gerona, 1st weekend October)

Pinolere Proyecto Cultural
Calle Germinal nº 36 Pinolere
La Orotava S/C de Tenerife 38310
www.pinolere.org
(late summer exhibition)

Portugal

Museu Nacional da Etnologia
Avenida Ilha da Madeira, Lisbon
www.lisbon-guide.info/historical_sights/
museums

The Nordic Lands

Sweden

The Lönsboda Punnet Museum
V Jarnvagsgaten, S-28070 Lönsboda,

Nordiska Museet
Djurgårdsvägen 6-16, Box 27820
115 93 Stockholm
www.nordiskamuseet.se

Norway

Historical Museum
Museum of Cultural History,
University of Oslo ,PO Box 6762 Olav's
place, 0130 Oslo
www.uio.no/english/about_uio/org

Norsk Folkemuseet (Norwegian
Museum of Cultural History)
Museumsveien 10, N-0287 Oslo
www.norskfolke.museum.no

Sunnfjord Museum
Movika, 6800 Førde Movik, 6800 Førde
www.sunnfjord.museum.no

Vefsn Bygdemuseum
Byhistorisk avdeling i Sjøgata 31b
Bygdetunet i Austerbygdveien 2
www.helgelandmuseum.no/ip/pages/
avdelinger/vefsn.php

Maihaugen Museum
Maihaugvegen 1, N-2609 Lillehammer
www.maihaugen.no

Finland

Luostarinmaki Handicrafts Museum
P.O. Box 286, 20101 Turku
www.turku.fi/maakuntamuseo

Denmark

Moesgaard Museum
Moesgård Allé 20 - 8270 Højbjerg
www.moesmus.dk
(Annual Festival, mid-August)

Germany

Deutsches Korbmuseum
Bismarckstraße 4, 96247 Michelau i.OFr
www.gemeinde-michelau.de

Ethnological Museum
Lansstraße 8, 14195 Berlin-Dahlem
www.smb.museum/smb/sammlungen

Wannenmacher Museum
Mühlenstraße 28-30, Emsdetten
www.emsdetten.de/staticsite/
staticsite.php

Volkskunde Museum Schleswig
Stiftung Schleswig-Holsteinische
Landesmuseen, Schloß Gottorf
Volkskunde Museum, 24837 Schleswig
www.schloss-gottorf.de/vkm

Dorfmuseum Schönbach
On Drachenberg 1, 04668 Schönbach
www.tv-schoenbach.de

Staatliche Berufsfachschule für
Flechtwerkgestaltung Lichtenfels
Kronacher Straße 32, 96215 Lichtenfels
www.lichtenfels-city.de

Lichtenfelser Korbmarkt, Lichtenfels.
(Three-day fair held the 3rd Sunday in
September)
http://korbmarkt.lichtenfels-city.de

Alpine Regions

Switzerland

Schweizerisches Freilichtmuseum
Swiss Open-Air Museum Ballenberg
PO Box, CH-3855 Brienz
www.ballenberg.ch

Schweizerisches Landesmuseum Zurich
Museumstrasse 2, 8021 Zürich
www.landesmuseen.ch/d/zuerich

Austria

Landesmuseum Joanneum
Landwirtschaftliche Sammlung
Schloss Stainz, Schlossplatz 18510 Stainz
www.museum-joanneum.at

Bad Tatzmannsdorf Freilichtmuseum
Eliabeth-Allee 2, A-7431 Bad
Tatzmannsdorf
www.freilichtmuseum-
badtatzmannsdorf.at

Salzburger Freilichtmuseum
Hasenweg , A-5084 Grossgmain
www.freilichtmuseum.com

Österreichische Freilichtmuseum
Stübing
A-8114 Stübing
www.freilichtmuseum.at

Landesmuseum Burgenland
Museumgasse 1-5, 7000 Eisenstadt
www.burgenland.at/landesmuseum

Ethnographisches Museum
Schloss Kittsee
Dr. Ladislaus Batthyányplatz 1
A - 2421 Kittsee
www.schloss-kittsee.at

Stadtmuseum Friesach
Fürstenhofplatz 1, A-9360 Friesach
www.friesach.at

Freilichmuseum
Domplatz 3, A- 9063 Maria Saal
www.tiscover.at/at/guide/5,en,SCH1/
objectId,SIG2098at,season,at2,selectedEn
try,sights/intern.html

Tiroler Volkskunstmuseum
Universitätsstraße 2, A 6020 Innsbruck
www.tiroler-volkskunstmuseum.at

Slovenia

Slovene Ethnographic Museum
Metelkova 2, SI - 1000 Ljubljana
www.etno-muzej.si

Cebelarski Muzej (Apicultural Museum)
Linhartov trg 1, 4240 Radovljica
www.muzeji-radovljica.si

Ptuj Regional Museum
Muzejski trg 1, SI-2250 Ptuj
www.pok-muzej-ptuj.si

Italy

Centro Tradizioni Popolare della
Provincia di Lucca
Palazzo Ducale, Piazza Napoleone, Lucca
www.centrotradizionipopolari.it

Centro Etnografico della Civiltà Palustre
Piazza Tre Martiri
48020 Villanova di Bagnacavallo RA
www.racine.ra.it/erbepalustri

Civico Museo Etnografico Romagnolo
G. Pergoli
c.so Repubblica, 72 47100 Forli

Museo della Vita e delle Tradizioni
Popolari Sarde
Via A. Mereu, 56, 08100 Nuoro, Sardinia
www.comune.nuoro.it

Museo Deledda
Via Grazio Deledda, 08100 Nuoro Nu
Sardinia
www.emmeti.it/Arte/Sardegna/
ProvNuoro/Nuoro/
museo_deleddiano.it.html

Museo Nazionale delle Arti e Tradizioni
Popolari
Piazza Marconi, 8/10 Rome
www.popolari.arti.beniculturali.it

Museo della Cultura Popolare Padana
Piazza Teofilo Folengo 1
San Benedetto PO 46027 (MN)

Museo del Vino - Fundazione Lungarotti
Corso Vittorio Emanuele, 31 06089
Torgiano (Perugia)
vino.lungarotti.biz

Museo Civico di San Ferdinando di
Puglia
Piazza Trieste, 11,71046 San Ferdinando
di Puglia (Fg)
www.vocedipadrepio.com/
itinerariculturali.php#sanferdinando

Museo dell'Intreccio Mediterraneo
Castello dei Doria via Marconi,
Castelsardo, Sardinia

Museo del Lavoro Contadino
Via Monticino 2 48013 Brisighella
www.sistemamusei.ra.it

Museo delle Tradizioni Popolari
Largo Maria de Mattias, 7 - Canepina
(VT)
www.prolococanepina.it

Museo Civico dei Costumi e delle
Tradizioni Locali
piazza della Repubblica, 7, Gurro
(Verbania)

Museo della Cultura Arbëreshe
via Regina Margherita, San Paolo
Albanese, (PZ)

Museo Lombardo di Storia
dell'Agricoltura S. Angelo Lodigiano
Secretary for guided visits: c/o Fondazione
Morando Bolognini Piazza Bolognini, 2 -
Sant'Angelo Lodigiano
www.museilodi.it

Poland

Pañstwowe Muzeum Etnograficzne w
Warszawie
00-056 Warszawa
ul. Kredytowa 1
www.pme.waw.pl

Museum Okregowe w Nowym Saczu
The Sacz Ethnographic Park
33-300 Nowy Sacz
ul. B. Wieniawy-Długoszowskiego 83b
www.muzeum.sacz.p

Carpathians

Hungary

Museum of Ethnography
1055 Budapest, Kossuth Lajos tér 12.
www.neprajz.hu

Magyar Mezögazdasági Múzeum
(Museum of Hungarian Agriculture)
1146 - BudapestVárosliget,
Vajdahunyadvár
www.museum.hu/museum/
index_hu.php?ID=57

Romania

Muzeul Satului (Village Museum) Kiseleff
Road 28-30 Bucharest 713211
Romania
www.muzeul-satului.ro

**Muzeul Tehnicii Populare (Museum of
Popular Technology)**
Muzeul Civilizatiei Populare Traditionale
ASTRA, Padurea Dumbrava, Sibiu
www.sibiu.ro/turism/ro/muzee.htm

Ethnographic Museum of Transylvania
Memorandum Street no. 21, 400114
Cluj-Napoca
and open-air exhibition: Ethnographic
Park Romulus Vuia, Taietura Turcului
Street n.n., 400221 Cluj-Napoca
www.muzeul-etnografic.ro

Maramurez Ethnographic Museum
Piata Libertatii nr. 15, Sighetu Marmatiei
www.ici.ro/romania/ro/cultura/
mz_maramures.html

Cimitir Vesel (Merry Cemetery)
Sapînta, Maramures
www.ici.ro/romania/ro/turism/
b_merrycemetery.html

Street stalls in Izvoru Crisului, West of
Cluj-Napoca (on the DN1 to Oradea)

Czech Republic

**Valasske Muzeum v Prirode (Open-air
Museum of Wallachia)**
Palackeho 147, 756 61 Roznov pod
Radhostem
www.vmp.cz

**Polabske Narodopisne Muzeum Prerov
nad Labem:(Ethnographic Museum of
the Labe Region)**
CZ 289 16 Prerov nad Labem
www.polabskemuzeum.cz

Balkans

Croatia

Etnografski Muzei
Mazuranicev trg 14, Zagreb
www.mdc.hr/etno

Bulgaria

National Agricultural Museum
30 Suhodolska Str, Sofia 1713

Ethnographic Institute and Museum
6A, Moskovska St, Sofia
http://hs41.iccs.bas.bg

Prolet (basketmaking company)
Shumen
http://prolet.icon.bg

Cyprus, Greece, Malta and Turkey

Greece

Historial and Folklore Museum
Ermou 1, Korinthos Beach, Corinth

**Folk Art Museum, Peloponnesian
Folklore Foundation**
1 Vas Alexandrou Str, 21100 Nafplion
www.pli.gr

Ethnological Museum of Macedonia
68, Vasilissis Olgas St, GR 54642,
Thessaloniki, Macedonia
www.museumsofmacedonia.gr/Folklore/
Laografiko_Thessalonikhs.html

Crete

Museum for Cretan Ethnology
Voroi Pyrgiotissis, 702 00 Herakleion
www.interkriti.org/timbaki/vorimus.htm

Malta

Folklore Museum
Bernardo de Opuo Street, The Citadel
Victoria VCT 104, Gozo
www.heritagemalta.org/
folkloremuseum.html

Index